Criminal

This new text will encourage students to develop a deeper understanding of the context and the current workings of the criminal justice system.

The first part offers a clear, accessible and comprehensive review of the major philosophical aims and sociological theories of punishment, the history of justice and punishment and the developing perspective of victimology. In Part II, the focus is on the main areas of the contemporary criminal justice system – including the police, the courts and judiciary, prisons and community penalties.

The active engagement of students with the material covered distinguishes this text from others in the area and makes it a real teaching resource for lecturers and tutors. There are regular reflective question breaks which enable students to consider and respond to questions relating to what they have just read.

Criminal Justice is particularly geared to undergraduate students following programmes in criminal justice and criminology. It will also prove a useful resource for practitioners who are following vocationally based courses in the criminal justice area – for instance, social work, youth justice and police training courses.

Ian Marsh is Programme Leader for Criminology at Liverpool Hope University College and is a widely published textbook author. His recent publications include *Theory and Practice in Sociology* and *Sociology: Making Sense of Society*. **John Cochrane** is Lecturer in History and Criminology at Liverpool John Moores University. **Gaynor Melville** is Lecturer in Sociology and Criminology at Liverpool Hope University College.

Criminal Justice

An introduction to philosophies, theories and practice

Ian Marsh
with John Cochrane and Gaynor Melville

 Routledge
Taylor & Francis Group

LONDON AND NEW YORK

First published 2004 by Routledge
11 New Fetter Lane, London EC4P 4EE

Simultaneously published in the USA and Canada
by Routledge
29 West 35th Street, New York, NY 10001

Routledge is an imprint of the Taylor & Francis Group

© 2004 Ian Marsh, with John Cochrane and Gaynor Melville

Typeset in Univers and Rotis by Graphicraft Limited, Hong Kong
Printed and bound in Great Britain by Bell & Bain Ltd, Glasgow

British Library Cataloguing in Publication Data
A catalogue record for this book is available from the British Library

Library of Congress Cataloging in Publication Data
Marsh, Ian, 1952–
    Criminal justice : an introduction to philosophies, theories and practice
    / Ian Marsh, with John Cochrane and Gaynor Melville.
        p. cm.
    Simultaneously published in the USA and Canada by Routledge.
    Includes bibliographical references.
    1. Criminal justice, Administration of.   2. Criminal justice,
    Administration of—Philosophy.   3. Criminology.   4. Criminology—Philosophy.
    5. Police—Great Britain—History.   I. Cochrane, John.   II. Melville, Gaynor.
    III. Title.
    HV7419.M35 2004
    364—dc22   2003018479

ISBN 0–415–33301–6 (hbk)
ISBN 0–415–33300–8 (pbk)

Contents

Preface

The intention of this book is to provide students (and tutors) with an introduction to the study of criminal justice. Its central aim is to encourage students to develop a deeper understanding of the context and current workings of the criminal justice system.

Content

The book is divided into two main sections. Part I provides an examination of the philosophical, theoretical and historical contexts of criminal justice and Part II focuses on the major agencies of the contemporary criminal justice system in England and Wales.

In Part I, Chapter 1 considers the basic question 'Why should offenders be punished?' It does this by looking at the justifications for punishment and the philosophies that lie behind them. There are various plausible justifications for punishment and there are different ways of categorising them. Here these justifications are examined under three main headings: deterrence, retribution and rehabilitation. The contradictions and tensions between the different philosophies of punishment are highlighted through examples of different forms of punishment at different periods of history. Chapter 2 focuses on explanations for punishment and, in particular, addresses the question 'What have social theorists said about the role of punishment in society?' The main theoretical approaches that are examined are Durkheim's argument that punishment produces social solidarity; the Marxist tradition that punishment is part of a class-based process of economic and social regulation; and the more recent theorising of Foucault emphasising the interrelationship between punishment, power and regulation. Chapter 3, written by John Cochrane, relates and applies these and other theoretical approaches to the history of the policies and practices of crime and justice. Essentially it tries to understand this history in terms of the nature of the particular governments and societies responsible for introducing these policies and practices. Chapter 4, written by Gaynor Melville, shifts the focus to an examination of the role of the victim within the criminal justice system. It charts the emergence of the discipline of victimology and considers the main theoretical positions within it. In doing this, it distinguishes between victims of different forms of criminal behaviour, with a particular focus on victims of domestic violence (private crime) and of corporate crime (public crime).

The three chapters in Part II examine the major different elements and agencies of the contemporary criminal justice system. Chapter 5 looks at police and policing, setting the context for an examination of police culture through a consideration of how historical changes, and especially those of the post-1960 period, have shaped the current form and style of policing. Chapter 6 turns to the courtroom and examines issues around the trial and sentencing of offenders, in particular issues of impartiality, focusing on gender, ethnicity and class bias. After this, it looks at those who sentence offenders – the magistrates and the judges – considering their backgrounds, appointment and ideologies. Chapter 7 looks at prison, the most severe penalty available in our criminal justice system; it provides data that enable a consideration to be made of the extent to which the current prison system is in 'crisis', and looks at some of the issues facing the prison service – including overcrowding, security and the different needs of long-term and other prisoners. The chapter concludes by examining the background to and success of community sentences. Issues of inequality – in particular in terms of gender, ethnicity and class – are raised and discussed in relation to each of the main agencies of the criminal justice system that are examined in Chapters 5, 6 and 7.

Features

Criminal Justice: An Introduction to Philosophies, Theories and Practice adopts an interactive approach that aims to actively engage the reader with the material being examined, so as to encourage reaction to and reflection on it. There are question breaks throughout the text that offer opportunities for reflection. These question breaks might encourage students to consider a particular case study or example of writing and respond to questions on it; or in some cases are just short stop-and-think type questions. The text makes use of extracts from academic sources and the contemporary press to encourage students to read a range of original sources. At the end of each chapter there are suggestions for further reading and research, including key texts on the particular area and, where appropriate, useful Web sites.

This book has been a collaborative venture, and the authors would like to thank James McNally and his colleagues at Routledge and the various anonymous reviewers who have commented on it.

Ian Marsh
Liverpool Hope University College
January 2004

Acknowledgements

The publishers would like to thank Penguin Books, Editions Gallimard and George Borchardt Inc. for permission to reprint material from Michel Foucault's *Discipline and Punish: The Birth of the Prison* (Penguin, 1991), first published as *Surveiller et punir: naissance de la prison* (Editions Gallimard, 1975).

Part I

History and theories of crime and punishment

1 Why punish? Philosophies of punishment

Introduction: studying punishment

The basic question that this chapter will be considering is 'Why should offenders be punished?' In addressing this question it will look at the aims and justifications for punishment and at the philosophies that lie behind them. Before it does this, and by way of an introduction, some general points about the sociological study of punishment will be raised.

The sociological study of punishment examines the relationship between crime, punishment and society. It looks at punishment as a social phenomenon and, in particular, the role of punishment in social life. While punishment occurs in a variety of different contexts – in the home, at school and at work, for instance – the focus here is on the legal punishment of offenders. This legal punishment is a complex process that involves the making of laws, the trial, conviction and sentencing of offenders, and the administration of particular penalties. Given this complexity, it is not surprising that legal punishment can have various aims. However, it is likely that a majority of people would see the reduction or containment of crime as the major purpose of punishment, with punishment seen as a means to an end – that of controlling crime. Although crimes still occur, and in ever-increasing numbers, it would perhaps be unfair to say that punishment has therefore 'failed'; rather, it is arguably an unrealistic aim and expectation of punishment that it control rates of crime.

Until comparatively modern times there was little attempt to use punishment to reform wrongdoers and there was little pity wasted on law-breakers, with punishments tending to be quick, harsh and public. The history of crime and punishment (examined in detail in Chapter 3) demonstrates that there have been attempts to reform criminals but they have not detracted from the general motif of punishment as needing to be severe and exemplary. Reform and rehabilitation as 'aims of punishment' gained perhaps their widest support in the late 1950s and 1960s, providing a different sense of purpose for punishment and leading to a general optimism about the possibilities of punishment. This was reflected in various new methods of punishment introduced in Britain and elsewhere in this period, including parole, suspended sentences, community service orders and day training centres. The optimism of the 1960s soon gave way to a more sceptical perspective: rising crime rates and high rates of reoffending led to criticisms of the new methods of punishment as being too soft. The emphasis moved away from reform, with senior politicians advocating a hardline approach to punishment that was reflected in 'short, sharp shock' sentences being introduced in the early 1980s, and more recently the introduction into Britain of policies based on American 'boot camps' and 'three strikes and out' policies.

However, these newer, harsher initiatives have similarly had little effect on the size of the prison population or on rates of recidivism. Without going into great detail, some overall figures will help illustrate the pressures on the prison system in Britain and provide a context for considering the different philosophies of punishment. The prison population in Britain has continued to rise pretty steadily over the past few decades, with over 71,000 people in Prison Service establishments in 2002 (Home Office data, *Social Trends* 33, 2003). The number of people given immediate custodial sentences in 1999 was over 105,000 compared to just under 80,000 four years previously (Home Office data, *Annual Abstract of Statistics*, 2002). (The reason that the number of people sent to prison each year is greater than the prison population is that most prisoners are sentenced to short sentences of less than one year and so not all would be in prison when the annual figure is calculated.) As regards repeat offenders, it would seem that a relatively small number of offenders are responsible for a large proportion of offences. Of the 97,800 males who entered prison in 1999, almost 68 per cent had had previous convictions for 'standard list offences' (which include all indictable offences plus some of the more serious summary offences), with 46 per cent having had three or more previous convictions (Home Office data, *Annual Abstract of Statistics*, 2002).

These kinds of figures and the obvious concerns they highlight about justice and punishment raise questions about the aims and philosophies of punishment, which we will now turn to.

QUESTION BREAK: 'HARD' AND 'SOFT' APPROACHES

In the introduction to the chapter, reference was made to the support for 'hardline' approaches to punishment in response to criticisms of reformative approaches to punishment as being too 'soft'. The terms 'hard' and 'soft' are routinely used to indicate polarised positions in the debate about punishment.

Former Home Secretary (and, in 2003, leader of the Conservative Party) Michael Howard has been a strong advocate of the 'hard position', and is particularly renowned for his 'prison works' comments: 'Prison works ... it makes many who are tempted to commit crime think twice. ... This may mean that more people will go to prison. I do not flinch from that' (at the Conservative Party Conference, 1993).

While Howard's predecessors as Home Secretary (including Kenneth Clarke, Kenneth Baker, David Waddington and Douglas Hurd), as well as key figures involved in running the criminal justice system (including Lord Woolf, now Lord Chief Justice), have favoured a reduction in prison sentences, for minor offences at least, the hardline approach tends to be popular with the wider public and certain sections of the mass media. In contrast, any perceived 'softness' on crime tends to be seen as a sign of political weakness; and when we hear of horrific crimes occurring it is easy to see how a hardline, 'hang 'em high' approach will gain considerable sympathy and support.

It is not surprising, then, that the hardline approach has been regularly advocated by politicians. Former Prime Minister John Major, commenting on the supposedly lenient treatment of juvenile offenders, said that 'We should understand a little less and condemn a little more.' The Labour government that replaced his administration has promised to be 'tough on crime and tough on the causes of crime' and to give 'zero tolerance' to crime and criminals.

The 'debate' between the 'hard' and 'soft' positions can be illustrated by the comments made by the Lord Chief Justice, Lord Woolf, in December 2002 when he told judges and magistrates that burglars facing a sentence of up to 18 months should not go to prison but be given a non-custodial sentence, and even where a prison sentence was imposed it should be no longer than necessary. This 'soft' position led the leader of Britain's Chief Constables, Sir David Phillips, to say that such a move would undermine the morale of the police, who had successfully focused on burglary for a number of years – an attack on Lord Woolf's proposals that was supported by the Police Federation, which represents rank-and-file officers, who felt that such comments would only encourage burglars.

Question

Why do you think that (a) the reformative approach might be unpopular with the general public; and (b) a tough approach might be more popular?

The aims of punishment

While punishment and the institutions associated with it are generally accepted as being a necessary part of any orderly society, that does not mean punishment is unproblematic. As Garland (1999, p. 5) puts it:

> The modern institutions of punishment are especially prone to conflicts and tensions that tend to undermine their effectiveness and legitimacy as instruments of social policy. These conflicts – between condemnation and forgiveness, vengeance and mercy, the sanctity of the law and the humanity of compassion, social defense and individual rights, the urge to exclude and the dream of rehabilitation – set up complex, ambivalent sentiments that colour the day-to-day experience of those caught up in penal relations, whether as administrators and officers, inmates and clients, or as members of the public.

Given these and other tensions, it is little surprise that the history of punishing offenders has been one of 'reform and reaction, of false dawns and disappointed optimism' (Garland 1999). Garland also points to the ambitious expectations held for our modern criminal justice system. It is viewed not just as being about 'doing justice' through law enforcement and punishing offenders, but also as having a wider remit to reduce crime through reforming offenders and deterring others from offending. And, as the expectations of reducing crime have not been met, so issues about the aims and success of punishment become a focus for public concern.

It is not surprising, then, that various different aims of punishment have been advocated or that different commentators adopt different ways of categorising these aims. Moreover, the philosophies that underpin the reasons for punishing offenders are an important area to consider, perhaps at the most basic level because punishment will involve some form of compulsion (forcing something on someone) which, typically, involves hardship. Decisions to punish inevitably raise fundamental issues of moral justification, of what are the reasons for doing it.

QUESTION BREAK: JUSTIFYING PUNISHMENT

Before we consider the major aims of punishment, the following exercise asks you to reflect on what you think the justification for punishment should be.

Read the two brief fictional case studies and then answer the question at the end.

Case 1

James has been found guilty of fraud. Over a number of years he embezzled funds from the city bank at which he worked; he opened false accounts and used them to finance a lifestyle way beyond what would have been possible on his regular salary. As well as a large country house in Britain, he owned a small villa in Spain and an apartment in New York. He justified his wealth to his colleagues by claiming he had been left money by a rich spinster aunt which he had invested successfully. The court heard that he stole over £2 million between 1977 and 1999.

Case 2

Paul has been found guilty of burglary. He broke into a house while the residents were at work and stole a VCR, a number of CDs and videos and cash – to the value of some £500 in all. He had one previous conviction for burglary, for which he had received a six-month probation order, which he had successfully completed.

Question

As a judge, you have to punish the two offenders. For both James and Paul (separately) decide which of the following approaches would be your personal motivation in determining the appropriate punishment. (You can choose only one.)

1   The punishment must be unpleasant enough to discourage James/Paul from committing another crime.
2   The punishment must be in line with the punishment others would get for a similar crime and be of sufficient severity to match the crime.
3   The punishment must provide opportunities for James/Paul to make better choices in the future so that he is unlikely to want to commit another crime.

Discussion

Consider what your answer tells you about your 'philosophy of punishment' – did you lean to punishment as a deterrent (answer 1), or as retribution (2), or rehabilitation (3)?

Probably the requirement to choose only one answer restricted you. Often there will be more than one philosophy at play; and the philosophy that guides your own decisions may well change if you get to know more about the circumstances of the offence, the characteristics of the offender, and so on.

This exercise illustrates the point that there are various plausible justifications for punishment, and that difficulties can arise for sentencers because these justifications can and do conflict with one another. In particular, and as the comments from Garland illustrate, there is a basic tension between protecting the rights of offenders (not punishing them more than they deserve) and protecting the rights of the public not to be victims of crime.

In the rest of this chapter, we will examine the major aims of punishment. As mentioned earlier, there are different ways of listing and categorising these aims. Hudson (2003) suggests two basic groupings: aims concerned with preventing future crimes and those concerned with punishing crimes already committed. Those focused on future prevention could be seen as utilitarian, as having a certain degree of 'usefulness' for the wider society; thus if a punishment deters someone from reoffending or discourages others from offending or 'reforms' offenders so that they do not offend again, its utility is clear. These future-oriented aims of punishment have been called reductivist by some commentators, as their aim is to reduce crime (Cavadino and Dignan 2002). Past-oriented aims and approaches to punishment are known as retributivist in that their focus is on exacting retribution from offenders, the blame is placed squarely on the offender and the future conduct of that offender is not seen as the major issue – punishment is essentially about blame and repayment.

QUESTION BREAK: CRIMINAL RECORDS

There is clearly a conflict between these two broad aims of punishment. As Hudson (2003, p. 5) comments:

[I]f a person is assessed as likely to commit a further offence, should s/he be punished more severely than someone who commits the same offence but is not assessed as likely to reoffend? Conversely, should someone who commits an offence and has a record of previous offences be punished more severely than someone committing the same offence for the first time?

Question

What priority do you think should be given to someone's criminal record and what to the actual offence? Give reasons for your answer.

Deterrence

Deterrence is a future-oriented aim in that the intention behind it is to reduce crime. It could also be seen, therefore, to have a utilitarian rationale. As already mentioned, 'utility' would be apparent if a punishment deterred an offender from reoffending or if it discouraged others from offending in the first place. This comment indicates that there are two basic ways in which deterrence can work: either at an individual or at a general level (Cavadino and Dignan 2002). Individual or specific deterrence involves the punishment showing the offender that her/his action was undesirable because it brought her/him more pain than pleasure; so the fear of punishment would prevent the individual from repeating the offence. General deterrence works by showing others who may consider a criminal act that they will suffer painful consequences if they commit the offence.

Before we try to assess the effectiveness of deterrence as a basis for punishment, it would be useful to explore the relationship between the utilitarian philosophy that underpins deterrence and punishment. While utilitarian approaches to punishment are not exactly synonymous with reductivist approaches, recent theories of punishment that focus on crime reduction are clearly linked with the theorising of the Enlightenment thinkers Cesare Beccaria (1738–1794) and Jeremy Bentham (1748–1832), the classic exponents of utilitarian theory. Essentially, the utilitarian argument is that actions are moral if they are useful, and so punishment can be morally justified only if the harm and suffering it prevents is greater than the harm it inflicts on offenders; and unless punishment reduces future crime then it would add to rather than reduce the sum of human suffering. When Beccaria published *An Essay on Crimes and Punishments* in 1764 he advocated a system of justice and punishment as much as an explanation of crime and, in similar vein to the British philosopher Bentham, proposed that punishment should be used to achieve some greater good for society – with a reduction in crime being a clear example of such a good. Beccaria proposed that a graduated system of penalties with the particular punishment appropriate to the crime would work as a deterrent. Prior to the move to democratic, constitutional governments (as opposed to monarchies) in Europe in the eighteenth and nineteenth centuries, punishment was often arbitrary and down to the whims of the nobility and monarchy. Bentham developed what has become known as the 'classicist' penal code based on the classic ideas of the Enlightenment. He stressed the importance of human reason rather than notions such as the divine right of monarchs as a means of governing. As regards punishment, he argued that this should be rationally based. Bentham saw the criminal as an individual with free choice who could therefore be deterred by the threat of future punishment. He also argued for a strict link between crime and punishment: once a crime was committed it should be punished accordingly, with no room for mitigating circumstances to be taken into account. For both theorists, then, the crime issue was basically the punishment issue; and punishment should be rational, fair and just. They argued that excessive and violent punishments were barbaric and not worthy of civilised nations, and that each particular form of punishment must impose just enough pain and suffering to outweigh the pleasure that may come from committing the specific crime.

In summarising Bentham's approach, Hudson (2003) highlights three ways in which he suggests an individual can be deterred from reoffending: first, through taking away the individual's ability and power to offend; second, by taking away the individual's desire to offend; and third, by making the individual afraid to offend. The first of these would involve some form on incapacitation; the second refers to a reformist or rehabilitative approach, which we will consider later; while the third, deterring someone through fear of the potential punishment, is the meaning that is conventionally attached to deterrence.

Now an obvious way in which deterrence might work would be to have very draconian punishments that were so severe that people would be bound to be put off committing crimes. This sort of approach could not be called utilitarian, in that there is no attempt to limit the amount of pain as there would be no limit on the severity of punishment. While life imprisonment for driving over the speed limit or for shoplifting might lead to a dramatic reduction in those offences, and while 'get tough', 'hard' approaches to punishment may be attractive to politicians because of their appeal to the wider public, the notion of very severe punishment for any but very serious crimes would be held by most to be unacceptable from a human rights point of view. A compromise position is the notion of passing 'exemplary sentences' – sentences that are more severe than would usually be given for a particular offence because they aim to get over a message that such behaviour is being taken especially seriously. The notion of such 'exemplary' penalties raises the interesting point that for punishment to work as a general deterrent it is not necessary that only guilty people are punished. While the punishing of innocent people would, hopefully, be rejected by all ethical systems, there may be some justification, in terms of general deterrence, for punishing people for something they have not yet done but may be likely to do in the future.

The focus of the deterrence philosophy is, essentially, on frightening people into not offending; and it is, therefore, generally associated with severer penalties such as long prison sentences. One problem with this notion is that what one person may feel to be severe might be viewed by another as mild. Another is that for general deterrence to be effective, the punishment has to be severe, and painful, enough to outweigh the potential pleasure that the particular offence might give the offender – a difficult assessment to make. It is also necessary that there is adequate publicity so that would-be offenders are aware of the particular punishments meted out. Indeed, any publicity that leads to an increased awareness that many crimes are not being solved or that highlights an increase in what are seen as lenient punishments can work against the effectiveness of deterrent punishments.

It seems fair to say that there is little evidence that deterrence 'works', and we will conclude this section with a brief assessment of the effectiveness of deterrence as a justification for punishing offenders.

It might seem reasonable to suppose that offenders who had received a harsh punishment would be less likely to reoffend than offenders who had received a less severe punishment. However, there is little evidence that this is the case – the figures on repeat offenders that were given at the start of the chapter certainly raise questions about the deterrent effect of punishment, while young offenders who served custodial sentences under the stricter regimes of detention centres in the 1980s were just as likely to reoffend as those who had not been subject to such regimes.

This does not mean that harsh punishments never deter, but does indicate that the basic notion of deterrence is difficult to measure and assess. Walker (1991) points out that individuals can be deterred from committing offences at certain times and in certain places, but merely commit that (or another) offence elsewhere – and that such 'displacement' of offences hardly constitutes deterrence. He also points to the effectiveness of 'on-the-spot' deterrents, which pose practical difficulties for would-be offenders, but which again may only serve to 'displace' offences. Furthermore, deterrence can work 'at a distance'; for instance, the potential 'stigma' of being known as a shoplifter might put many people off from even considering such an offence. These sorts of examples indicate that the likely form of punishment is certainly not the only possible consequence that will influence a would-be offender.

Deterrence, then, involves would-be offenders weighing up a range of possible consequences of future offending. For it to have an effect, individuals have to be tempted to offend in the first place; deterrence cannot be applied to a person who is not tempted to offend. However, it can 'work' in an indirect way – refraining from committing an offence because the individual would reproach him/herself at some future date demonstrates a deterrent effect. Walker (1991) argues that the crucial factor in assessing the effectiveness of deterrent punishments is that the individual believes in the deterring consequences, even if they are not very likely to occur. For instance, many people stopped buying and eating British beef in the 1990s because of the remote possibility of contracting the human form of 'mad-cow disease'. Furthermore, the deterrent effect will vary as an individual's state of mind varies; people who would not normally consider breaking the law may become undeterrable and commit offences when they are influenced by drink or drugs, or when driven to do so by anger or jealousy, for example.

It may be that people are just not that rational and calculating; and if their behaviour is determined not by free will but rather by biological, psychological or social factors, then they are not going to be deterred by the potential punishment. We have highlighted the difficulties with applying and assessing the notion of deterrence not in order to dismiss the notion but to question the extent to which the type or severity of punishment influences how effective it is. Some people would be unlikely to commit any offence, however harsh the punishment attached to it might be – the fear of being caught and stigmatised would be enough to deter them. For others, the punishment may be accepted as part of the risk: 'If you can't do the time, don't do the crime.' This is not to say that punishments cannot have a deterrent effect. As mentioned earlier, and slightly tongue-in-cheek, massively severe penalties for relatively minor offences would have a general deterrent effect and significantly reduce those offences. However, aside from extreme examples, there is little evidence that the type or severity of punishment has much influence as a general deterrent. This argument is supported by a case that is often referred to whereby a Birmingham youth received a 20-year detention sentence for a mugging offence in 1973. Although this exceptional punishment was given widespread media coverage, comparisons of rates of mugging before and after this 'exemplary' sentence found it had no effect on the rate of such offences (cited in Cavadino and Dignan 2002).

QUESTION BREAK: EXEMPLARY SENTENCES

Suggest some (a) positive benefits and (b) negative consequences of 'exemplary sentences'.

List any crimes that you have committed or have considered committing. What would deter you from committing them again (or in the first place)?

Why do you think that young offenders who have been subject to a strict punishment regime might be more likely to reoffend?

There is a danger that deterrence can outdo itself as a justification for punishment, with too severe a punishment for a relatively minor offence pushing the offender into committing more serious ones – 'might as well be hanged for a sheep as for a lamb'. And while offenders do always run the risk of being caught, the chances of getting away with an offence (chances which are often pretty good, given the estimated amount of unrecorded and unsolved crime) will greatly weaken the deterrent effect of any punishment.

In concluding, then, it would seem fair to suggest that deterrence is a rather limited basis for penal policy. As the White Paper which preceded the 1991 Criminal Justice Act put it:

> Much crime is committed on impulse, given the opportunity presented by an open window or unlocked door, and it is committed by offenders who live from moment to moment; their crimes are as impulsive as the rest of their feckless, sad or pathetic lives. It is unrealistic to construct sentencing arrangements on the assumption that most offenders will weigh up the possibilities in advance and base their conduct on rational calculation. Often they do not.
>
> (Home Office 1990)

Impulsive offences are clearly a problem for a penal strategy of deterrence, and it could well be argued that many, if not most, crimes are not rationally premeditated.

If it were possible to measure the crime rate accurately and if there were a reduction in crime according to the statistics, it would still be difficult to relate this to the effect of particular punishments. Hudson (2003) uses driving with excess alcohol to illustrate this point. This might seem an offence which could be targeted by deterrent sentencing; and it is clear that sentences have become much harsher for this offence, with fewer fines and more prison sentences (and not just in Britain). It would also seem to be the case that less driving with excess alcohol now occurs, with the common, and police, view seeming to be that only a hard core of drunk drivers remain. However, Hudson questions whether this change in behaviour is due to the increased punishments, because as well as tougher penalties there has also been an extensive educational and moral campaign highlighting the dangers of drink-driving. She suggests that 'there seems to have been a change in public consciousness about the activity, rather than, or as well as, a fear of tougher penal consequences'. More recently, there has been similarly hard-hitting television advertising over the dangers of speeding, and it will be interesting to see if this has an effect on the public view of breaking the speed limits and on the extent of that offence.

The difficulties we have highlighted with the notion of deterrence as a justification for punishment have lent support to the argument that the probability of conviction is the one deterrent factor that is likely to have any great effect – offenders' own estimates of whether they will 'get away with it' would seem to be the crucial influence on whether an offence is committed. The actual punishment would seem to have less deterrent influence.

QUESTION BREAK

As well as the difficulties with the notion of deterrent sentencing that we have highlighted above, there are also moral objections. For example, the offender might be punished in excess of what is deserved by the offence, and, also, this approach would allow for the punishment of offences which have not been committed on the grounds that they may be in the future.

Make a case for and against an approach that would allow for some people being overly (or wrongly) punished on the grounds that this may prevent more future crime.

Retribution

In contrast to the future-oriented, utilitarian emphasis of deterrence, retribution as a philosophical justification for punishing offenders is clearly based on the past. The retributivist approach is based on the revenge motive – expressed in the supposed logic of 'an eye for an eye and a tooth for a tooth'. Historically, retribution was related to the paying back of a debt, while in the penal context it has referred to the idea of deserved punishment. It is easy to see how it is often regarded as the most important aim of punishment – certain offences deserve certain punishments, and if offenders did not receive their 'proper', deserved punishment, then surely law and order would break down? Linked with this basic notion of retribution is the belief that punishment should also demonstrate a society's condemnation of particular offences and of particular offenders; and that those offences which excite the strongest condemnation merit the most severe of punishments. While it is accepted that punishment cannot undo the harm done by an offender, it can have the potential to make victims of crime (including indirect victims such as families and friends of victims) feel better and can perhaps enable people to make sense of the senseless (in cases such as child abuse, for example).

Retributivists emphasise the denunciation aspect of punishment. The passing of a sentence acts to denounce the particular offence and can be seen as a public statement of disapproval – with the severity of the punishment demonstrating the degree of this disapproval. And it is only by pronouncing a proper and proportionate penalty that the offence can be given the disapproval that it merits.

QUESTION BREAK: PUBLIC PUNISHMENT?

The emphasis on revenge and public condemnation and disapproval suggests a case for public punishments – which used to be commonplace in previous times.

Question
What arguments can you suggest for and against public punishments?

Before considering some of the issues around the retributionary justification for and philosophy of punishment, we will refer to the way in which retribution has come back into vogue and manifested itself in recent years. For much of the twentieth century, and certainly up to the 1970s, as the study of crime and the discipline of criminology developed and spread, retribution was seen as being rather an unprogressive approach to punishment that was largely based on vengeance. The emphasis of criminal justice policy and practice during this period was on doing something positive to rehabilitate and re-integrate offenders. During the 1970s there was a return to the old retributive ideas and by the 1980s a new sort of retributionary approach, under the banner of 'just deserts', became the most influential aim of and justification for punishment. In part this was due to a feeling that the rehabilitative initiatives and efforts of the previous decades had been too lenient and partly to the concern that the indeterminate sentencing approach associated with rehabilitation (giving offenders a custodial sentence which they were only released from when they had demonstrated that they had been 'reformed') was making a mockery of sentencing (issues surrounding indeterminate sentences will be returned to when we look at rehabilitation later; see p. 22). This indeterminate sentencing, although no doubt based on admirable intentions to reform offenders, meant in practice that some offenders convicted and sentenced for relatively minor offences ended up spending excessively long periods in custody – and often longer than much more serious offenders who managed to play the system and demonstrate that they were 'reformed'. Hudson (2003) highlights how the disparity in sentences, resulting from the discretion that those working in the criminal justice system had to decide when offenders were, or were not, 'reformed', led to a strong 'back to justice' movement in England, Wales and elsewhere.

The emphasis on rehabilitation and reform of offenders in prison had an unsettling effect on the running of prisons. The fact that prisoners did not know when they would be released, and their consequent dependence on 'experts' saying that they were fit to be released, increased the tensions in prisons, particularly in the United States, where indeterminate sentences were used as a matter of course in the 1950s and 1960s.

So, by the 1970s there was a situation where 'rehabilitative' punishments were seen by some, perhaps the more critical, commentators as overly oppressive and by others, more politically to the right, as soft and ineffective. All of this helped a swing against rehabilitation and reform and towards retribution in the 1970s and beyond. As Hudson puts it:

the primary principle of new retributivism is that punishment should be commensurate to the seriousness of the offence . . . the modern version interprets commensurate as *proportionate*. What is required is that there should be a schedule of punishments in which the most serious is reserved for the most serious offences, and that penalties should be graduated throughout the scale according to offence seriousness.

(2003, p. 40)

The retributivist approach is known as *tariff* sentencing and in practice usually involves bands of sentence – for instance, the 'band' may be between three and five years, depending on the particular circumstances of the offence.

This emphasis on the relationship between seriousness of offence and form of punishment leads to the obvious question of how offences should be ranked in terms of seriousness. In attempting to grapple with this issue, the 1991 Criminal Justice Act set out three broad divisions of seriousness: so minor that a discharge or fine is appropriate; serious enough to warrant a community punishment; and so serious that only a custodial sentence was appropriate.

QUESTION BREAK: 'JUST DESERTS'

While it may not be so hard to agree on those offences which are 'so minor' and those which are 'so serious', it is perhaps more tricky to try to rank those of medium seriousness. After all, most of us would be happy to rank rape as more serious than shoplifting, but would be less sure of ranking burglary in relation to embezzlement.

Question

What do you think should be the key factors that determine the seriousness of an offence?

Although there are different retributive approaches to punishment, there is a general agreement that punishment has to be backward-looking in important respects and that the infliction of suffering through punishment is justified because of what the offender has already done. Retribution as a justification for punishment requires that the amount of punishment must fit the wrong done and, therefore, that the offender should get no more than their 'just deserts'.

Walker (1991) sees retribution as offering the certainty that the deterrent and utilitarian approaches cannot provide. Punishments that are based on retribution will at the least ensure that offenders get what they deserve. However, while the retributive justification for punishment is clearly based on what an offender has done, it does not follow that it is unproblematic. As we have discussed above, the idea of deserved punishment implies that there should be an equivalence between the seriousness of the offence and the penalty received. In particular, the gravity of the offence, measured in terms of amount of harm done, is generally regarded as the key factor in determining the severity of penalty. Harm done, though, is not a clear-cut determinant. It is conventionally accepted that the extent to which harm was intended is a variable that should affect the sort of punishment received, so that an accidental killing is not punished as if it were murder even though the end result may be the same. Furthermore, there are offences that might cause only a minimal degree of harm yet which would be generally seen as meriting severe punishment: while an attempted murder or unsuccessful terrorist attack may not do any actual harm, such offences would be seen as deserving a punishment almost as severe as a successful murder or attack. As Walker eloquently puts it, 'incompetence does not mitigate'.

Although few would argue that some harms are clearly greater than others – injuries that cause permanent disabilities are obviously distinguishable from minor cuts or bruises, for instance – harm is not just a physical concept. The psychological harm that is caused to victims is less easy to quantify. While it may be possible to 'rank' thefts in terms of the amount of money involved, this ranking will not necessarily relate to the harm felt by the victim. Someone who loses all of their savings, however limited these may be, is likely to suffer more than better-off victims who lose a similar amount in real terms; and in a similar vein, stealing from a large shop or company is liable to cause very little in the way of personal suffering.

As well as it being difficult to quantify the harm experienced by the direct victims of offences, a by-product of punishment is that other 'innocent' people can unintentionally suffer from the punishment of an offender. Imprisonment will often cause hardship and distress to the innocent partners and/or children of an offender; and fines may lead to the dependants of offenders suffering perhaps to an even greater extent than the offenders themselves.

QUESTION BREAK: MITIGATING FACTORS AND SENTENCING

Although failing to succeed in committing a crime through incompetence would not normally be seen as a mitigating factor that should lessen the severity of a punishment, there are other factors which are taken into account when sentencing offenders.

Give examples of the sort of factors which you feel should be taken into account when punishing offenders; and explain why you feel they should affect a sentence.

You might consider factors that relate to (a) the offender; (b) the victim; and (c) the offence itself.

We have tried to highlight some of the difficulties with applying the retributive approach to punishment and with the notion that certain crimes deserve certain punishments. Before moving on to examine the idea that punishment can be used to reform or rehabilitate the offender, we will consider a more general concern about and criticism of retribution – that it is nothing more than vengeance.

Both retribution and vengeance share what Nozick (1981) has termed 'a common structure'. They both involve dispensing harm and/or deprivation for a reason. He does, though, distinguish between the two in that retribution is done in response to a crime or some other wrongdoing while revenge can follow something that is not necessarily intended (e.g. an accidental injury). Also, there is usually some limitation placed on the extent of retribution, while revenge can be unlimited; retribution involves punishment but also offers protection from over-punishment through the just deserts model. Retribution could, then, be thought of as a sort of vengeance, but one which is bound by a notion of proportionality and of the rights of the individual. In a similar vein, retribution should involve impartiality and should lack the personal element often implied in revenge. This personal element might even involve gaining pleasure, or at least satisfaction, from the suffering of the 'wrongdoer'.

Deterrence, retribution and capital punishment

Arguments over the effectiveness or otherwise of deterrent sentences have been a central element in the debate over capital punishment. Advocates of capital punishment have argued that the death penalty would have a deterrent effect and would, as a result, lead to a reduction in serious crime, and at a simple, common-sense level many might feel that it would be a better deterrent than any other penalty. However, this view presupposes that the potential murderer rationally calculates the advantages and disadvantages of murder and would be deterrable if the disadvantages were believed to be sufficiently strong. A problem with this view is that many, if not most, murders are not planned or calculated but are committed on impulse, perhaps during a fight or while in a fit of rage, and would probably be little affected by the threat of capital punishment. And even the supposedly rational murderer – the terrorist, or the person who kills in the course of a robbery, for instance – is not necessarily easily deterrable. In most cases such would-be murderers will believe they have a good chance of getting away with their crime.

These problems with justifying capital punishment on the grounds of its deterrent potential does not mean that such a punishment has no deterrent effect – there is, though, a lack of reliable evidence of just when deterrence might work, and there is little evidence that long-term imprisonment would be a weaker deterrent than capital punishment. However, there are other arguments concerning capital punishment that have nothing to do with its deterrent potential, and these arguments relate to the retributionary aim of punishment. Indeed, capital punishment can perhaps more easily be justified in terms of retribution – someone has killed and so deserves to be killed themselves. In his examination of arguments over capital punishment, Wolfgang (1998) questions whether any real equilibrium would be achieved by the 'life for a life' approach to such punishment. Retribution could be said to require an equal pain being inflicted on offenders, which raises the question of how the state could inflict an equal kind of pain – the sort of torturous executions that happened in the past would be out of line with modern, Western ideas (in the United States, for instance, the killing of offenders is done clinically and under medically protective circumstances). Taking this argument further, Wolfgang asks whether societies would tolerate other punishments of the body in response to what offenders have done – for instance, stabbing or throwing acid in the face of people convicted of assault-type offences would be considered completely inappropriate, which, he argues, would seem to question a retributionary rationale for the death penalty.

Of course, the 'just deserts' retributionary approach does not mean the punishment should be exactly like the crime; it means that there should be equivalencies of seriousness of punishment. In Britain, equivalencies of pain in kind are looked for; and the common commodity of pain is deprivation of liberty measured in lengths of time spent in prison. And in terms of pain, it would be argued that death ends all pain and the pain of imprisonment is greater, with the lingering reminder of deprived liberty providing a more enduring pain – a point made by the famous Enlightenment thinker Beccaria in the eighteenth century: 'the death penalty expends its total influence in a single moment . . . many look on death with a firm and calm regard . . . [however, in prison] the evildoer begins his sufferings instead of terminating them' (cited in Wolfgang 1998).

Wolfgang finishes his discussion by highlighting a comment made by Sister Helen Prejean after her eyewitness account of the death penalty, where she says, 'you could say "they deserve to die", but the key moral question is "do we deserve to kill them?" '.

QUESTION BREAK: RETRIBUTION AND THE DEATH PENALTY

The death penalty is perhaps the most obvious example of a retributionary punishment which clearly meets the desire for revenge – if someone has killed, then it can be argued that they deserve to be killed themselves. And murder is a crime totally condemned by society and so generally seen as requiring the severest possible punishment. However, the retributionary argument is not generally put forward as the most important reason for the re-introduction of capital punishment; in spite of the uncertainties over the deterrent effect of punishment, it is that issue that has tended to be the focus of the death penalty debate.

Questions

List the philosophical arguments for and against capital punishment and consider which of the aims of punishment they most closely relate to.

What other arguments are there for and against this punishment (e.g. you may consider practical rather than philosophical points).

To what extent have your views on capital punishment altered since you started studying criminal justice?

Rehabilitation

As with deterrence, and in contrast to retribution, rehabilitative aims of punishment can be seen as future oriented and, therefore, having a utilitarian rationale and appeal. The rehabilitative approach is based on the belief that people can change, that they are never beyond reform. Thus offenders can be taught how to be 'normal', law-abiding citizens; and punishment can be organised so that they will be less likely to reoffend. In these brief introductory lines the terms 'rehabilitation' and 'reform' have been referred to, and in the rest of this section those terms will be used regularly and, to a certain extent, interchangeably. Strictly speaking, however, the terms refer to different approaches and processes. Reform relates to an individual offender being given the opportunity and space to change him- or herself, and being persuaded to do so, while rehabilitation involves a more planned, regulated and imposed treatment, perhaps in the form of a supervisor overseeing an offender pursuing a training or employment programme and monitoring his or her progress. Thus reform has some similarities with deterrence in that it works through the will of the individual offender, whereas rehabilitation implies that the offender is not acting from his or her own free will but is expected to respond to attempts from outside to change him- or herself. A difference with both these approaches is that reform and rehabilitation aim to make the offender a more useful, productive and 'better' member of society, whereas deterrence is primarily concerned with whether the offender commits further offences.

In general terms, the focus of these approaches and philosophies is on how punishment can be used to 'correct' an offender's behaviour; and Walker (1991) uses the term 'correction' in preference to either rehabilitation or reform – as he puts it, 'correction is a very non-committal word, very wisely adopted by penologists in the United States'. Here, though, we will stick to the more conventional and generally used terms of reform and rehabilitation.

The broad aim of reform became of increased importance in the British penal system in the late eighteenth and early nineteenth centuries. In this period of the Industrial Revolution and the move from absolutist to more democratic forms of government in Europe, there was a growing demand for labour (particularly in the new factories of early industrial Britain), and so punishments which equipped offenders with self-discipline and a desire to work were popularly advocated. It was around this time that the notion of imprisonment as a punishment developed, with the prison changing from being a place that just held people awaiting trial or deportation towards being a method of punishment in its own right, as an alternative to the death penalty, transportation and other sentences. Since the Middle Ages, local jails had performed this holding function – including holding debtors until they were able to pay their debts, as well as those awaiting trial or exile. These jails were privately run, with deplorable conditions the norm, particularly for those who could not pay their jailers for services. There was no segregation of women and men or of tried and untried prisoners, with racketeering and extortion rife. (See pp. 187–192 for a fuller discussion of the history of imprisonment.)

In the face of the appalling conditions and abuses, the authorities were persuaded that 'a well-ordered, disciplined, clean and properly managed form of confinement was required' (Mathews 1999). This led to the development of new, refurbished prisons in the early nineteenth century and to a different view of the purpose of imprisonment. Sentencing offenders to a period of imprisonment was seen as offering the potential for reform as well as being for punishment; this contrasts with the contemporary view that sees 'reformative' punishments such as community orders and probation as 'alternatives to prison', with the implication that reform and imprisonment do not go hand in hand. The prisons built in the major industrial cities in Britain and elsewhere in the nineteenth century were designed to reform as well as incarcerate. It was believed that this reform would occur through a combination of work and solitary contemplation, and the model for these prisons was based on a sort of monastic ideal, with individual cells allowing time for reflection and penance after the prisoner had finished a hard day's labour in a prison workshop.

The monastic style of the new prisons was one element of the strong religious influence on the methods and forms of punishment; and this influence has usually emphasised the reform of the offender. However, the early, religiously motivated attempts to reform often caused as much hardship for prisoners as they had faced under the previous, corrupt prison regimes. The early Victorian reformers, for instance, felt that prison should be a place where the offender might became a reformed and God-fearing person. Thus they advocated long periods of solitary confinement during which time the prisoners could examine their souls and consciences, spend hours in prayer, read (if they could) the Bibles that were made available in all cells and emerge purified.

The differing interpretations for the development of prisons and imprisonment at this period will be considered later (in Chapter 7); however, it would be useful to say a little about the early prison reform developments here. The work of John Howard, who examined and then described and catalogued the state of prisons in the late eighteenth century, was a major impetus for prison reform. His detailed account of prison life painted a graphic picture of squalid, disease-ridden conditions and led him to recommend sanitary and separate accommodation for prisoners, the introduction of useful labour and the banning of alcohol in prisons. Howard's pioneering survey of prison conditions was a major influence on the sort of new prisons that emerged in the nineteenth century. As Priestley puts it:

> In order to understand why so many Victorian prisoners were locked up in these gloomy rooms and forced to endure absolute solitary confinement that might last anything from a few days to eighteen months . . . it is necessary to look back at what went on in the unreformed prisons of the late eighteenth and early nineteenth centuries.
>
> (1985, p. 33)

QUESTION BREAK: VICTORIAN PRISONS – THE SEPARATE SYSTEM

Read the extract from Priestley's study *Victorian Prison Lives* and consider the questions below:

> The 1835 Select Committee on Gaols and Houses of Correction closely questioned the governor of Newgate about stories that 'there was gambling carried on all day long' . . . and that prisoners were 'boasting of their former robberies, some cursing and swearing, telling of obscene stories, and some singing vile songs. . . . Here and there these ribaldries were lubricated with quantities of beer. . . .

> It was a desire to remove these sources of corruption that led the 1835 committee to propose fundamental changes in the English prison system. Their views were not in the least revolutionary; their origins can be located in a tradition that predated the work even of John Howard. . . . Condemnation of these evils [of prison life] was so widespread as to constitute an almost unanimous expression of enlightened opinion in the early part of the nineteenth century. . . .

The recommendations of the select committee started with the proposition that 'One uniform System of Prison Discipline be established in every Gaol and House of Correction in England and Wales'....As to the nature of the 'uniform system' the committee wished to see established, the intellectual climate of the time presented them with 'two principal plans...the silent and the separate'....Under the Silent System the prisoners are collected in masses for work and other purposes, but are forbidden to speak or hold any intercourse; under the Separate System they are precluded from intercourse, by being kept not only in silence, but separation at all times....

The Separatist plan 'won'...with a decision to construct a new national penitentiary at Pentonville along 'separate' lines....The design of the new penitentiary was entrusted to Captain Joshua Jebb....In his eyes, the virtue of the separate system was that 'in depriving a prisoner of the contaminating influences arising from being associated with his fellow prisoners, all the good influences which can be brought to bear upon his character are substituted for them'....

One of the reasons for the immediate success of the 'separate' system was its capacity to appeal simultaneously to different and often conflicting constituencies of interest.

(Priestley 1985, pp. 33–37)

Questions

What do you think the 'different and conflicting constituencies of interest' that Priestley refers to in the final sentence of the extract might be?

How might the 'separate' system (a) help reform offenders; (b) work against such reform?

More recent advocates of the rehabilitative philosophy of punishment have promoted a treatment, rather than a spiritual, model of reform. Alongside the establishment of the 'human sciences' of psychology and sociology as reputable academic subjects in the late nineteenth century, the new and distinct discipline of criminology emerged. This reflected a greater interest in studying the reasons why particular people offended and in the classifying of offenders into various categories and types. This new scientific knowledge could then be applied for the purpose of reforming such offenders. The work of Cesare Lombroso, who is generally agreed to be one of the key founders of the science of criminology, was particularly important in assessing and creating typologies of criminals. Lombroso was an Italian army physician who argued, in his famous study *L'uomo delinquente* (1876), that criminals were 'born so', and claimed his research proved that the criminal was a throwback to primitive, aggressive human types who could be recognised by their physical characteristics, particularly facial characteristics such as prominent foreheads, large jaws and ears, and shifty eyes. Lombroso's work, and his rather bizarre descriptions of criminals, has been criticised and dismissed by modern theorists – and his method of examining only those offenders who were in prison and then basing a general theory of crime around this evidence is clearly methodologically flawed. However, the growing development of a science of criminology and the growing role of doctors and psychiatrists in diagnosing and treating offenders illustrated the move to a treatment model of reform and rehabilitation and away from the old religiously motivated and driven approaches. As Mathews (1999) put it, 'Crime, like madness, was seen by many medical professionals as arising from a lack of self-control, and as a deviation from the path of reason.'

The development of the 'new' punishment of imprisonment along with the growth of the scientific study of crime provided a strong impetus for the introduction of more constructive and humane punishments both within and outside of the prison. The prison rules that were established in the early prisons invariably required that prisoners be engaged in useful work. While the extent to which the work was useful might be debated, there was a clear commitment to instilling in prisoners the discipline of regular work – so much so that where productive and useful labour was not available, a range of 'work for the sake of it' practices and schemes were devised and introduced. The treadmill, for instance, was widely used in nineteenth-century prisons; it was attractive to prison authorities because, as Mathews (1999) points out, 'it provided a form of exercise that could be used by the uneducated, while the pace and resistance of the wheel could be controlled'. The lack of skill and education of prisoners did, though, cause difficulties in providing useful work, as did the fact that many prisoners were sentenced to relatively short spells of imprisonment: according to Mathews, nearly two-thirds of those sentenced by magistrates in the 1860s were given terms of a month or less.

Although short sentences and the lack of skills of the prison population are still evident, even if to a lesser degree than in the mid-nineteenth century, the impetus towards more constructive forms of punishment has continued and has gained strong support from important and influential pressure groups such as Amnesty International and the Howard League, which have campaigned against unjust and inhumane punishments in more recent times. However, in spite of the promotion of rehabilitation and reform, revenge and deterrence as justification for punishment are still widely supported, and public anxiety and panic is easily aroused over any supposed 'softness' in modern punishments. Whenever there are moves to release, or even discuss the release of, widely condemned prisoners there is invariably and immediately a massive, media-orchestrated public outcry. Before her death in November 2002, any consideration of parole for Myra Hindley, the Moors murderer, caused so much public and media anger that it is unlikely any Home Secretary would have contemplated it. It would seem to be the case that rehabilitation is associated by many with softness, which in turn is associated with political weakness, and which arguably has not given it much of a chance as a philosophical underpinning for punishment.

We will now consider briefly some of the criticisms of the rehabilitative aim of punishment.

First, there is a danger that offenders are dealt with in a degrading, or at the least patronising, manner – almost as if they are animals to be trained. Given that the medical or treatment models of rehabilitation are based on the idea that criminal tendencies can be 'cured' by changing the personality of offenders, and in particular by restricting or taking away their capacity for moral choice, it is hardly surprising that such methods can appear to be demeaning. Although treatments based on behaviourist techniques, such as aversion therapy, as well as more clearly medically based approaches, such as chemically reducing the libido of offenders, might be provided in the name of treatment, and so be for the offender's own good, they can still be criticised as inhumane.

As well as the sort of approaches mentioned above, which might be seen as 'assaulting the personality' of offenders, the rehabilitative approaches to punishment invariably involve indeterminate sentences. These are open-ended sentences where the length of time that is spent in custody is dependent on the judgement of prison administrators and other experts. Here the punishment is less closely related to the particular offence committed and more about deciding whether and when the offender is rehabilitated and so harmless, or at least able to be returned to 'normal' society. Although it is more a feature of the system of criminal justice in the United States, there are elements of this approach in the way the parole system works in Britain, with prisoners released on licence ahead of their expected release date on the advice of professional experts. A danger with these sort of sentences is that they can encourage offenders to 'play the system', to do all they can to show those who decide on release that they are reformed – with there being an obvious temptation for such offenders to be less than honest and to try to give the impression they are reformed.

QUESTION BREAK

To what extent do you think that an offender's behaviour during a sentence (for instance while in prison) should determine when s/he is released?

Suggest arguments for and against the use of indeterminate sentences.

Of course, it is extremely difficult to assess how effective rehabilitative approaches are. It is clear that there are some successes, but the 'success' of a programme or initiative for a particular offender can never be guaranteed; something may work for some offenders but not others. We will look at initiatives in 'restorative justice' as an example of rehabilitation shortly, after a general comment on the way in which the policies adopted towards the punishment of offenders have demonstrated a balance or see-sawing between reform/rehabilitative and retributivist themes. One or other of these broad themes or approaches has tended to become fashionable and dominant at particular times. In the 1950s and 1960s, for instance, the rehabilitative model was in vogue and a range of new, reform-based approaches to dealing with offenders were introduced, including parole, suspended sentences and community service orders. However, there was no hard evidence that these 'reformist' initiatives were any more effective in reducing reoffending than more obviously punitive measures. By the late 1970s the notion of rehabilitation had become discredited, with the emphasis on policy moving away from reform, a move reflected in the hardline approach to punishment advocated by politicians and government ministers and characterised by the introduction of 'short, sharp shock' sentences in detention centres in 1980 and, more recently, the support for adopting hardline initiatives from the United States such as 'boot camps' and 'three strikes and you're out' legislation.

The concern in the 1970s in particular about the extent to which rehabilitation was 'working' led to the emergence of what has been termed the 'justice' or 'just deserts' model of punishment. As mentioned on p. 13, rehabilitative, treatment-based approaches had led logically to indeterminate sentences, based on the notion that when a treatment had been shown to 'work', the punishment could end. This was seen as giving too much discretion to 'experts' working in the criminal justice system, and the justice model argued that punishment should be based on the seriousness of the offences, so that all offenders received their 'just deserts'. In addition, the rehabilitative approach was seen as inherently unfair in that it treated offences of similar seriousness in very different ways – so, for instance, two offenders could be found guilty of the same offence (indeed, they could be co-defendants in the very same case) and end up receiving quite different sentences and, in some cases, spending widely differing lengths of time in custody. As evidence of the impact of the justice model on penal policy in Britain, Cavadino and Dignan (2002) highlight the abolition in 1982 of indeterminate Borstal sentences for young offenders (who were released any time between six months and two years, according to how they had 'responded' to their punishment) and their replacement with fixed-term sentences.

In recent years there has been a revival of rehabilitative approaches, but according to Cavadino and Dignan the claims made for them are now more modest. The idea that methods of punishment could work almost independently of the offenders has been replaced with an emphasis on how a particular punishment can be used to help offenders improve their behaviour. These ideas characterise the notion of restorative justice, which we will consider here as an example of newer rehabilitative initiatives. Restorative justice is most closely associated with the principle of reparation – based on the notion that crime affects communities and victims, who should therefore have a part to play in administering justice. This approach usually involves the offender being brought face to face with someone they have harmed and thereby confronting what they have done.

When serving as Chief Constable of Thames Valley Police, Charles Pollard introduced a community conferencing scheme which gave victims 'a part to play in the system', and he was a strong advocate of restorative justice. He saw the Thames Valley initiative as a

> hugely powerful thing. . . . This is about coming face to face with the harm they have caused, and that has the impact of shaming the offender. But what's important is that it is private and is what we call reintegrative shaming which means that once that person has really understood the impact they have had on others they are very ready to really think about how they are going to change their behaviour in future. They are ready to think about the damage to the people they have harmed whether by compensation, certainly by apologising, maybe doing some work for them.
>
> (Pollard 1998, p. 14)

Pollard goes on to point out that the criminal justice system does not have a mechanism for people to apologise for their behaviour; and that an apology should be the first and most important part of any reparation.

With regard to compensation more generally, it would seem to be logical to try to compensate the injured party and for the offender to do that in some way – and if there is no clearly identifiable or individual victim, then the community can be compensated through some sort of community service undertaken by the offender or by a fine paid into public funds. However, this notion of reparation or compensation is not always easy to apply. Offenders may not have the means to repay the victim; and the extent to which parents should be responsible for compensating for the behaviour of their children is debatable. However, such an approach can be appropriate in certain situations. In many offences the offender and victim will know one another, and if they are brought together to reach a settlement it can be better for all parties, as well as cutting down on court workloads. It is an approach that is probably particularly suited to minor crimes but, like other new approaches to punishment, is not likely to gain favour with the general public or the popular media, who will see it as too soft a response to crime.

This sort of critical response to new, rehabilitative approaches to punishment highlights a basic problem that is faced by any penal system: the lack of success of harsh, retributive punishments might encourage reform measures, but in turn these are liable to be felt by many to be not a 'proper' response to the harm caused by offenders. As a result, there tends to be the see-sawing between reform- and retributive-based punishments that we referred to on p. 22.

In assessing the extent to which rehabilitation 'works', Walker (1991) points to the difficulty of ever being sure why a particular offender ceases to offend. There are all sorts of possible reasons: the stigma of being caught, the unpleasant memory of the punishment, the influence of family, friends or social workers. Even offenders who appear to have changed their behaviour may well still be involved in offending but are better able to avoid detection. However, the difficulty with assessing these approaches to punishment does not mean that 'nothing works', but rather that there is no guarantee that particular punishments work as they are intended to and that some approaches may work with some offenders but not with others. This is illustrated by the methods used at Grendon Prison. Grendon was established in the 1960s as an institution that would treat and rehabilitate serious offenders; it attempted to bring a therapeutic approach to the treatment of non-psychotic recidivist offenders. Although its success rate in reducing repeat offending among serious offenders is better than that in more conventional regimes, it worked only with some offenders: 40 per cent of the prisoners who had been through the Grendon programme reoffended within two years (*Behind Bars – Grendon Prison*, BBC television programme, 2000).

Summary

In this chapter we have considered some major aims and philosophies of punishment and the issues and debates they have raised. Perhaps not surprisingly, this discussion has uncovered a great deal of uncertainty as to what works and how; and perhaps it is unrealistic to hope to find one approach to punishment which will be generally seen as just and effective and so widely supported. A basic reason why punishment poses such dilemmas is that it involves treating other people unpleasantly. We have seen that there are a number of grounds and justifications that can be put forward for punishing offenders, including to deter others, to denounce, because it is deserved and to reform or rehabilitate. It is this last one, the focus of the final section of this chapter, that is especially tricky because it is seemingly for the benefit of offenders yet still involves forcing them to do something – and something which will be inconvenient and probably not chosen voluntarily (pursuing some form of treatment programme or undertaking work for no financial reward, for instance). This ambivalence is particularly illustrated when attempts are made to rehabilitate offenders within custodial institutions.

So, there are no clear answers to the question of 'why punish?'. Punishment involves using legal authority to do things which would otherwise be morally wrong – and with no guarantee that those things will achieve what they are intended to. The basic justifications we have considered here both contradict and overlap with one another. Retribution looks back and aims to punish in proportion to the offence committed; deterrence and rehabilitation look forward and aim to reduce future offending. And these different rationales can exist together within particular punishments – so that a prison sentence can be passed with the intention of being retributionary, of deterring offenders and of offering rehabilitation.

QUESTION BREAK: THE *OBSERVER* CRIME AND JUSTICE DEBATE

Tough on crime, tough on the causes of crime. But that was only half of it. Tough on criminals – there's the full story. Lock them up (71,000 of them). Make sure the good-for-nothings are so far from home and family that regular visits are near impossible or, at least, financially crippling. Cut the training and education budget, so that their spell inside will really brand them second-class citizens incapable of holding any job apart from sweeping streets or washing cars. . . .

Mete out this kind of treatment to the average healthy Anglo-Saxon, and you'll find they develop a bit of an attitude problem; but about half of prisoners have the reading skills of an 11-year-old, and more than 70 per cent suffer from at least two mental disorders: when these people come out after a spell inside, is it any wonder that, in two out of three cases, they are re-convicted of another crime within two years?

This is a primitive, short-sighted prisons policy, as Cherie Booth warned in *Inside Time*, the newspaper for prisoners. . . . Today's prisoners will one day sit next to you on the Tube, or fix your car. If their time inside has offered them nothing but hardship and humiliation, how will they view you?

Given the certainty that prisoners will be recycled in our society, Cherie Booth's warning should be heeded. But in Britain's culture of retribution . . . [it] is sure to give rise to cries of horror. . . . They're guilty, aren't they? Let them rot in hell. They've been tried and convicted: we've done our duty by them. . . .

This indifference to the prisoner's future is shown in our failure to invest in programmes or schemes that can enable inmates to turn their lives around.

A few work apprenticeship schemes exist . . . but our failure to reproduce such schemes throughout the prison system, or to protest the repeated budget cuts that have shrunk education programmes behind bars, have reduced rehabilitation to an empty word, and turned every prison sentence into the first step in a campaign of retribution. . . .

It's an eye-for-an-eye mentality that betrays how, beneath the civilised arguments of defence and prosecution, an Old Testament heart beats within the body of British justice. It's an attitude betrayed by the hysterical headlines every time the debate about Myra Hindley's release resurfaces; and by the row over the freeing of James Bulger's murderers, when threats to the boys' lives prompted police to move them and their families, and issue them with new identities. No-one believed in their redemption: no matter how many years Myra languished inside, no matter how young Robert Thompson and Jon Venables had been when they perpetrated their crime. Given their faith in this tough and unforgiving philosophy, can we really expect people to lobby for more schemes to train prisoners? Can we hope for a more generous budget for education behind bars? Once you've been convicted, it would seem, you've forfeited all rights to our concern.

(C. Odone, *Observer*, 7 July 2002)

Questions

What evidence is provided to demonstrate the popularity of the retributive mentality?

Why do you think that rehabilitation does not easily gain public support?

What might be done to change the public's attitude to rehabilitation?

How might retribution and rehabilitation coexist within a criminal justice system?

Further reading

Hudson, B. (2003) *Understanding Justice: An Introduction to Ideas, Perspectives and Controversies in Modern Penal Theory*, Milton Keynes: Open University Press. This is the second edition of a very successful text that summarises the major philosophical ideas of retribution, rehabilitation and incapacitation and discusses their strengths and weaknesses.

McLaughlin, E., Fergusson, R., Hughes, G. and Westmarland, L. (2003) *Restorative Justice: Critical Issues*, London: Sage. This edited collection traces the development of restorative justice (which was introduced in the discussion of rehabilitation in this chapter) and includes examples of current practices and policies from around the world.

Walker, N. (1991) *Why Punish?*, Oxford: Oxford University Press. A short, thought-provoking book that considers the different justifications for, and aims of, punishment, grappling with the moral issues and dilemmas that they raise.

The journal *Punishment and Society: The International Journal of Penology* was launched in 1999 and is an excellent source of recent research and theorising that is relevant to the topics examined in this chapter and in Chapter 2 on theories of punishment.

2   Theories of punishment

Introduction

In this chapter the focus moves from the philosophical justifications for punishment to a consideration of some of the theoretical explanations for punishment. In particular, we will examine what social theorists have said about the nature and the role of punishment in society.

While moral and legal philosophers have examined the different aims or justifications for punishment, social scientists have centred their explanations on the relationship between particular societies and the forms of punishment – or penal system – that characterise them. In considering this issue, the major social theorists have tried to explain a movement from physical punishments (punishments of the body such as execution and mutilations) to punishments of the mind and soul (especially, forms of custodial punishment). They have explored the role and purpose of punishment in relation to the forms of authority prevalent in different societies, an approach which has involved a consideration of the law and legal authority. As we will see later, early, classic social theorists such as Durkheim and Weber emphasised how punishment and the law helped to hold societies together, while Marx saw it as supporting and maintaining the interests of the powerful.

Hudson points out that philosophical approaches to punishment have not concerned themselves with

> why, in different places or at different times, societies use different kinds of penal strategy. Why, for example, did punishments such as ducking stools and stocks go out of fashion? Why have so many industrial democracies given up capital punishment? Why has imprisonment become such an important form of punishment?
>
> (2003, p. 95)

It is questions such as these, about penal strategy, that are the central concern of sociological theories of punishment. And social theorists have tried to relate these questions to some of the philosophical justifications for punishment considered in the previous chapter. Why, for instance, has retribution seemed to fit the mood of the day at certain times, while at other times rehabilitation has been favoured? Why at some periods is there a greater tolerance and optimism while at other times vengeance comes to the fore?

Although the theorists mentioned above are not solely sociologists, in this chapter we will look at what are generally taken to be the major sociological theories of punishment. The approaches we will look at are:

- the role of punishment in promoting social solidarity – the work and influence of Durkheim and Weber;
- punishment as a part of a class-based process of economic and social control – the Marxist approach;
- the relationship between punishment, power and regulation – Foucault.

These theoretical approaches examine punishment in social terms, rather than as a mechanism for the control of crime. In his comprehensive discussion of theories of punishment, Garland (1990) points out that the specific forms and institutions of punishment, such as prisons or community service orders, are social artefacts that reflect particular cultural standards and styles. Just as styles of building or music cannot be explained solely in terms of their obvious purposes – of providing shelter or entertainment – so punishment has to be considered in a historical context and as a cultural and social phenomenon.

What the sociology of punishment shows us is that penal policies and goals have to be seen in relation to other areas of social life, such as the economic system of society or the form of government that has evolved. As Hudson puts it:

> Sociological writing on punishment has been focused on penal change and development; on the relationship between punishment and other aspects of social life; on the functions punishment performs for various sections of society; and on the ideas and expectations people have of punishment.
>
> (2003, p. 96)

It is important to keep these general notions and points in mind when considering the theories of punishment that have been developed by social theorists. The work of Durkheim, Foucault and others has to be seen as part of a more general interest in and questioning about the way in which order and authority are maintained in society. Indeed, questions of social order, and how it is maintained and transmitted from one generation to the next, have always been at the core of sociological theorising in general.

The role of punishment in promoting social solidarity: the work and influence of Durkheim and Weber

Emile Durkheim is one of the key founding figures in sociology; in particular, he was one of the first scholars to differentiate sociology from other branches of social and political philosophy. A brief overview of his general sociological perspective and an introduction to some of the key terms he used in his work will help provide some background and context for discussing his analysis of punishment. His approach to understanding society was to look at how it had an existence and a reality apart from the individuals who made it up. For instance, he looked at how social rules and relationships influence the behaviour of the individual members of society, at how people behave in accordance with social rules (even when no one is observing them), and at how the existence of social rules forms a culture which gives each society its distinctive character. These general points illustrate the central idea behind Durkheim's sociology and, therefore, his theorising: that the individual is born of society, rather than the society of individuals. For Durkheim, then, the society has primacy over the individual. This can be seen in his emphasising the priority of the whole over the parts and his argument that individual phenomena had to be explained by the state of the collectivity (or society).

In looking at the nature of modern industrial society, Durkheim focused on the moral basis of social order and stability – the basis of what he termed social solidarity. He argued that without the regulation of society, individuals would attempt to satisfy their own desires and wishes without regard to their fellows. This societal regulation had, he believed, to be based on a set of shared values; and a working society required that the individuals within it accepted these common values. Durkheim called this common set of values the collective conscience, which he defined as 'the totality of beliefs and sentiments common to average citizens of the same society'.

For Durkheim, the achievement of social life among people, the existence of social order and social solidarity, is ensured by collective standards of behaviour and values. Such social solidarity is crucial for the existence of society; however, the particular form of solidarity is not fixed and will vary with the changing forms of society. Durkheim explored the changing nature of social solidarity from early, pre-modern societies to complex, modern ones in his first major study, *The Division of Labour in Society* (1960 (1893)).

Within this general approach to theorising about the nature of society, punishment was one of the central objects of Durkheim's sociological analysis. He saw punishment as representing the collective conscience of society at work, and a detailed examination of it would, he argued, provide an insight into the moral and social life of the particular society. Durkheim focused on punishment because he felt that the ways in which a society chooses to punish would provide an important indicator to that society's culture – punishment was viewed as one of the key indices of a society's culture. He was also interested in the functions that punishment might fulfil for the maintenance of social order and for the reinforcement of the culture of a society. The punishing of lawbreakers, then, was not just, or even mainly, about controlling crime.

So, for Durkheim, social order was based on a core of shared values and moralities; and punishment provided a clear illustration of this moral nature of social order. These ideas about social order and punishment were first elaborated by Durkheim in *The Division of Labour in Society*, with changes in the nature of punishment seen as reflecting changes in the nature of social morality and social solidarity. His analysis of the relationship between the punishment of crime and the maintenance of moral and social order begins by looking at crime and, although our focus is on theories of punishment, it is useful to consider briefly his discussion of crime. Crimes are acts which violate the society's collective conscience; they violate its moral code, and this violation produces a punitive reaction. To put it another way, crimes are seen as moral outrages which lead to a demand that they be punished. In Durkheim's words, 'crime brings together upright consciences and concentrates them'; it provides the occasion for the collective expression of shared moral feelings.

Crime, then, can be understood only in relation to the particular social context; it is simply an act that is prohibited by the collective conscience of the particular society. And the relative nature of crime means that it can be defined only in terms of the state of the collective conscience of the society in question; as Aron (1970) points out, the fact that an act which one society called a crime might seem quite innocent to observers several centuries after the event, or observers belonging to a different society, is of no importance to Durkheim.

> Sociologically, to call someone a criminal does not imply that we consider him guilty in relation to God or our own conception of justice. The criminal is simply the man in society who has refused to obey the laws of the city.
>
> (Aron 1970, p. 28)

Durkheim's approach to crime and the collective conscience of society is considered in the following question break.

QUESTION BREAK: CRIME AND THE COLLECTIVE CONSCIENCE

In the first place crime is normal because a society exempt from it is utterly impossible. Crime consists of an act that offends certain very strong collective sentiments. . . . Imagine a society of saints, a perfect cloister of exemplary individuals. Crimes will there be unknown; but faults which appear venial to the layman will create there the same scandal that the ordinary offense does in ordinary consciousness. If this society has the power to judge and punish, it will define these acts as criminal and treat them as such. For the same reason, the perfect and upright man judges his smallest failing with a severity that the majority reserve for acts more truly in the nature of an offense. . . .

Crime is, then, necessary; it is bound up with the fundamental conditions of all social life, and by that very fact it is useful, because these conditions of which it is a part are themselves indispensable to the normal evolution of morality and law. . . .

Crime itself plays a useful role in this evolution. Crime implies not only that the way remains open to necessary changes but that in certain cases it directly prepares these changes. According to Athenian law, Socrates was a criminal. However, his crime, namely, the independence of his thought, rendered a service not only to humanity but to his country. . . . Nor is the case of Socrates unique, it is reproduced periodically in history. It would never have been possible to establish the freedom of thought we now enjoy if the regulations prohibiting it had not been violated. At that time, however, the violation was a crime. . . . From this point of view the fundamental facts of criminality present themselves to us in an entirely new light.

> Contrary to current ideas, the criminal no longer seems a totally unsociable being, a sort of parasitic element. On the contrary, he plays a definite role in social life.
>
> (Durkheim 1964 (1895), pp. 67–72)

Questions

What positive and useful functions of crime are suggested by Durkheim?

Suggest any other social functions that crime might perform.

To return to Durkheim's analysis of punishment. The existence of social morality and social solidarity makes punishment inevitable and necessary, in that it reaffirms and strengthens the moral and social bonds. Of course, punishment is not the only process that does this; religion, education and family life all help to strengthen the collective conscience and to promote social cohesion. However, formal punishment is given a special place in Durkheim's analysis.

So far, we have considered Durkheim's general approach to punishment and its role without relating it to particular societies and the notion of social change. Durkheim acknowledged that the nature and to some extent the importance of punishment would change as society changes. In general terms, he saw punishment as being more important as a means of reinforcing moral and social order in less complex societies with a less developed division of labour. However, while methods of punishment change over time, the essential functions of punishment remain constant. Although the collective conscience of a society changes over time and people are outraged by different activities, punishment as a social process has an unchanging character.

In contrasting simpler societies based on what he termed mechanical solidarity with modern societies based on organic solidarity, Durkheim suggested that the former were characterised by more severe and intense forms of punishment. To elaborate on this a little, in *The Division of Labour in Society* Durkheim described simpler societies as having a mechanical sort of social solidarity whereby individuals would, he argued, feel the same emotions, hold the same values and the same things sacred and where, essentially, there would be little differentiation between them. In contrast, more modern societies would have an organic form of social solidarity characterised by increased differentiation between individuals; there would still be a collective conscience but of a slightly weaker nature.

In comparing the forms of solidarity and consciousness in these two types of society, Durkheim examined the role of the law and legal phenomena and distinguished between two kinds of law, each of which was characteristic of one of the basic forms of social solidarity. *Repressive law* was found in simpler forms of society which exhibited mechanical solidarity, and the punishments associated with it revealed and reflected the force of common sentiments. *Restitutive law* is typical of more advanced societies, where the focus is not just to punish but to re-establish the state of things, in accordance with justice (Aron 1970, p. 29). Durkheim goes on to suggest that the intensity of the collective conscience of society (indicated by the form of social solidarity) is reflected in the intensity of punishment. In more modern, advanced societies, collective sentiments are less demanding and there is more scope for diversity and interdependence. In those societies, punishments for violation of the collective conscience (and more specifically the law) are consequently more lenient. So Durkheim argues that as the intensity of punishment reflects the strength of the collective conscience, then as a society develops, the severity of punishment will diminish. In *The Division of Labour*, he points to a progressive decline in the degree of repression as mechanical solidarity recedes and organic solidarity advances.

The link between punishment and morality is perhaps the key element of Durkheim's sociology of punishment. Punishment is seen as an important and necessary part of the moral order of society. It helps prevent the collapse of moral authority and demonstrates the strength of moral commands. For Durkheim, the primary function of punishment is the reassertion of the moral order of society. From this analysis, punishment is not an instrument of deterrence that aims to prevent the repetition of a guilty act; the threat of the unpleasant consequences of particular punishments are just practical problems that might stand in the way of the criminal's desires. Rather, it is a means of conveying moral messages and of indicating the strength of feelings that lie behind those messages and the common consciousness. In practical terms, punishment may have to be unpleasant, but in terms of the role of punishment in society Durkheim sees that as incidental: the essence of punishment is the expression of moral condemnation.

QUESTION BREAK: PUNISHMENT AS MORAL CONDEMNATION

List the crimes that excite the greatest moral repugnance. Why do they?

In what ways can punishment express this moral condemnation and repugnance? (Think of punishments in a range of different societies.)

In introducing Durkheim's work on punishment we have focused on the arguments and points he made in his first major work, *The Division of Labour in Society*. Durkheim elaborated on his theory of punishment in an article published some years later, 'The Two Laws of Penal Evolution' (1984 (1901)). In this article he developed his argument that punishments become less repressive in modern compared to traditional societies, and built this into his 'two laws'. The first law relates to the 'intensity' of punishment, which is seen as 'greater in so far as societies belong to a less advanced type – in so far as the central power has a more absolute character'. In developed, modern societies collective sentiments exist but they are constituted by the laws rather than enshrined in religion, and the law is seen as a human rather than a divine construction. As a consequence, crimes are seen as transgressions against fellow humans rather than offences against a god or gods and so do not arouse the same outrage and indignity. Also, there is likely to be more human sympathy for offenders as the punishment does not have to be undertaken to appease the god or gods. Durkheim argued that in the more modern forms of society, retribution is tempered by mercy. The evidence for this first law can be found, Durkheim argued, in the changes in the forms of punishment over time. In particular, he refers to the decline of aggravated capital punishment, where death was accompanied by rituals of mutilation and torture. As examples of this greater leniency, he contrasts the barbarity of imperial Rome and of pre-revolutionary France with the more democratic republican regimes that followed them.

The second law also relates to the 'lesser intensity' of punishment as society develops and as imprisonment becomes the main means of punishment. 'Deprivation of liberty and of liberty alone, for periods of time varying according to the gravity of the crime, tends increasingly to become the normal type of repression.' Durkheim saw this second law as dependent on the first.

These laws, and Durkheim's theory of punishment, led him to consider why it is that punishments become milder as societies move from less to more advanced types. His explanation centred on the relationship between punishment and crime, and in particular on the changes in the ways in which collective sentiments respond to crimes. This point is explained by Lukes (1973) in his detailed study of Durkheim's life and work. Durkheim classified crimes into two basic categories: those directed against 'collective things, such as religion, tradition and public authority', and those directed only against individuals. The first he called 'religious criminality' and the second 'human criminality'. As societies evolved, so the religious crimes declined and crimes against the individual gradually took their place. The former, often seen as sacrileges, inspired greater passion and fear, and left little room for pity for the criminal. However, when the individual was the object of the crime, collective sentiments were less aroused and less fearful. As a consequence, as crime became less religious and more human, so punishment became less severe.

Another variable in Durkheim's discussion of crime and punishment is that of political power, which he refers to in the first law of penal evolution in claiming that as governments become more absolute, so the collective sentiments become stronger and more imbued with 'religiosity'. Absolute governments, he suggested, treated political offences as sacrilegious and repressed them with greater violence.

To summarise, Durkheim explained punishment and changes in penal practice in terms of the changes in collective sentiments and beliefs that occurred with the evolution of societies and social practices and institutions. Durkheim also emphasised the necessity for punishment; it would not disappear as societies evolved further. As Lukes puts it, 'the penal system was ultimately a function of the moral beliefs of society, and it was fair to predict that the list of human crimes would lengthen, and they would be punished less severely, but punished nonetheless' (1973, p. 262).

QUESTION BREAK: THE RITUALS OF PUNISHMENT

In seeing punishment as a means of conveying moral messages and fostering social solidarity, Durkheim emphasised the importance of the rituals associated with the punishment, rather than the actual details of the particular punishment. With the decline in public punishment such as floggings or executions, these rituals tend nowadays to centre around the courtroom. They include the wearing of wigs and gowns and the process of the trial and the passing of sentence. There are rituals associated with particular punishments. In his famous study of total institutions, Goffman (1959) highlighted the initiation rituals that helped to 'mortify the self', including the shaving of heads of prisoners and the restrictions on contact with the outside world. These rituals, however, are undertaken for an internal audience rather than the general public. As a consequence of the decline in public punishment, the focus of public and media interest tends to be on the courtroom drama and the trial of offenders – on 'who gets what' rather than on the detailed workings of the processes of punishment.

Questions

Consider some recent criminal trials that have received detailed media coverage.

How would you describe the media reporting of these trials?

To what extent might such trials and the reporting of them help to strengthen the 'collective conscience'?

Court cases and punishments can provide a range of other responses as well as social solidarity. What other responses might these recent trials have provoked?

Durkheim and punishment: comment and criticism

The historical changes examined by Durkheim are described in very general and sweeping terms and have been criticised as over-simplistic. His description of simple societies characterised by a mechanical form of solidarity, and advanced societies characterised by organic solidarity, provides no real account of the range of intermediate possibilities. Garland (1990) suggests that the historic transition from simpler societies with more severe forms of punishment to advanced ones with more lenient punishments is assumed by Durkheim rather than actually demonstrated in any sort of detailed historical account.

In a similar vein, Garland also raises questions about Durkheim's application of the notion of the collective conscience. The fact that there is a certain degree of order and agreement in society does not necessarily mean there is a generally held commitment to shared moral norms. People follow rules and laws for a variety of reasons, some of which might be purely practical (to avoid punishment, for instance) rather than because of any deeply held moral commitment. This raises the issue as to whether violations of the criminal law do really break genuinely held moral sentiments. Of course, there is some link between popular sentiment and the law: laws protecting a person's safety or property, for instance, are widely and generally supported. However, while there may be general agreement that rape, burglary and so on are morally repugnant, there is much less agreement over what should be the 'proper' punishment for such behaviour. And there is even less agreement over criminal offences which do not offend such strongly and widely held moral sentiments: crimes such as drug use, tax evasion or infringing copyright laws do not excite the same sort of general moral repugnance. It would seem that it is those punishments which deal with the most shocking and serious crimes, such as child murder, that provoke the sort of collective moral outcry that Durkheim described. This is not to say that punishment of crime does not produce emotive responses – the general fascination with crime and criminals evidenced in the popularity of films, books, magazines and television programmes on serial killers, for instance, demonstrates that. However, crime and criminal behaviour and the punishment of it perhaps cover too broad a spectrum to be generalised about with the confidence of Durkheim.

This raises the question of the extent to which punishment is functional for society. There is likely to be little disagreement with the argument that it performs some functions – that it legitimates some forms of authority and restrains some types of behaviour. However, what is functional from one point of view or for one group in society might prove to be dysfunctional for others. This sort of criticism can be applied to the work of Durkheim, and to the general functionalist perspective that developed from his work. It takes issue with the idea that there is a general agreement over what is functional or not and what should and should not be valued and appreciated in society. As regards punishment, there are dysfunctional consequences as well as functional ones; in this context Garland refers to Mead's argument that the passions and emotive responses engendered by crime can encourage societies to direct their energies to denouncing certain individuals, rather than to doing anything about wider social conditions that might give rise to crime. The directing of anger at particular evil perpetrators might also encourage the scapegoating and consequent harassment of certain groups.

The emphasis given to the notion of a collective conscience and a general moral agreement also takes little account of the obvious power differentials involved in the business of maintaining order in society. Is the law reflective of general interest or rather the interests of those who are in positions of power and authority? Durkheim's work seems to underplay the fact that individuals are members of groups that can and do have opposed interests; it neglects the conflict between interest groups. This point raises questions as to the extent to which Durkheim's theory is relevant to modern, advanced societies with complex divisions of labour and where the moral order is not necessarily universal.

In spite of these critical comments, Durkheim's work has highlighted and encouraged a detailed examination of the social processes of punishment; his work explored the symbolic and emotional elements of the punishment process, rather than just the narrow technical side of it. And in his arguing that punishment was necessary and func-tional for society, Durkheim was well aware that it had only a limited ability to control criminal behaviour. It is this apparent contradiction – that punishment was politically and socially functional yet had little effect on actual criminal behaviour – which illustrates, for Garland, the crucial characteristic of punishment: 'This sense of being simultaneously necessary and also destined to a degree of futility is what I will term the tragic quality of punishment' (1990, p. 80).

Max Weber: rationality and punishment

Before moving on to the second major sociological approach to punishment, theoretical work influenced by the writings of Karl Marx, we will look briefly at the third of the classic, founding theorists in sociology, Max Weber, in terms of his contribution to the sociology of punishment. Although Weber did not study or write about crime or punishment specifically, his work was wide-ranging and covered areas that can be applied to that area. In particular, he examined and categorised different forms of authority in different types of society and argued that modern, advanced societies were increasingly characterised by more rational and formalised social structures and institutions.

In his study *Economy and Society* (1978 (1920)), he examined the social institutions of modern capitalist societies and described the forms of authority and rational organisa- tion associated with them. Weber distinguished authority from power in terms of the extent to which consent was present. Power he saw as the ability to get things done or to compel others to comply with demands, whereas authority also involved the ability to get things done but in contexts where the particular order is seen as legitimate and accepted by those to whom it is applied. So authority is legitimated power or power by consent, in contrast to power exercised through coercion. Power and authority are closely related concepts, but for Weber the notion of legitimacy is the important distin- guishing feature. Having made this initial distinction, Weber then defined and classified three types of authority which were based on different types of legitimacy. These three types were traditional, charismatic and rational-legal authority and were, he argued, found in one degree or another in all forms of society.

With *traditional* authority there is an unquestioning acceptance of the distribution of power. The leader has authority by virtue of the traditional status of the office that she or he holds; legitimacy is not doubted, because things have 'always been so'. *Charismatic* authority is based on commitment and loyalty to a leader because of that leader's excep- tional qualities. In this situation, the word of the leader is seen as all-important. This form of authority tends to be unstable, as it depends on a leader keeping the loyalty and sup- port of the masses and because it is difficult to pass on from one generation to the next (why should the successor of a charismatic leader have the same exceptional qualities?). Furthermore, the authority of the charismatic leader tends to become routinised over time; she or he will almost inevitably have to involve other staff as the job of leader extends and evolves. *Rational-legal* authority is based on a legal frame- work which supports and maintains the distribution of power in the society. This form of authority is characterised by bureaucracy, where there is an emphasis on rules rather than on the individual qualities of the leader (charismatic) or the customs of the society (traditional).

In broad historical terms, Weber believed that the third form of authority was the most appropriate form of rule for modern industrial societies. Traditional and charismatic forms of authority, which were common in earlier, pre-industrial societies, would become redundant as a general rationalisation occurred (by this Weber means the increased application of scientific thought and the influence of science on behaviour). Authority, then, would become increasingly rational-legal, based on formal rules – specifically, the law. And in practice, the most typical form of rational-legal authority would be bureaucracy – which was, for Weber, the characteristic form of administration in modern society, not just confined to the political arena but common across all areas of society, including education, religion and, as regards our concern in this discussion, crime and punishment.

Bureaucracy he saw as a system of authority based on proceeding according to strictly laid down rules and with individuals following clearly defined roles. We won't go into the details of Weber's definition of bureaucracy here, but consider how it relates to developments in penal practice and policy.

QUESTION BREAK: BUREAUCRACY AND PUNISHMENT

Consider the sort of punishments that are typical of modern societies such as Britain. To what extent are they based on the idea of rational-legal authority?

Look up Weber's definition of bureaucracy (in a sociology dictionary or introductory textbook). In what ways is the punishment of offenders bureaucratised?

Weber's general argument about the increasing rationalisation of society can, then, be applied to punishment. Indeed, there can be instances when the public criticise any move away from a rule-based, bureaucratic approach to punishment. Hudson (2003) refers to the concerns and criticism made of judges who pass individualistic sentences that seem to be based on their own views and beliefs rather than according to the facts of the case and the rules of due process.

It would certainly seem to be the case that over the past two hundred or so years punishment has become increasingly rationalised and bureaucratised, the makeshift, *ad hoc* punishments of the past having been replaced by a centrally administered system of punishments. In part this has been due to the population growth since the eighteenth century, along with the rising rate of crime. In general terms these have led to a greater uniformity of punishments and to the development of a penal infrastructure. Garland (1990) has argued that these developments have led to a 'professionalisation of justice', with a range of professional groups now working in the area of punishment, including social workers, probation officers, psychiatrists, police and prison officers. With the increasing complexity of punishment, different approaches to the treatment of the punished, and of prisoners in particular, have been instituted. At the same time, those who are professionally involved in the penal system have come to see offenders in different terms – to see them as either good or bad inmates on account of their institutional behaviour, rather than as evil or wicked on account of the crimes that they are being punished for. These changes, Garland suggests, have taken the emotion out of the punishment of offenders, with punishment being administered by paid officials rather than the general public or even those personally affected by the offenders' actions. All of this affects the form (and length) of punishment; for example, how an inmate behaves in prison will affect the time he or she spends in prison.

The rationalisation and professionalisation of justice has clearly altered the meaning and the practices of punishment in modern society. The institutions of punishment have become less accessible and more secretive as specialised professions have taken a greater role. This trend towards rationalisation would seem to run counter to Durkheim's emphasis on the emotional nature of punishment – on punishment as reflecting an outrage to the moral sentiments of a society. The lack of involvement of the public in the day-to-day business of punishing offenders may help to explain why the public do from time to time vent their anger and frustration at the closed nature of the penal system, as evidenced in the outrage of hostile mobs of people who gather to hurl abuse at those involved in crimes against children, or by the campaigns to ensure that the child killers of toddler James Bulger remained in prison, or the massive opposition to any suggestions that Moors murderer Myra Hindley be considered for early release on parole (prior to her death in November 2002).

QUESTION BREAK: PUBLIC OUTRAGE

The sort of public outrage described above was graphically illustrated in summer 2002 after the arrests of Ian Huntley and Maxine Carr in connection with the murders of 10-year-olds Holly Wells and Jessica Chapman in Soham, Cambridgeshire. Crowds gathered outside Peterborough Magistrates' Court as Maxine Carr was remanded in custody.

Hate fills the air as public vents feelings

Explosion of rage outside court as Maxine Carr is remanded . . .

It was the mothers who led the ugly chorus, jeering and shouting at a woman they could not see. . . .

'I've never done anything like this before,' said Nicola Warrener, a 24-year-old hairdresser from Peterborough . . .

She added: 'I didn't know I could feel like this . . . but I'm actually shaking with rage. I have been thinking of starting a family, but now I am not so sure. I think I would be too afraid to leave them with anyone.'

(*Guardian*, 2 August 2002, 'Hate Fills the Air')

Into the gauntlet of hate

Mob hurls abuse and eggs at caretaker's girlfriend after court appearance

As the vehicles swept by, the boos rose up, turning into a feverish cacophany of screams. Eggs were thrown as young mothers with crying children yelled obscenities. Accusations of 'sick cow' and 'murdering bitch' were hurled at Ms Carr. A banner proclaiming 'rot in hell forever' summed up the mood.

Earlier, television crews from across the world had tried to catch a glimpse of a woman who in just a few days has become a figure of hate.

(*The Independent*, 22 August 2002, 'Into the Gauntlet of Hate')

Question

How does this sort of reaction relate to the work of (a) Durkheim; and (b) Weber?

Punishment as part of a class-based process of economic and social control: the Marxist approach

The practices and institutions for the punishment of offenders were not analysed or written about in any detail by Karl Marx, or his collaborator Friedrich Engels. Neither did they write much on crime or criminals, and they did not develop a theory of crime and punishment in the same manner as Durkheim. So, we have to look at the writing of later Marxist-influenced writers to provide us with a Marxist analysis and theory of punishment.

As with Durkheim, the context and background for the Marxist approach to punishment come from Marx's general theoretical writing and analysis. This analysis sees the economy as the key locus of power in society, with the economic system determining all other areas of social life, including, in this context, the legal system. Those groups who have economic power are able to ensure that social institutions work in a way that is consistent with their own interests. Thus the various institutions of the law and punishment come to reflect and represent the interests of the dominant economic groups. Consequently, a Marxist analysis of punishment has tended to focus on the way in which elements of the superstructure (essentially, the rest of society, apart from the economic base) support the powerful ruling groups in society – how, for instance, the law works in the interest of some groups more than others, an analysis that is reflected in the adage 'There's one law for the rich and one for the poor.'

The Marxist approach argues that market relations, and in particular the economic relations that involve some groups in society exploiting and others being exploited, condition all other social institutions, including the laws but also other institutions such as the education system, the mass media and the family. As Hudson puts it:

> All social institutions, according to Marxists, have as their prime function the maintenance of the capitalist system. Laws will protect rights to property necessary for capital accumulation; families reproduce workers, and give workers motivation to work for wages; education gives potential workers the skills that are needed in the workforce, and instils attitudes of respect for authority.
>
> (2003, pp. 114–115)

As regards the social institution of the law, it is seen by Marxists as performing functions that are either *regulatory* (mechanisms for keeping the system working effectively) or *repressive* (imposing penalties on those who do not accept and keep the rules of the capitalist system) or *ideological* (ensuring that the workforce and the population in general believe that society and social arrangements and differences are fair and work in the interests of everyone).

Punishment, and more generally the law, are seen from a Marxist perspective as serving all three of these kinds of function. Legislation concerning health and safety or the rights of employees, for instance, might seem to be specifically serving the interests of workers and thereby acting as a sort of curb on capitalist exploitation. However, such legislation can have a regulatory function that works in the interests of capitalism;

it might help prevent individual capitalists from damaging the overall system, and so help maintain the smooth running of capitalist economies.

QUESTION BREAK

Think of other areas of legislation – for example, laws regarding fraud and forgery or illegal drug use – and consider how they might fulfil regulatory, repressive and ideological functions.

As regards the repressive function of law and punishment, the Marxist analysis of punishment centres on the notion of class struggle and the ways in which the relationship between social classes determines the form of punishment present in any particular society.

These brief introductory comments have presented what is basically the orthodox or classic Marxist view. Garland (1990), among others, has highlighted the work of Rusche and Kirchheimer as the clearest example of this Marxist interpretation of punishment. Rusche and Kirchheimer's major text, *Punishment and Social Structure*, was first published in 1939 but was not widely referred to by Western theorists until its reissue in 1968. Since then, their work has been taken up by Marxist criminologists and become much more widely known and referred to.

Rusche and Kirchheimer provide a detailed history of punishment which emphasises how the economy and, in particular, the labour market influences the methods of punishment adopted by different societies. They suggest that the severity of punishment is influenced by the value in which labour is held. Its value is higher when labour is scarce and, as a consequence, punishments become relatively more lenient; by contrast, when there is a surplus of labour, punishments tend to become more severe. They illustrate this argument in their account of the development of punishments such as galley slavery, transportation and hard labour. These emerged as 'new' punishments in the sixteenth and seventeenth centuries alongside the early developments of a capitalist economic system. At this time, labour power was increasingly seen as a vital resource, and the harsh physical punishments, such as whipping, branding, mutilation and execution, were replaced by punishments that involved some form of productive, hard labour – and particularly work that 'free' people would be less willing to undertake.

Transportation demonstrates this shift in the emphasis of punishment. At this period there were vast amounts of land in the colonies that needed to be worked, and the penalty of transportation was introduced to help develop these areas. It was initially offered as a commutation of capital punishment but by the early eighteenth century was regularly used as a specific sentence for a range of quite minor offences. As an indication of its popularity, around 30,000 people were transported to the American colonies between 1718 and 1775. When the transportation of convicts to America declined, an alternative punishment of confinement in old vessels, known as hulks, was introduced. Offenders punished in this way were given hard labour to do in the daytime – dredging the Thames and other rivers, for instance – and returned to the vessels at night to eat and sleep. Concern over the conditions in these hulks was such that they did not figure as a major method of punishment for long.

After American independence and the consequent ending of transportation there, the focus of transportation shifted to Australia, with the first fleet of ships setting off for Botany Bay in 1787. Conditions on the ships taking the convicts to Australia were appalling and the death rate was as high as 25 per cent. By 1852, transportation to Australia and Tasmania (Van Diemen's Land) was finally abolished, with a 'ticket of leave' scheme offered in place of it to convicted offenders (a scheme which foreshadowed the development of parole as a means of punishment). It was, essentially, the growing prosperity in the colonies that led to the decline in this form of punishment: those people who emigrated of their own free will to Australia and elsewhere were not too happy about convicts and criminal labour undercutting their wages, while the authorities felt that the punishment of transportation was becoming little deterrent to criminals.

So for Rusche and Kirchheimer, the severity and the form of punishment were related to the value of labour, and they examined the link between demand for labour and forms of punishment in different periods to history. In the medieval period around the thirteenth century, the labouring population was small in relation to the land that had to be utilised for production; as a result, punishments that limited labour power were not used, with fines or doing penance being more popular penalties. And as we have seen, in the early days of capitalism, in the sixteenth and seventeenth centuries, demand for labour led to more 'productive' punishments, such as transportation and workhouses. By contrast, when there was a surplus of labour, and it was no longer necessary to employ offenders, the punishments tended to leave them with nothing to do. This, Rusche and Kirchheimer argue, raised a dilemma as to the purpose of imprisonment and brought the repressive and deterrent side of punishment and imprisonment to the fore. In England and elsewhere, hard labour within prisons was introduced as a form of punishment rather than as a means to increase productivity or engender profit; and moral arguments were used to justify this sort of punishment within a punishment – arguments that hard labour was good for moral improvement and discipline, for instance.

Prison labour, then, became a method of punishment after the Industrial Revolution of the late eighteenth century and when there was a large industrial reserve army of labourers. Being sent to prison was not the complete punishment: punishment also happened within prison. Indeed, the authorities became pretty adept at inventing new forms of prison labour, including making prisoners carry huge stones from one place to another and then back again, or tread water mills which just sent water round in a circle for no useful purpose. The treadwheel was a sort of 'everlasting circle' that might be used to grind corn or might just grind nothing, and was widely used because it was a cheap and easy means of forcing prisoners to work and one that might also deter any who might feel prison was a place of potential refuge and rest.

Rusche and Kirchheimer argued that the move to incarceration and prison labour fitted in with the aims of a capitalist economy. It would help to create a submissive and regulated workforce, would contain working-class unrest and teach habits of discipline and order. Although humanitarian principles and ideas were advocated, the Marxist interpretation saw these as mere rhetoric. Prison conditions remained deplorable in the nineteenth century, characterised by meaningless and degrading work. Rusche and Kirchheimer saw the expansion of imprisonment as resulting from a combination of population increase and the emergence of industrial capitalism creating a depressed labouring class; the aim of the prison was, then, to teach the discipline of labour and to encourage the poor to accept whatever conditions were imposed on them by their employers. It was taken as evident that conditions in prisons had to be worse than those faced by even the worst-off 'free' workers, and as a result, prisons developed and intensified the punishments they imposed on their inmates – based around forms of hard labour.

Put simply, the 'Marxist thesis' is that during the Industrial Revolution the rationale for punishment changed from being directly economic (a need for productive labour) to being something much more repressively punitive, with prisons being used as means for inflicting control and intimidation.

In his discussion of the work of Rusche and Kirchheimer, Garland summarises the key points that they make (see Box 2.1). He highlights the most quoted sentence in their study *Punishment and Social Structure* as being 'Every system of production tends to discover punishments which correspond to its productive relationships.' In modern industrial societies, the 'corresponding punishment' is clearly imprisonment. Garland considers why Marxists such as Rusche and Kirchheimer argue this. For them, prison was a source of labour and therefore became the dominant mode of punishment at a time when the emerging capitalist system produced an almost insatiable demand for labour. This, though, raises the question of why imprisonment has persisted when the economic need is less obvious: the number of 'free' people who are able to work does not need to be supplemented with convict labour. The answer for Rusche and Kirchheimer and others is to emphasise the role of the prison in creating a regulated and submissive workforce.

BOX 2.1

Garland's summary of Rusche and Kirchheimer's theoretical approach highlights the following points:

- Punishments have to be viewed as historically specific phenomena that appear in particular forms at different periods. This principle of historical specificity distinguishes Marxist accounts from Durkheim's view of punishment as something that performed essentially similar functions in all societies.
- The mode of production is the major determinant of specific penal methods in specific historical periods. Different systems of production will produce different methods of punishment.
- The particular forms of punishment are, therefore, social artefacts or constructions.
- Penal policy is one element within a wider strategy for controlling the poor. Punishment is seen almost exclusively as aimed at the control of the 'lower orders'. Rusche and Kirchheimer suggest that there were clear similarities between the way criminals were treated and the policies aimed at controlling the labouring masses. In the early industrial period the regime and organisation of prison life was similar to the way workers were treated in factories and beggars and vagrants in workhouses.

- Punishment is a mechanism deeply implicated within the class struggle: 'the history of the penal system is the history of the relations between the rich and the poor' (Rusche 1933).
- Although punishment is generally and conventionally seen as an institution which benefits 'society as a whole', for Marxists, in reality it supports the interests of one class against another. Punishment is (another) element and example of control that is hidden within ideological veils.

Source: Adapted from Garland (1990, pp. 90–92)

So far, we have referred to the regulatory and repressive functions and role of punishment and prison; we will now consider the role of *ideology* in the Marxist approach to punishment. In the context of Marxist theory, an ideology refers to a set of ideas which influence and govern people's perception of the world. In capitalist societies, ideas which support the capitalist relations of production are seen by Marxists as essential for ensuring the continuation of that form of society. Here we will look at how the Marxist approach to punishment and the law relates to this notion of ideology.

The law, and punishment for breaking it, is important to the maintenance of capitalist society in that it seems to express values of equality and thereby give credibility to the state's claims that it is ruling in the interests of all citizens, rather than just one group or class. Althusser, for instance, sees the law as part of what he terms the 'ideological state apparatus', working along with the education system, the mass media and so on to ensure the continuing domination of the ruling, capitalist class.

The law, then, is seen as functioning at both the ideological and the repressive levels. For example, the large, symbolic prisons built in working-class areas of the major towns and cities as capitalism developed, served as a stark reminder to everyone that if the discipline of the factory was ignored or rejected, workers might face an even more austere and rigid discipline within the prison. The differing importance given to either the ideological or the repressive role of punishment is essentially a difference in emphasis for Marxists; punishment is seen as having both an ideological and a repressive role and function.

In recent years, and particularly since the 1970s, Marxist criminologists have tried to explain the rise of a 'law and order' ideology which has seen prison numbers grow and grow while there has been a cutback on social welfare institutions. In part, this has been explained as a mechanism of social control, a way of creating specific groups to blame for economic downturn and depression: illegal immigrants, welfare scroungers and criminals, for example. Concerns and fear over economic recession become less urgent in the face of fear of crime. It is debatable whether economic depression does lead to any increase in crime. However, Hudson argues that

> what is not debatable is that in times of recession the vocabulary of justice becomes harsher [and that in this context] [b]lame is attached to individuals, and social

responsibility for crime is denied; lack of investment in areas of high unemployment is blamed on crime rates rather than on the flight of capital.

(2003, p. 125)

In such a climate, theories of justice will emphasise punishment rather than treatment; incapacitation rather than deterrence or rehabilitation will come to the fore. Policies of containment of persistent offenders will gain support and influence, with the rights of offenders being of less and less concern. Hudson refers to the 'three strikes' laws passed in California, whereby a third offence of any sort can lead to an immediate 25-year term of imprisonment with no parole, as illustrative of this development in penal philosophy and strategy.

The Marxist approach: comment and criticism

The priority given to economic explanations by Marxist writers such as Rusche and Kirchheimer has been criticised for understating the importance of non-economic factors – political, religious and humanitarian influences on the development of punishment are accorded only secondary importance, for example. Furthermore, the emphasis given to class and class relationships tends to ignore popular attitude to punishment. There is widespread support among the working classes for harsh punitive policies and little evidence that the working class are any more sympathetic towards criminals than are other social groups, points which Garland (1990) suggests cast doubt on a simple class conflict approach to analysing punishment. However, these comments do not necessarily refute the Marxist argument of Rusche and Kirchheimer that economic relationships and the labour market can exert an important influence on penal policy and that the institutions of punishment can be seen as part of a wider strategy for managing the poor and working classes.

The essence of the Marxist argument is that the approach to, and form of, punishment are influenced by the strategies that the dominant, ruling groups adopt towards the working classes. Punishment is determined not just by the extent and pattern of crime but by the perception of the working classes, and particularly the poor, as a social problem. Rusche and Kirchheimer argue that the working classes have little commitment to the law or to the dominant moral order in general and that it is therefore important that the criminal law and the punishments attached to it do all they can to ensure that crime does not pay. For this reason, punishments have to be severe and institutions of punishment such as prisons have to be unpleasant – and certainly more unpleasant than the conditions that the general working population are able to live in.

QUESTION BREAK

Think of recent criminal cases that have received a lot of publicity. Consider different sorts of crime – for example, the murder of Holly Wells and Jessica Chapman in Soham in 2002 or the conviction of Jeffrey Archer for perjury.

Questions

How big a part do you think class plays in public reaction to crime and criminals?

To what extent do you think it is fair for Rusche and Kirchheimer to suggest that the working classes have little commitment to the law?

In contrast to Durkheim's view that punishment expresses the interests of the society as a whole, the fairly basic review of the Marxist approach to punishment that we have presented here sees punishment as expressing only the interests of the dominant, ruling groups. Although the criminal law and punishment do provide protection for the working classes as well as the ruling classes – protection against assault and burglary, for instance – they do not, according to Marxists, 'protect' against economic domination and oppression.

Marxism, gender and punishment

The Marxist approach to punishment emphasises how it works in the interest of some groups more than others and, in particular, how punishment is imposed on and directed against the working class and, more specifically, sections of the working class. The argument that punishment can reflect the interests of some sections of society more than others should, Hudson (2003) suggests, encourage an examination of the treatment of groups other than the working class and lead to a 'recognition of the significance of gender for the sociology of punishment'. In this context, feminist approaches have been concerned with the penal treatment of women, although such work has tended to remain 'on the margins of penology and criminology'. We have seen how the traditional Marxist approach highlights the relationship between the labour market and methods of punishment. In relating this to the issue of gender and punishment, women have been seen by Marxists as part of a 'reserve army of labour' – encouraged into the workplace at certain periods and discouraged at others. If we adapt the Marxist argument, there should, then, be a link between rates of imprisonment of women and the labour market situation of women. Hudson points to the limited research in this area, which does, however, emphasise women's importance to the capitalist system as reproducers of labour power – in both the biological and the sociological sense (in terms of their socialising and educating roles). Research on the imprisonment of women has shown that having a family to look after does encourage leniency in punishment (Eaton 1986, cited in Hudson), in line with the Marxist notion of the family as reproducing a disciplined and essentially submissive workforce. In the context of the relative penalties given to women and men, an issue which the Marxist approach does not really address is that of why women offenders are more liable to be seen as mad rather than bad, and punished accordingly. (See pp. 175–177 for fuller discussion of this point.)

QUESTION BREAK: RICH LAW, POOR LAW

The sociological study of business crime lends support to the Marxist argument that the extent and severity with which the legal system is applied varies between different social groups. Dee Cook (1989) examined the different responses to tax and supplementary benefit fraud. She cited the following examples of judicial responses to defrauding the public purse by two different means: by defrauding the Inland Revenue by evading tax and defrauding the DHSS by falsely claiming supplementary benefit:

Two partners in a vegetable wholesalers business admitted falsifying accounts to the tune of £100,000. At their trial the judge said he considered they had been 'very wise' in admitting their guilt and they had paid back the tax due (with interest) to the Inland Revenue. They were sentenced to pay fines. A chartered accountant who defrauded taxes in excess of £8,000 was sentenced to pay a fine as the judge accepted, in mitigation, that his future income would be adversely affected by the trial.

An unemployed father of three failed to declare his wife's earnings to the Department of Health and Social Security (DHSS). He admitted the offence and started to pay back the £996 he owed them by weekly deductions from his supplementary benefit. He was prosecuted a year later and sentenced to pay fines totalling £210, also to be deducted from his benefit. Magistrates told him that 'this country is fed up to the teeth with people like you scrounging from fellow citizens'. A young woman defrauded the DHSS to the tune of £58: she served three months in custody as magistrates said she 'needed to be taught a lesson'.

(Cook 1989, p. 1)

In looking at why the law does not treat white-collar crime in the same way as conventional crime, Hazel Croall (1992) points out that white-collar crime is subject to different regulatory arrangements and these tend to be more lenient than those of the criminal justice system. Regulatory bodies are less worried about securing convictions and more keen on settling disputes with a minimum of fuss and, often, publicity. Burglars, for example, are more likely to be prosecuted and imprisoned than are fraudsters, whose offences usually involve much larger sums of money. This point is supported by Steven Box's comments on the deterrents for would-be corporate criminals:

For the most part corporate crimes are not/do not fall under the jurisdiction of the police, but under special regulatory bodies. . . . In the UK, there are numerous inspectorates, commissions and government departments. . . .

Corporate executives contemplating the possibility of being required to commit corporate crimes know that they face a regulatory agency which for the most part will be unable to detect what is going on, and in the minority of cases when it does, it will have no heart and few resources to pursue the matter into the criminal courts. . . .

Criminal laws aimed at regulating corporate activities tend to refer to a specific rather than a general class of behaviour . . . they focus purely on the regulation broken and not on the consequences of that broken regulation. Thus the company responsible for the hoist accident at Littlebrook Dee power station were not prosecuted for the fact that five men died, but for the fact that the machinery was not properly maintained or inspected. For this they were fined £5000. In conventional crime ... a person is charged with the consequences of his/her action; if someone dies as a consequence of being stabbed, the assailant is more likely to be charged with a homicide offence rather than 'carrying an offensive weapon'. The point of this fracture between the regulation broken and its consequences is that it facilitates corporate crime; executives need only concern themselves with the likelihood of being leniently punished for breaking regulations.

(Box 1983, pp. 44–58)

White-collar offenders are usually better off and can use their superior resources to avoid detection, prosecution and severe punishment. They can emphasise that they are respectable business people who have made one mistake and don't deserve severe punishment. The law itself encourages such compliance strategies and allows for out-of-court settlements.

Questions

What are the key differences between corporate and conventional crime?

To what extent do you think that they provide a justification for the differential treatment of white-collar and business criminals?

Punishment, power and regulation: the work of Michel Foucault

Foucault (1926–1984) was a French philosopher whose major works were published in the 1970s. His writing focused on issues surrounding knowledge, power and the human body, and was not confined to the area of crime and punishment. However, as regards our interest here, his emphasis was on the emergence of 'crime' in the early nineteenth century. The turn of the nineteenth century was the period of the Industrial Revolution and the aftermath of the democratic revolutions in France and the United States. It was a time of hectic social change that was accompanied by widespread concern over the threat to social order that would result, it was feared, from an emerging industrial working class whose members would be less likely to respect traditional hierarchies. It is not surprising that this period also excited a great deal of comment and analysis from social and political theorists, philosophers and other commentators. Indeed, the attempt to understand the significance of the changing nature of the new industrial society of the nineteenth century led to the emergence of sociology as a new area of study and discipline.

Although writing a hundred or so years after the key founding social theorists such as Karl Marx, Max Weber and Emile Durkheim, Foucault also examined and analysed the social changes brought about by the emergence of modern industrial society. In this context, his main theme was that of the 'disciplinary society' and of the pervasive nature of social control. In his detailed study of the prison system that was established in the early nineteenth century he emphasised that the methods of dealing with criminals in the modern penitentiaries of that time were part of a wider process of control and regimentation in society. The criminal was no longer viewed just as a lawbreaker who should be punished, but rather was seen as a pathological individual who required close surveillance and expert supervision in order to be returned to 'normality'.

Discipline and Punish (1977), one of Foucault's later works, focused on what he saw as the 'problem' of knowledge and power, and has become one of the key texts in the sociology of punishment. Foucault saw punishment as a system of power and regulation which is imposed on people – an analysis that overlaps with the Marxist approach considered earlier and contrasts with Durkheim's argument that punishment is embedded within collective sentiments and therefore conveys moral messages. Where Foucault differed from both of these 'grand theories' was in his methodological approach. He focused on the specific working of penal institutions, on how they were organised and structured and how they actually imposed and exercised control. This approach moved away from an examination of society as a coherent whole that could be analysed by structural methods, and to that extent Foucault's work could be described as phenomenological rather than structural, or Marxist. To elaborate on this point, as with the other social theorists we have looked at, such as Durkheim and Rusche and Kirchheimer, Foucault was also concerned with the historical transition in the forms of punishment, from the harsh physical penalties of pre-industrial societies to the more regulated sanctions of industrial capitalist societies. So, *Discipline and Punish* followed the same broad themes as other social histories of punishment but differs in the methodological approach that is used. Foucault did not adopt the grand theory, 'top-down' approach that characterises the work of Durkheim, Marx and other classic social theorists, but developed his theoretical argument on the basis of a detailed examination of specific penal practices. This building of theoretical explanations from the detailed descriptions of specific things and events and the patterns that emerge from such descriptions illustrates the phenomenological approach of Foucault. To a certain extent, then, and as Garland (1990) argues in his discussion of Foucault's work, it is not so much the originality of Foucault's themes but rather the method that he used in examining and analysing them that is perhaps his major contribution to the sociological study of punishment.

To return to Foucault's study, the historical issue that he set out to explain in *Discipline and Punish* was the disappearance of punishment as a public spectacle of violence and the emergence of the prison as the general form of modern punishment; indeed, the subtitle of *Discipline and Punish* is 'The Birth of the Prison'. This change in the basic form of punishment took place between the mid-eighteenth and early nineteenth centuries, when, Foucault argued, the target of punishment changed – the emphasis moved towards changing the soul of the offender rather than just the body, towards transforming the offender, not just avenging the particular crime. Foucault saw these developments as reflecting how power operates in modern society, with open physical force and the ceremonies and rituals associated with it being replaced by a much more detailed regulation of offenders, with troublesome individuals removed from their society and, hopefully, resocialised, rather than being broken and destroyed.

In trying to explain why imprisonment so quickly became the general method of legal punishment, Foucault considered the developing role of the human sciences. The prison practice of isolating and monitoring inmates encouraged the idea that they should be responded to and studied as individuals with their own characteristics and peculiarities. To an extent, then, prison was seen as leading to the discovery of the 'delinquent' (a person distinct from the 'normal', non-delinquent) and, according to Foucault, to the rise of the science of criminology. Foucault also argued that the 'creation' of delinquency has been a useful strategy of political domination that encouraged divisions within the working class, and enhanced and guaranteed greater powers for the police. Delinquency itself generally consists of relatively minor attacks on authority and is not a particular political danger, and so can, within limits, be tolerated by the authorities. In addition, it produces a group of known, habitual criminals who can legitimately be kept under surveillance.

As regards his history of punishment and the basic change in punishment between the eighteenth and nineteenth centuries, Foucault described the punitive phenomena which he argued characterised each period: public execution (and specifically aggravated capital punishment) in the eighteenth century and the timetabled regime of a modern nineteenth-century young offenders' institution. These descriptions are used to start his book *Discipline and Punish*; the two types of punishment that are detailed define particular 'penal styles' and have to be seen in relation to the different social contexts in which they occurred. These are, respectively, the public execution of the *ancien régime* in pre-revolutionary France and the new prison system characteristic of modern industrial capitalist society. For Foucault, the overthrow and passing of the *ancien régime* is also the passing of public execution, and the emergence of the industrial factory society is the emergence of the imprisoning society.

QUESTION BREAK: *DISCIPLINE AND PUNISH*

Read the following edited extract from the start of Foucault's *Discipline and Punish* and consider the questions at the end of it.

On 2 March 1757 [Robert] Damiens the [attempted] regicide was condemned 'to make the *amende honorable* before the main door of the Church of Paris', where he was to be 'taken and conveyed in a cart, wearing nothing but a shirt, holding a torch of burning wax weighing two pounds'; then, 'in the said cart, to the Place de Greve, where, on a scaffold that will be erected there, the flesh will be torn from his breasts, arms, thighs and calves with red-hot pincers, his right hand, holding the knife with which he committed the said parricide, burnt with sulphur, and, on those places where the flesh will be torn away, poured molten lead, boiling oil, burning resin, wax and sulphur melted together and then his body drawn and quartered by four horses and his limbs and body consumed by fire, reduced to ashes and his ashes thrown to the winds'.

'Finally he was quartered', recounts the *Gazette d'Amsterdam* of 1 April 1757. 'This last operation was very long because the horses used were unaccustomed to drawing; consequently, instead of four, six were needed; and when that did not suffice, they were forced, in order to cut off the wretch's thighs, to sever the sinews and hack at the joints. . . .

'It is said that, though he was always a great swearer, no blasphemy escaped his lips; but the excessive pain made him utter horrible cries, and he often repeated: "My God, have pity on me! Jesus, help me!"' . . .

Bouton, an officer of the watch, left us his account: 'The sulphur was lit, but the flame was so poor that only the top skin of the hand was burnt, and that only slightly. Then the executioner, his sleeves rolled up, took the steel pincers, which had been especially made for the occasion, and which were about a foot and a half long, and pulled first at the calf of the right leg, then at the thigh, and from there at the two fleshy parts of the right arm; then at the breasts. Though a strong, sturdy fellow, this executioner found it so difficult to tear away the pieces of flesh that he set about the same spot two or three times. . . .

'After these tearings with the pincers, Damiens, who cried out profusely, though without swearing, raised his head and looked at himself; the same executioner dipped an iron spoon in the pot containing the boiling potion, which he poured liberally over each wound. Then the ropes that were to be harnessed to the horses were attached with cords to the patient's body; the horses were then harnessed and placed alongside the arms and legs, one at each limb.

'Monsieur Le Breton, the clerk of the court, went up to the patient several times and asked him if he had anything to say. He said he had not; at each torment, he cried out, as the damned in hell are supposed to cry out, "Pardon, my God! Pardon, Lord." . . .

'The horses tugged hard, each pulling straight on a limb, each horse held by an executioner. After a quarter of an hour, the same ceremony was repeated and finally, after several attempts, the direction of the horses had to be changed, thus: those at the arms were made to pull towards the head, those at the thighs towards the arms, which broke at the joints. This was repeated several times without success. He raised his head and looked at himself. Two more horses had to be added to those harnessed to the thighs, which made six horses in all. Without success. . . .

'After two or three attempts, the executioner Samson and he who had used the pincers each drew out a knife from his pocket and cut the body at the thighs instead of severing the legs at the joints; the four horses gave a tug and carried off the two thighs after them, namely, that of the right side first, the other following; then the same was done to the arms, the shoulders, the arm-pits and the four limbs; the flesh had to be cut almost to the bone, the horses pulling hard carried off the right arm first and the other afterwards.

'When the four limbs had been pulled away, the confessors came to speak to him; but his executioner told them that he was dead.' . . .

Eighty years later, Leon Facher drew up his rules 'for the House of young prisoners in Paris':

'Art. 17. The prisoners' day will begin at six in the morning in winter and at five in summer. They will work for nine hours a day throughout the year. Two hours a day will be devoted to instruction. Work and the day will end at nine o'clock in winter and at eight in summer.

Art. 18. *Rising*. At the first drum-roll, the prisoners must rise and dress in silence, as the supervisor opens the cell doors. At the second drum-roll, they must be dressed and make their beds. At the third, they must line up and proceed to the chapel for morning prayer. There is a five-minute interval between each drum-roll.

Art. 19. The prayers are conducted by the chaplain and followed by a moral or religious reading. This exercise must not last more than half an hour.

Art. 20. *Work.* At a quarter to six in the summer, a quarter to seven in winter, the prisoners go down into the courtyard where they must wash their hands and faces, and receive their first ration of bread. Immediately afterwards, they form into work-teams and go off to work, which must begin at six in summer and seven in winter.

[...]

Art. 27. At seven o'clock in the summer, at eight in winter, work stops; bread is distributed for the last time in the workshops. For a quarter of an hour one of the prisoners or super-visors reads a passage from some instructive or uplifting work. This is followed by evening prayer.

Art. 28. At half past seven in summer, half past eight in winter, the prisoners must be back in their cells after the washing of hands and the inspection of clothes in the courtyard; at the first drum-roll, they must undress, and at the second get into bed. The cell doors are closed and the supervisors go the rounds in the corridors, to ensure order and silence.'

Questions

How would you describe the aims of the two styles of punishment?

What might the likely effect of those punishments be on the rest of the society?

What, if anything, do you think the style of punishment can tell us about a society?

In both the forms of punishment characterised by Foucault, the body of the offender remains central, but in the second example the body is incarcerated rather than muti-lated and the soul of the body becomes the focus for reform. There is a change in the objective of punishment – away from being a display of the awful consequences that accompany a crime against the Crown and towards instilling discipline and ensuring that the offender's body and soul function in a regular manner that helps the smooth running of the prison. So, the modern prisons regulated their inmates by detailed control of all activities so as to ensure standardised, uniform conduct.

As regards the history of these different punishments, Foucault did not propose a simple theory of historical progress; and he was well aware that there was not a sudden change from one form of punishment to another in all societies at a specified time. He stressed the discontinuities and complexity of historical change: the ending of public execution, for instance, was not a single event but a series of changes and counter-changes brought in as governments became more or less punitive at different periods between the mid-eighteenth and the nineteenth centuries.

Foucault's major concern was with power, and in particular, power over the body. Public execution is a clear demonstration of the application of this power. Foucault also tries to show that the imposition of punishment in modern societies illustrated the differences and asymmetries of power just as much as it did in the *ancien régime*, even though infliction of physical pain was rejected and replaced with punishments that involved the suspension of rights, through the deprivation of liberty and control over the individual's time and space. The modern forms of punishment might even involve withdrawal of the right to live – in situations where societies still use the death penalty, for instance. However, in these situations the death penalty is administered in a medicalised and closed sort of way – through lethal injection, gas chamber and the like – and there even tends to be a good deal of concern over how to ensure that the capital punishment avoids any unnecessary agony for the executed.

Although Foucault did not develop a 'grand theory' in the manner of classic social theorists such as Karl Marx, his work shares a Marxist appreciation of the importance for capitalism of labour power. In the context of punishment he considered how methods of punishment could be used to turn rebellious subjects into productive ones. For instance, in charting the emergence of prisons and prison regimes in the nineteenth century, he emphasised how they produced a new kind of individual 'subjected to habits, rules and orders'. This investigation of the development of prisons in the early nineteenth century was utilised by Foucault to help him explore the general themes of domination and how that is achieved, and of how individuals are 'socially constructed'.

Foucault saw an extension of power and domination occurring through the methods of surveillance that were part of the design of the new prison buildings of this time. The Panopticon designed by Bentham was a prison building constructed so as to allow for the constant observation and monitoring of 'progress' of all its inmates – essentially it was a circular building built around a central axis that allowed the guards to observe the inmates without themselves being observed. The aim of this design was to induce in the inmates the belief that they were under constant surveillance, and although that classic sort of panopticon was never fully instituted, the ideas and basic approach behind it were integrated into the architecture of the new nineteenth-century prison buildings. Foucault, then, saw the prison as illustrating the basic principle of punitive and disciplinary power:

> The perfect disciplinary apparatus would make it possible for a single gaze to see everything constantly . . . the major effect of the panopticon: to induce in the inmate a state of conscious and permanent visibility that assumes the automatic functioning of power.
>
> (1977, pp. 173 and 201)

To elaborate on this a little, the 'panopticon principle' is the principle of disciplinary regulation, and for Foucault this is the fundamental principle of social regulation in modern society. He sees society as a 'carceral archipelago' – essentially a chain of institutions with all members subject to an overarching disciplinary regulation, including being liable to the suspension of their rights across all aspects of their lives. While such disciplinary regulation is most obviously and fully realised in the prison, it is also dispersed out from the prison to other areas of society. There are, of course, many other social institutions and organisations that regulate us and that could also be said to be in the business of surveillance. As well as obvious examples such as the police and security companies, schools and colleges monitor our educational progress, the Inland Revenue checks to see whether we have paid our taxes, and social service agencies keep records on citizens' uptake of services, to name but a few. And all of these forms of checking and surveillance have been massively helped by advances in video and computer technology that have extended the range and the ease with which information from people can be gained, stored and utilised.

It is this argument that disciplinary regulation underpins the whole web of social interaction and relationships – and that prisons, factories, schools and other institutions differ only in the degree to which they are permeated by such disciplinary regulation – that is perhaps Foucault's most controversial claim. Foucault's analysis dissolves the differences between punitive and non-punitive institutions and presents a view of society that is a mesh of disciplinary relationships – as he puts it, citizens of modern society are 'inhabitants of the punitive city within the carceral archipelago'. The prison is just one end of a continuum in which regulation and surveillance are normal. As mentioned above, the very term 'carceral archipelago' implies that a chain of institutions stretches out from the prison; and Foucault's whole argument conjures up images of totalitarianism and a 'Big Brother' society that does not sit easily with our notion of Western, liberal, democratic values. Indeed, this critical edge to Foucault's work perhaps explains why he has become so much in vogue in academic circles over the past few decades.

QUESTION BREAK: DISCIPLINARY OBSERVATION

The extract from *Discipline and Punish* that follows illustrates Foucault's analysis of how 'disciplinary power' works by using a series of simple instruments, including what he termed hierarchical observation. He describes how architectural planning can be used to help the surveillance of individuals in a wide range of social institutions, including hospitals, schools and working-class housing estates. He discusses how the power of observation operates in a more insidious and subtle manner than conventional means of exercising power, such as the use of force.

Hierarchical observation

The exercise of discipline presupposes a mechanism that coerces by means of observation: an apparatus in which the techniques that make it possible to see induce effects of power and in which, conversely, the means of coercion make those on whom they are applied clearly visible. Slowly, in the course of the classical age, we see the construction of those 'observatories' of human multiplicity for which the history of the sciences has so little good to say. . . .

These 'observatories' had an almost ideal model: the military camp – the short-lived artificial city, built and reshaped almost at will. . . . In the perfect camp, all power would be exercised solely through exact observation; each gaze would form part of the overall functioning of power. The old, traditional square plan was considerably refined in innumerable new projects. The geometry of the paths, the number and distribution of the tents, the orientation of their entrances, the disposition of files and ranks were exactly defined; the network of gazes that supervised one another was laid down: 'In the parade ground, five lines are drawn up; the first is sixteen feet from the second; the others are eight feet from one another; and the last is eight feet from the arms depots. . . . All tents are two feet from one another. The tents of the subalterns are opposite the alleys of their companies. The rear tentpole is eight feet from the last soldiers' tent and the gate is opposite the captain's tent . . .' For a long time this model of the camp, or at least its underlying principle, was found in urban development, in the construction of working-class housing surveillance. The principle was one of 'embedding' (*encastrement*). The camp was to the rather shameful art of surveillance what the dark room was to the great science of optics.

A whole problematic then develops: that of an architecture that is no longer built simply to be seen (as with the ostentation of palaces), or to observe the external space (cf. the geometry of fortresses), but to permit an internal, articulated and detailed control – to render visible those who are inside it; in more general terms, an architecture that would operate to transform individuals: to act on those it shelters, to provide a hold on their conduct, to carry the effects of power right to them, to make it possible to know them, to alter them. . . . In this way the hospital building was gradually organized as an instrument of medical action: it was to allow a better observation of patients, and therefore a better calibration of their treatment; the form of the buildings, by the careful separation of the patients, was to prevent contagions; lastly, the ventilation and the air that circulated around each bed were to prevent the deleterious vapors from stagnating around the patient, breaking down his humors and spreading the disease by their immediate effects. The hospital – which was to be built in the second half of the century and for which so many plans were drawn up after the Hotel-Dieu burnt down for the second time – was no longer simply the roof under which penury and imminent death took shelter; it was, in its very materiality, a therapeutic operator.

Similarly, the school building was to be a mechanism for training. It was as a pedagogical machine that Paris-Duverney conceived the École Militaire, right down to the minute details that he imposed on the architect, Gabriel. . . . The very building of the École was to be an apparatus for observation; the rooms were distributed along a corridor like a series of small cells; at regular intervals, an officer's quarters was situated, so that 'every ten pupils had an officer on each side'; the pupils were confined to their cells throughout the night; and Paris had insisted that 'a window be placed on the corridor wall of each room from chest level to within one or two feet of the ceiling. Not only is it pleasant to have such windows, but one would venture to say that it is useful, in several respects, not to mention the disciplinary reason that may determine this arrangement.' In the dining room was 'a slightly raised platform for the tables of the inspectors of studies, so that they may see all the tables of the pupils of their divisions during meals'; latrines had been installed with half-doors, so that the supervisor on duty could see the head and legs of the pupils, and also with side walls sufficiently high 'that those inside cannot see one another'. This infinitely scrupulous concern with surveillance is expressed in the architecture by innumerable petty mechanisms. These mechanisms can only be seen as unimportant if one forgets the role of this instrumentation, minor but flawless, in the progressive objectification and the ever more subtle partitioning of individual behaviour. The disciplinary institutions secreted a machinery of control that functioned like a microscope of conduct; the fine, analytical divisions that they created formed around men an apparatus of observation, recording and training. How was one to subdivide the gaze in these observation machines? How was one to establish a network of communications between them? How was one so to arrange things that a homogeneous, continuous power would result from their calculated multiplicity?

> The perfect disciplinary apparatus would make it possible for a single gaze to see everything constantly. A central point would be both the source of light illuminating everything and a locus of convergence for everything that must be known: a perfect eye that nothing would escape and a center toward which all gazes would be turned.
>
> (Foucault 1977, pp. 170–177)

Questions

Consider the institutions that you have come into contact with (such as schools/colleges, places of work, leisure centres, hospitals, etc.). To what extent does their design and architecture help to impose discipline and control?

What do you think are the main strengths and weaknesses of Foucault's argument that observation can be used as a means of regulation and control?

Foucault: comment and criticism

There is no disputing the fact that Foucault's much broader approach to the analysis of power and domination has changed the way in which social scientists think about those concepts. Foucault placed power at the centre of social life and has encouraged an examination of how power operates no longer through a centralised body, such as the state, but as a network without a centre. Power is invested in all the relationships that make up social life. However, in spite of the importance of these general ideas, the emphasis on 'hierarchical observation' and disciplinary control has raised concerns and been subject to specific research that has questioned some of Foucault's arguments.

In a paper that he entitled 'What Would It Matter if Everything Foucault Said about Prison Were Wrong?', Alford (2000) drew upon research that he undertook in a maximum-security state prison in Maryland, USA, to contrast Foucault's account of how power operates within prison with his own experience. Although Foucault emphasised the ways in which surveillance, categorisation and classification, and regimentation characterised the disciplinary nature of prisons, Alford did not find this to be the case in his research. Not only were those disciplinary practices absent, but he found almost the opposite to exist. The prison authorities in the prison he was based in did not spend their time constantly observing the prisoners, because they didn't have to. As long as the entrances and exits were controlled, there was no need to constantly monitor what was happening inside. As Alford points out, this approach is hardly new and is captured in the populist sentiment, 'lock 'em up and throw away the key'. So rather than excessive supervision, he found an absence of supervision to be the norm in US prisons. Close surveillance and supervision might still occur in the wider society but not within prisons: as Alford puts it, 'The panopticon might be a bad way to run a prison, but a good way to run a society, at least from the perspective of knowledge/power.'

Real power, for Alford, would involve not having to bother to look; indeed, having to look is a sign of the limits of power: '[I]f you have to look, you do not really control. If you are in control, you do not have to look.' What is important in controlling inmates within prison is the count – one inmate is exactly like another and all that needs check-ing is that none has escaped. '[T]he count is the ultimate in human superfluity, each inmate's like every other. But the count is not unique. It finds its tally in everyday life in bureaucracy.' Alford coins the term 'nonopticon' rather than panopticon as best describing what goes on in prisons. It is not that guards have a greater respect for the prisoners' privacy; rather, they don't care. One aspect of this not caring is the lack of concern with how prisoners spend their days and nights – as long as there is no trouble, what they do is immaterial. He argues that there is nowhere where time is less structured and people more idle than in prison.

While increased surveillance in general and the growing use of CCTV specifically can be and is criticised as attacking individuals' civil liberties and privacy, research into the use of CCTV inside police stations has produced some interesting findings that seem to offer 'support' for such monitoring from inmates and offenders themselves. Newburn and Hayman (2001) evaluated the use of CCTV within custody suites by the Metropolitan Police. Cameras have been introduced into booking areas and cell corridors as well as a small number of cells for 'vulnerable' prisoners. Newburn and Hayman found that the major worry that the inmates felt about the use of cameras was the invasion of privacy, with the filming of their use of the toilet a particular concern. They also found that the officers in the police stations were themselves bothered about the constant filming: as well as not being able to switch off images of people they had detained going to the toilet, they were concerned that the films might be used to check up on their behaviour too. However, the inmates did see some benefits from the use of cameras in police cells: they felt it increased their safety from physical threats, particularly in the case of those who had been assaulted when in custody previously. As one of the detainees said to Newburn and Hayman, 'They [police officers] wouldn't risk beating you up if they knew there were people watching the camera. The cameras are there for my benefit rather than theirs. I'm less likely to get a kicking.' So the detainees were aware of the benefits as well as being concerned about the intrusive nature of the cameras. Newburn and Hayman conclude by arguing that CCTV can be both a means of social control and a means of safeguarding individuals' rights, and can do these two things simultaneously: individuals may face a loss of privacy but they may also feel that they are better protected.

Summary

The sociological theories of punishment we have considered have tried to explain the form and role of punishment in society and to relate these to the changing nature of society. In introducing our discussion of these theories we referred to Garland's (1990) argument that styles and institutions of punishment have to be studied as social con-structions. We will finish this overview of such theories by considering the concluding comments that Garland makes in his more detailed study.

In spite of the hopes and claims that inevitably accompany the introduction of new forms of punishment, it is clear that no form of punishment has ever managed to control crime or to achieve high rates of reform of offenders. And Garland argues that it is unrealistic to expect anything else. Punishments are bound to 'fail' because they can never be much more than a back-up to the mainstream processes of socialisation. Acceptable standards of behaviour have to be learned; they cannot be forced on people. As Garland puts it, 'Punishment is merely a coercive back-up to those more reliable social mechanisms, a back-up which is often unable to do anything more than manage those who slip through these networks of normal control and integration' (1990, p. 289).

He suggests that maybe we should expect less from policies on punishment, which, while sometimes necessary, is inevitably beset by contradictions and tensions:

> However well it is organized, and however humanely administered, punishment is inescapably marked by moral contradictions and unwanted irony – as when it seeks to uphold freedom by means of its deprivation or condemn private violence using a violence which is publicly authorized.
>
> (1990, p. 292)

It is appropriate to finish the chapter by referring to Garland's work, as he is arguably the key modern commentator on theories of punishment, and in his work he has tried to move away from the tendency for one or other theoretical position to be the current 'flavour of the month'. While Foucault is understandably a major force in the area, Garland argues that we need the insights of all the major theorists for a fuller understanding of punishment. From the Marxist approach and from Foucault we can gain complementary but distinct appreciations of the relations between social institutions and the power dynamics of society; Durkheim's arguments demonstrate how punishment and the law are both part of and help to make up the moral character of a society; and Weber enables us to see the processes and policies of punishment in relation to broader issues concerned with the rationalisation of modern society.

Further reading

Cavadino, M. and Dignan, J. (2002) *The Penal System: An Introduction*, 3rd edn, London: Sage. Although this is a general introductory text that examines the workings of the contemporary criminal justice system, chapter 3, 'Explaining Punishment', provides a clear and accessible introduction to the main sociological theories of punishment.

Garland, D. (1990) *Punishment and Modern Society: A Study in Social Theory*, Oxford: Clarendon. This is a comprehensive introduction to the sociological study of punishment, which critically examines punishment as an instrument of ideology and as a means of class control. It includes a detailed assessment of the work of Durkheim and Foucault and of Marxist analyses.

Valier, C. (2002) *Theories of Crime and Punishment*, Harlow: Longman. While there are plenty of texts introducing criminology and criminological theory, this book provides a critical introduction to the main theories of both crime and punishment from the late eighteenth century to the present day.

The journal *Theoretical Criminology* is an interdisciplinary, international journal that focuses on the theoretical aspects of criminology, including research and comment that relates to the philosophies, theories and history of punishment.

3   The history of crime and justice

Introduction

The historical development of a state's criminal justice system can be viewed simply as a series of rational responses to 'criminality', as variously defined by successive governments through time. Alternatively, the criminal justice system can be described as the policies of a political executive (be it monarch, chief minister, council or parliament) which happened to hold power during the period under review. It is sometimes assumed that the historian relies on the collection and description of factual information to depict policy and its often lurid impact on those unfortunate enough to be ensnared by it. Tales of execution and blood on the axe and block vie with Dickensian stories of incarceration in Newgate, the Fleet prison or 'Bedlam' for the attention of the reader seeking fascinating tales of crime and punishment. Yet this is an inadequate means of understanding the meaning of criminal justice and punishment through the ages, and it disguises rather than examines the underlying structural issues. It is particularly weak as an explanation of policy. It fails to indicate the central importance of the range of interpretations and theoretical models that historians and sociologists of state punishment have established in their attempt to understand the development of a criminal justice system, its administration, and the impact on governors and governed alike. This chapter will select a variety of examples of state initiatives in penal policy from the medieval to the modern period and show how social theory can be effective in their examination.

This theoretical approach will consider two related themes: first, predominant sociological theories that are central to the interpretation of past policies on crime and punishment; and second, some of the contemporary theories of government, authority and punishment which conditioned policy action in the periods under review here. Consequently, this chapter builds on the discussion of theory established in Chapter 2; the theories of Marx, Durkheim, Weber and Foucault will be used variously to explain major policy changes, and modern writers such as Ignatieff, Cohen, E. P. Thompson, Hobsbawm, Sharpe and Ballinger will be used to show how modern research has developed earlier theoretical paradigms. Essentially, the chapter seeks to understand the history of crime and punishment in terms of the nature, structure and power matrices of the governments and societies responsible for such policies.

Of course it is possible to deny or at least play down the existence of crime in the past. The 'common-sense' view that crime is more prevalent and 'worse' in our modern society has been critically examined to great effect by Pearson (1983). He has shown how every generation feels threatened by contemporary society (especially its youth) and looks back, erroneously, on a 'golden age' in which crime was not such a problem. In this utopia all front doors remained open and 'everyone' was secure in the knowledge that the felons simply did not exist who would dare disturb a peace to which all subscribed. Such folk memories are not empirically verifiable, yet popular perceptions of criminality are an important area of analysis. Writers such as Pearson and also Cohen (1980) have used the idea of the 'moral panic' to show how perceptions of threat, which have little basis in fact, can have a real impact on the legislative process and produce important changes in the criminal law and penal policy. There are many examples of 'deviancy amplification' as a moral panic spirals out of control sufficiently to legitimise the increased severity of a state's punishment regime. Examples range from medieval Christian concern about schismatic sects, Protestant reactions to 'popery' after the Reformation, to nineteenth-century fears of 'Outcast London' and the garrotting panic of the 1860s. More modern crises include 'mods and rockers' (Cohen's classic work on the 1960s) and the threat of the black mugger in the 1970s. The concept of moral panic is important in assessing not just popular assumptions (i.e. 'bottom-up' understanding) but also the reasons for initiatives in state policy carried by governing elites ('top-down' action).

When complemented by state concern for the unity and stability of society and the security of the political system, moral panics are part of a significant force for the extension of punishment. This was especially recognised by Durkheim (see pp. 28–35), as he saw punishment as central to the establishment of the moral authority of the state and its social solidarity in order to preserve what he termed the 'conscience collective'. Of course, the 'moral authority' is imposed with greater force when a new institution of power has captured the state apparatus, and the policies of theocratic states in the medieval and early modern periods show this.

QUESTION BREAK: RELIGIOUS JUSTIFICATIONS FOR PUNISHMENT

The supporters of [religious] coercion looked . . . to the writings of St. Augustine who had done more than anyone else to legitimise the use of force in religion. . . . [H]e wrote a series of famous letters justifying the persecution of the Donatists [who] . . . were a purist, schismatic sect who had separated from the Catholic church. . . . His arguments carried the day, or rather the millennium, for his position became the established orthodoxy of Western Christendom, both Catholic and Protestant. . . . Elizabethan bishops, mid-seventeenth-century Puritans and Restoration Anglicans all justified their drive for uniformity by referring their readers to Augustine's famous epistles against the Donatists. . . .

[I]n the next two centuries the capital punishment of heretics was to become widespread across the continent. . . . The medieval Inquisition was established to counter the threat of these groups and the fourth Lateran Council of 1215 codified the theory and practice of persecution. The greatest medieval theologian Thomas Aquinas summed up the standard medieval position when he declared that obstinate heretics deserved 'not only to be separated from the church but eliminated from the world by death.' The condition of the Jews also worsened dramatically in these years, as massacres occurred in a number of areas of Europe, and vicious anti-semitic stereotypes developed. Eventually, in 1478, an Inquisition was established in Spain which aimed to destroy all remnants of Jewish faith in the land. Finally, from the mid-fifteenth century, we find the first outbreaks of the witch-hunts that were to claim more than 30,000 lives over the next three centuries.

The sixteenth-century Reformation did little to end these persecutions. Indeed, by presenting a new and more powerful threat to the unity of Christendom than medieval heresies, the Reformation served to intensify persecution by Catholic regimes. . . . [They] fully embraced Augustine's vision of the coercive role of the Christian magistrate, and many shared Aquinas' belief in the legitimacy of the death penalty for heresy.

Yet the theorists of uniformity were not just concerned about religious truth and church unity, but also about political order. . . . [They were] much more concerned with political power and the preservation of stability. . . . There can be no doubt that defenders of uniformity were convinced that religious pluralism would have disastrous political consequences. . . .

Most early modern Englishmen assumed that some form of religious uniformity was absolutely essential for the unity of the nation. . . . To tolerate different religions, therefore, was to commit political suicide. . . .

Those who supported persecution constantly stressed the seditious character of religious deviants. Sir William Cecil [in Elizabethan England] was emphatic in his assertion that Catholics were only executed for sedition, not for their religion.

(Coffey 2000, pp. 22–38)

Questions

Summarise the views of St Augustine and suggest why they had such a significant impact on state punishment policy.

Explain the severity of state punishment for 'religious deviants' in this period.

Why did Catholic regimes 'intensify persecution' during the Reformation?

Why do you think the toleration of different religions might be seen as 'political suicide'?

Early history: before the 'Bloody Code'

Thus punishment in the medieval and early modern state was a direct function of concern by elites for political and social stability. It also represented a clear endorsement of the dominant religious and political beliefs of the day. There were elements of a 'moral panic' in the reactions of state authority to religious diversity in the period. Of course, there were fundamental challenges to religious orthodoxy, and it is not the intention here to relegate the Reformation to a moral panic. However, it is equally clear that politico-religious authority at this time was exceptionally sensitive to any group or movement that seemed to constitute an alternative faith, new intellectual paradigm or political threat. As in all the cases we consider in this chapter, the correlation between the actual, as opposed to the perceived, threat is variable, but the impact on penal policy is consistently demonstrated.

The role of the prison in the early modern period provides another example where sociological theory can be applied to historical change. Peters (1998) refers to this as the 'prison before the [modern] prison', and he describes the increase of imprisonment as a complement to forms of penalty such as mutilation, the wheel, the rack and other forms of execution. Peters emphasises the custodial role of prisons as pre-trial holding stockades rather than the punishment itself:

> When Henry II issued the Assizes of Clarendon in 1166, he ordered that sheriffs should build jails in each county to hold those accused of felonies until they could be tried by itinerant royal justices. . . .

> From the 1270s on, the number of prisons in England and of imprisonable offenses increased rapidly. By 1520 there were 180 imprisonable offenses in the common law.
> (Peters 1998, p. 31)

The increase in such offences and the extension of state punishment were a feature of the Tudor period in England. The high point of judicial excess was reached in the reign of the Catholic Mary I. 'Bloody Mary' ensured that over 300 Protestant heretics were burned alive in three years (1555–1558). Elizabeth I sentenced over 700 to death for supporting the Northern Rebellion, and it is estimated that there were over 1,000 executions a year in the Tudor period (1485–1603); 75,000 died in the period 1530–1630. If such a rate of judicial slaughter were replicated today in the United States, it is estimated that executions would run at 46,000 per annum (Coffey 2000; Jenkins 1986). Such executions were public theatre and often required that victims be disembowelled before death. Imprisonment, transportation (to America and Australia) and torture, especially the rack, were also used, not only against religious deviants but also against those convicted of treason (which was usually closely linked to the heretical) or indicted for a felony (homicide, highway robbery and burglary, for example).

An increase in the severity was also a central feature of Puritan punishment regimes (1640–1660) as 'popery' was targeted, and angry reactions to a massacre of Protestants in Ireland provoked Puritan attacks on Charles I and led eventually to the outbreak of civil war in England. Religious militancy once again determined criminal justice and was sufficiently important here to revolutionise the constitutional and political structure of the country.

After the traumas of the Civil War and the restoration of the monarchy under Charles II (1660), state punishment operated in a new context and there were significant changes in its nature and incidence. For example, it is clear that from the mid-seventeenth century the rate of execution in England shows a significant change, with imprisonment increasingly favoured as punishment (see Table 3.1).

QUESTION BREAK

Table 3.1 Capital punishment inflicted for felony: Palatinate of Chester, 1580–1709

Years	No. of executions
1580–1588	91
1600–1609	62
1620–1629	165
1640–1649	12
1660–1669	18
1680–1689	24
1700–1709	10

Source: Sharpe (1999, p. 91)

[T]he crucial issue is clear enough: in the century before 1640 English society was, and felt itself to be, under pressure.

By the 1660s this pressure had waned, and the late 17th and early 18th centuries experienced a period of relative social stability. Changes and conflicts still occurred, of course, but they did so within the constraints of a new equilibrium. For the historian of crime, the most important component of this equilibrium was the emergence of the poor as an institutionalized presence. The poor were not now the occasional beggar ... nor were they the sturdy beggars of Elizabethan drama. They were that third or so of the population who ... were unlikely to be able to support themselves from week to week without assistance. The propertied, however much they grumbled over the poor rates, and however much they despised the labouring poor, had learnt to live with them, and to fit them into their concepts of how society functioned. In such a context the poor house or the house of correction was a handier means of controlling the poor than ... frequent executions. ...

Disorder and division were still present, but they were less menacing than they had been ... and above all they were perceived as being less menacing by contemporaries. Most arguments on this point have revolved around elite culture and elite reactions: [and here] is an image of a 'settled and relaxed world' in the 18th century. The falling off of prosecution ... and the drop in executions ... must be regarded as symptoms of this massive shift. Behind it all ... there lies an unconscious psychological reaction as the wave of demographic expansion levelled off.

(Sharpe 1999, pp. 264–266)

Sharpe also shows that the percentage of felons receiving the death penalty fell dramatically in this period. In the mid-sixteenth century, about 25 per cent of cases brought the death penalty. By the early eighteenth century this was around 10 per cent. Also, the rate of acquittal rose. By the first decade of the eighteenth century, about 40 per cent of those accused were released; comparable figures a century earlier were about 25–27 per cent. In the period there was also a rise in the numbers transported, with figures of 20 per cent of cases reported. According to Sharpe, these figures illustrate a clear shift in state punishment policy.

There is another important question which needs addressing. Why did the use of the prison increase so? In Britain, a form of the prison called a 'house of correction' was used from the mid-sixteenth century, and its increase has also generated debates about the origins and purpose of such institutions. The 'house' represented an important change in the nature of state punishment in Britain. Sharpe believed that it 'provides an almost unique example of an institution which has been universally regarded as marking a new departure in such matters. The house of correction, of which the London Bridewell was the prototype, constituted an important shift in punishment policy' (1999, p. 256). The 'new departure' was the use of the prison for the reform of the criminal and to impose the discipline of labour. Inmates were put to work, in textile manufacture usually, and their output could be sold to generate profit for the institution. Given the regard for reform and rehabilitation, the house of correction can be seen as the ancestor of the modern prison, whose development is treated more fully below. Explanations for such shifts in penal policy include the important Marxist interpretation of the rise of the prison found in Rusche and Kirchheimer's classic *Punishment and Social Structure*, which was published in 1939 (see pp. 40–45). It is a key Marxist interpretation of the history of incarceration and its development up to the modern day. This Marxist approach looked at the rise of the prison (indeed, all criminal law) as the product of economic forces and the needs of an emerging capitalist mode of production. The prison, it is argued, is vital to the mature, capitalist economy because it retains and disciplines the labour force, secures adequate social control of labour units and perpetuates the exploitation of the workers in the interests of the bourgeois elites. The bourgeoisie thus remain the controllers of the 'means of production, distribution and exchange'.

QUESTION BREAK: THE RISE OF THE PRISON

Rusche and Kirchheimer ... argue that far from being motivated by humanitarianism, the establishment of houses of correction [and later prison regimes] reflected a growing demand for a regulated and disciplined labour force in the days of emerging agrarian capitalist and mercantile societies. In reviewing changes in forms of punishment from the late Middle Ages to the 1930s, they contend that:

Transformation in penal systems cannot be explained only from changing needs of the war against crime. Every system of production tends to discover punishments which correspond to its productive relationships. . . .

The rationale for the houses of correction . . . lies in the fact that they were primarily factories turning out commodities at a particularly low cost due to their cheap labour. Their use burgeoned . . . because the relative labour shortage in the general population coincided with the development of mercantilism [commercial expansion]. In short, to secure the development of an emerging capitalism, the labour of prisoners was to be exploited. . . .

It was the conditions of the local labour market which frequently determined . . . [that] valuable, able-bodied workers tended to be confined in houses of correction for as long as possible.

(Muncie 1996, p. 161)

Questions

What forms of emerging capitalism did the houses of correction resemble?

Given that the houses emerged in the sixteenth century and that their inmates were often vagabonds, army deserters and petty criminals, how might the Marxist link between imprisonment and capitalism be criticised?

Criticise the view that such houses were the direct forerunners of the modern prison.

The eighteenth century and the 'Bloody Code'

The eighteenth century was a period of considerable social, economic and political change. Population growth was spectacular. Stimulated by industrialisation, it doubled from about 5 million to over 10 million. Urban growth and migration became features of Britain's development: in the period 1700–1750, London attracted about half a million migrants, and as early as 1700, 25 per cent of the population of England lived in towns. The period saw political upheaval and rebellion as the succession to the throne remained controversial following the removal of the Stuarts. Great political disturbances shattered notions of an ordered society. Violence seemed endemic in politics and society, and the British were regarded as 'an ungovernable people'. Governments became acutely concerned about the preservation of social stability and the defence of property. They perceived the masses as increasingly dangerous, and fear of crime began to reach the dimensions of a moral panic.

Historians of criminal justice identify a direct connection between social upheaval, economic instability and depression, and increases in crime and perceptions of its threat by political elites and other propertied classes. Heightened perception of criminality leads to a more vigorous application of the criminal code and a strengthening of agencies responsible for crime and punishment. Certainly the economic trends discussed in the previous paragraph increased social polarisation and tension, and it is easy to understand how historians such as Hay and Thompson see the criminal justice system in this period as an ideological instrument preserving class hegemony, or at least, as Gatrell (1994) believes, securing the social hierarchy in the interests of the powerful and propertied. Debates about this and the eighteenth-century 'Bloody Code' are discussed in what follows, but it is clear that eighteenth-century law had the role of legitimising the political system that produced it and the distribution of political power and property upon which it was founded. The following example illustrates this important point.

In 1723 Parliament passed the 'Black Act'. It created about fifty new capital offences immediately and was passed by the Commons without any debate. The initial reason for the legislation was the sharp rise in attacks on cattle, deer and rabbits in Windsor Forest by thieves and poachers whose faces had been blacked to avoid detection. The list of offences was extended to include acts of arson and the cutting down of trees and breaking the heads of fish ponds. The historian of the Black Act, E. P. Thompson (1985), has shown how it enforced the Whig political ascendancy (Whigs had displaced Tories as the ruling party after the removal of the Stuart kings in 1688) and generalised the protection of property rights at a time when Whigs felt insecure in the face of their enemies the Hanoverians (who supported the new king, George I). Popular ideas that the masses had legitimate access to land and its product were also destroyed. The Act demonstrated the contrast between 'normative', or popular, notions of right and wrong, and the more powerful legal definitions imposed by law.

QUESTION BREAK: THE BLACK ACT

Thompson saw this law as an instrument of class power:

[The Black Act] is clearly an instrument of the ruling class: it both defines and defends these rulers' claims upon resources and labour-power. It says what shall be property and what shall be crime – and it mediates class relations with a set of appropriate rules and sanctions, all of which, confirm and consolidate existing class power. Hence the rule of law is only another mask for the rule of a class. . . .

But this is not the same thing as to say that the rulers had need of law in order to oppress the ruled, while those who were ruled had need of none. What was at issue was not property, supported by law, against no property; it was alternative definitions of property rights: for the landowner, enclosure; for the cottager, common [land] rights; for the forest officialdom, 'preserved grounds' for the deer; for the foresters, the right to take turfs.

(1985, pp. 259–261)

Questions
Suggest reasons for the great number of capital offences established.

In what sense can the Black Act be seen as an 'instrument of the ruling class'?

The eighteenth century was also the era of the 'Bloody Code'. The English criminal law was one of the most savage in Europe. The flow of capital statutes was the product of contemporary fears that a supposed criminal class was increasing its assault on respectable society. Governments indicated that harsh penalties were required to defend a society under attack. Yet here too there is debate. Many of these statutes, such as the Black Act, were passed without serious examination by the House of Commons and considered by its members to be a conventional response to the subversive masses. It was the defence of property and the state that was at the heart of such legislation, and the 'Bloody Code' was administered by political and social elites in their own interests to impose a measure of social control over the masses. From the 1750s there seemed ample evidence for those who felt that the collapse of civil society was imminent in the face of great increases in crime and civil disorder. Sir Henry Fielding, Chief Magistrate at Bow Street in London, suspected that the idle masses were increasingly a threat to 'respectable classes' and dangerously attracted to seditious schemes and treasonous designs. This was the time of the creation of the Bow Street Runners (the 'Thief-Takers') and horse patrols, and the increases in the establishment of watchmen and stipendiary magistrates. Fielding's brother, Sir John Fielding, demanded increases in the efficiency of magistrates across England.

Such panics were reinforced by dramatic outbreaks of civil disorder. London riots were provoked by support for John Wilkes's campaign for increased political representation (the cry was 'Wilkes and Liberty') in 1768, and the Gordon Riots of 1780 provoked a week of destruction in the capital as fears of uncontrolled popery ran wild. The powers of government were further placed in doubt by the loss of the American colonies by the mid-1780s and the unending, or so it seemed, list of strikes and food riots which increasingly challenged the coherence of the state and its powers to keep the peace. Even elements of the armed forces refused to comply, in 1783, when ordered to defend the American colonies in the final stages of the War of Independence. By the 1790s, an age of unreason seemed to threaten. The excesses and upheavals of the French Revolution appeared ready to cross the Channel. For treason, the Code indicated hanging, drawing and quartering; women murdering their husbands were burned at the stake. Persons found guilty of a felony (murder, theft, robbery, rape, forgery and burglary, for example) were hanged. In the late seventeenth century there were fifty capital offences. By 1800 this number had risen to over 200.

The period demonstrates an increase in the number of convictions, and the percentage of felons convicted. Pardons were increasingly refused, and the numbers of felons hanged rose to heights not reached in a century. In the 1780s the proportion of those condemned to death who were actually hanged leaped from a previous average per annum of 30 per cent to over 60 per cent, and in 1787 it is known that the figure reached 80 per cent. This seems to support traditional views of the impact of a 'Bloody Code' targeted by later nineteenth-century reformers as a barbaric and shameful expression of the arbitrary power of the criminal law in an unenlightened era. It also seems to support the view from the left that the 'Bloody Code' was a piece of 'class legislation'.

Revisionist historians have a different view. Langbein (1983) and Emsley (1996b), for example, have rejected the view that the eighteenth-century criminal code was the result of the self-regarding action of an identifiable, coherent and unified governing class committed to the manipulation and control of an equally distinct and identifiable class of the labouring, poverty-stricken and criminally inclined. Rather, they see the law providing for the resolution of disputes within and between a range of competing groups, and they reject the polarised model of social conflict indicated by left-wing historians such as Hay and his colleagues. According to this alternative explanation, the many capital statutes provided an alternative, lesser sentence which was left to the discretion of the judge. Transportation, under the Act of 1718, is such an example, and until the American War of Independence it was used increasingly as an alternative, secondary punishment for a growing list of property offences. Revisionists emphasise that many of the eighteenth-century capital statutes were in fact never used and that most convictions were achieved using older legislation. It would seem, from this standpoint, that Parliament was not really concerned about any perceived threat to the social and political fabric (there was little debate about such issues of criminal justice when Parliament sat), and the 'Bloody Code' has been misinterpreted.

QUESTION BREAK: THE 'BLOODY CODE'

Argue the case for and against the view that the 'Bloody Code' was a clear piece of 'class legislation'.

The birth of the prison: the late eighteenth century and beyond

The late eighteenth and early nineteenth centuries represented a turning point of great importance in punishment practices in Britain. Capital punishment declined in incidence, and public displays of hangings and ritual disembowelment were abandoned after centuries of practice. The public assault on the body of criminals was traditionally accepted as necessary to display the power and majesty of the socio-political system and especially to broadcast the limitless capacity of the monarchy to exercise ultimate control over life and death. This theatre of punishment had the most serious objective: the social control of the masses, by example. Yet the plan could misfire. Folk heroes on the scaffold could invite attempts at rescue or give a volatile crowd the opportunity to express opposition to the very forces of law there demonstrated. More frequently, the executions were occasion for the mixing of people from all walks of life, and the melodrama of death was often reinforced by impassioned speeches from the condemned. They attributed their downfall to drink, woman or their own idleness and misfortune, and expressed their regret and penitence while warning others who might be tempted to follow in their footsteps. A successful scaffold oration brought the condemned public acclamation, and a 'good end' was applauded and remembered in ballad and broadsheet. Copies of famous 'last words' were very popular and sold widely in the eighteenth century.

Yet by the late eighteenth century, public execution as a spectacle was being questioned. By the 1820s, after much debate, punishment was rationalised and was moved behind closed doors. It was a period of the rise of the modern prison and the establishment of the 'new' police, and debates about the role of incarceration rather than execution dominated contemporary debate. The issues were given greater urgency by the disappearance of the option of transportation as the American colonies gained their independence, and rising concerns about the cost of maintaining a penal colony in Australia led to the eventual abolition of transportation. Imprisonment in hulks tied in southern coastal waters was increasing by the 1790s as the transportation option receded. As it turned out, this constituted the first phase in the move over to incarceration as a major feature of public penal policy. Although the abandonment of transportation was not to be official policy until 1868, opposition to transportation had been mounting for some time as concerns over the efficacy of such punishment were added to the financial issues. This is discussed later when the philosophy of punishment in the emergent modern state of the nineteenth century is considered.

Calls for the reform of punishment and a less severe penal code and a more humane and rational system of punishment appeared in the historical literature. In particular, the origins of modern criminology can be traced to Cesare Beccaria's *An Essay on Crimes and Punishments*, published in 1764. Beccaria attacked uncontrolled use of execution as misconceived. For him, the severity of punishment should be governed by the nature of the crime rather than the criminal, and punishment should be sufficient for deterrence and based on rational grounds comprehensible to the public. The assumption in this 'classical theory of criminality' was that crime was the result of individual, rational choice and that the best policy was crime prevention rather than arbitrary and severe punishment. Such prevention would best be achieved by condemning the offender to hard physical labour in order to deter future offenders. Such theories were very much part of the period known as the Enlightenment, and Beccaria's rational approach to these issues was in keeping with the views of English reformers such as William Eden, Sir Samuel Romilly, John Howard and Elizabeth Fry (who attempted to reform conditions facing women prisoners in Newgate). It was Howard, campaigning in the 1770s and 1780s, who was responsible for the spread of the idea for the penitentiary as the preferred alternative to execution, and the rise of the modern prison dates from this period of debate and reform. A follower of Beccarian philosophy was Jeremy Bentham, whose Utilitarian approach to punishment involved the prison as a means of constant surveillance. His Panopticon of 1791 was a plan for such a prison and, although never built, it represents the changing nature of the debate about appropriate punishment (see pp. 52–53). Of importance for the new philosophy was Bentham's proposal that new prisons be financed by the labour of prisoners, who, it was hoped, would calculate that it was wiser to avoid offending rather than submit to such a prison regime.

Traditional interpretations of the rise of the prison in the nineteenth century (Radzinowicz 1968, and more recently McGowan 1998) as a departure from the barbarism of earlier punishment regimes are described as 'Whiggish' models of explanation. Here the prison is seen as the result of humanitarian reform and part of a whole package of advances in social reform which would lead to the greater welfare reforms of the twentieth century and the concept of the modern welfare state. Such an approach does not really withstand critical, or historical, scrutiny. Howard's reforming zeal and the ideals of Elizabeth Fry were not confirmed by subsequent policy, and the ideal of the humanitarian reformation of the prisoner remained a theoretical ideal to those responsible for administering Victorian prisons.

An important perspective which moved beyond traditional approaches to the history of punishment is that of the French philosopher Michel Foucault, already discussed in Chapter 2. His major work in this area is *Discipline and Punish: The Birth of the Modern Prison*, published in 1977. Foucault suggests that a 'carceral society' was being established at this time which moved punishment away from the public arena. The change occurred gradually, but the public ritual of execution was replaced by the greater subtleties of institutionalised punishment. For Foucault, the prison was one of many institutions created in the nineteenth century in order to develop a matrix of control that transmitted and circulated discourses of conformity and power that were internalised by the masses. Here the focus is on imprisonment, but mental institutions, hospitals, workhouses, schools and factories were, for Foucault, part of a complex which ensured the control of the body and the subjection of the mind in what are called 'power–knowledge' matrices that manipulated the masses. For Foucault, prisons demonstrated power over the mind and body and were concrete representations of social division and the normalising of incarceration as a means of social control (see pp. 47–56).

Foucault's analysis includes what at first seems the odd claim that the prison, as it developed in the nineteenth century, actually failed to achieve its goal of reforming offenders. Foucault, however, claims that this failure was actually a central part of the state's penal strategy. In effect, tolerated recidivism would mean the continued recycling of offenders through prison and back to society. The state prison would be publicly legitimised as the defender of the community as it acted to incarcerate the 'dangerous classes'. The masses, therefore, could be 'provoked' (a key Foucauldian concept) into obedience. In this way the Victorian state, officially bounded by liberal principles of *laissez-faire* and the ideology of the minimalist nature of state intervention into the lives of its citizens, could extend the administration and rationalisation of the emerging prison system.

Foucault does not identify a specific source of power and control. Marxists, however (Rusche and Kirchheimer, for example), regard the prison as a function of industrialisation with the precise aim of controlling the labour force in the interests of the capitalist class. In this view, capitalists created the prison as a factory of repression to hold a reserve army of labour ready to be used as the business cycle dictated. Thus the prison was part of an apparatus of social control and discipline that preserved the dominance of the bourgeoisie. Here too the failure of the prison to eradicate crime completely was not necessarily catastrophic, as fear of crime and recidivist (working-class) criminals would divide the working classes as they feared for their own security. Thus they would become more dependent than ever on the paternalist bourgeois state. It is central to Marxist thinking that the criminal justice system is required to endorse a capitalist social structure itself determined by economic change and industrialisation. Criminal justice is designed to protect property, control the labouring masses and preserve the class hierarchy.

In Michael Ignatieff's important work, the prison is explained as a new strategy of punishment emerging in the early nineteenth century following disillusionment with the effectiveness of traditional rituals of public punishment. Ignatieff does not offer a pure Marxist perspective but does see the prison as a successful exercise in social control as elites responded to fears of crime waves and the social disruption in a period of dramatic economic, social and political change in the period 1780–1850. Ignatieff feels that the prison was not just an attempt to control crime:

> The persistent support for the penitentiary is inexplicable so long as we assume that its appeal rested on its functional capacity to control crime. Instead, its support rested on a larger social need. It had appeal because the reformers succeeded in present-ing it as a response, not merely to crime, but to the whole social crisis of a period, and as a part of a larger strategy of political, social and legal reform designed to re-establish order on a new foundation. As a result . . . the penitentiary continued to command support because it was seen as an element of a larger vision of order that by the 1840s commanded the reflexive assent of the propertied and powerful.
>
> (1978, p. 210)

There are links with ideas of class power and discourses of social control, but Ignatieff adopts a revisionist stance in that he avoids Marxist notions of economic determinism and focuses on the process of reform in its social context. The transformation of punishment policy in Britain was extensive. The 1779 Penitentiary Act began the building of new prisons in London, and Millbank Prison, with capacity for 1,000 inmates, was opened in 1816. Peel's Gaol Act of 1823 attempted to impose uniform standards of administration and inspection across the country and to improve the health and treatment of prisoners. The culmination of reform was the opening of Pentonville in 1842 (see p. 188). As we have seen, such reform can be explained as the result of the efforts of social reformers such as John Howard and William Eden and the humanitarian impulses of the day. However, Ignatieff's explanation is more radical. He dismisses Whiggish notions of humanitarian reform and emphasises the importance of social control theories. Ignatieff places his explanation for the rise of the prison firmly in the context of nineteenth-century social and economic upheavals. Social peace and stability was perceived by both traditional, landed elites and the new-rich factory owners and capitalists to be endangered. Such powerful opinion makers, including many middle-class property owners, saw what they felt to be the critical balance of classes that had once secured social stability directly threatened. The spread of industrialisation, increased population growth and movement, growing urbanisation, the impact of faster travel as the railways were laid from 1830, changes to the labour market and the increase in the volatility of labour relations were forces that posed new questions about social control. There were transformations in the social structure as the period saw what the social historian E. P. Thompson has called 'the making of the English working class'.

Clearly, Ignatieff's model has the marks of a Marxist thesis, as the emergence of capitalism and changing class relations are central to his explanation for rise of the prison. Other social historians have also used the concept of social control to explain the trans-formation in penal policy as the product of the tensions between social classes. Garland (1985) explains penal policy in the Victorian period to 1890 as the outcome of a growing concern of the state, and those classes who directed it, to control a mix of targeted communities. Such groups were the stuff of innumerable Victorian panics throughout the period and included the working classes, the poor, the criminal, the 'alien' (Irish especially), the prostitute, the unemployed and the itinerant. Garland sees the incarceration of such groups as an example of social control policy founded upon contemporary ideas of a moral divide. Those classes beneath respectability were morally bankrupt at best and criminally dangerous at worst. The respectable part of the working class could be saved by the Methodist mission, the savings bank, mechanics' institutes and Samuel Smiles's gospel of 'self-help'. Those beneath constituted an underclass requiring control and incarceration. Garland writes:

> [There was] a definite gulf between 'respectable' and 'rough' elements of the working classes, a separation clearly understood by the individuals involved. . . . This division, and the respectable life-styles, responsible opinions and respectful attitudes that it upheld, were the major achievements of the forces of discipline and moralisation. The practices of penality, the poor law, the charities and so on ensured that these divisions were maintained by the threat of punishment or pauperisation for those who traversed the moral divide. But this separation once established, was by no means secure. . . . There was thus a continuing problem of containment and quarantine. Once concentrated in this small class, criminality and its related vices had to be kept there, within its fixed and manageable bounds.
>
> (1985, p. 39)

There are links here with Foucault's model of a nineteenth-century 'carceral society' with its archipelago of disciplinary institutions ranging from its centrepiece, the prison, to the police, poor law workhouses, elementary and charity schools, hospitals, mental institutions and the operation of the labour market. Clearly, the prison and the 'new' police as they developed from 1830 represented the strengthening of the power of the modern state and its legal–rational, legitimate force. The state was equipped with the power to control its own population in the interests of social stability and the defence of the constitution.

The police and the emergence of the criminal justice system

The creation of the police was a major development in the evolution of the nineteenth-century Criminal Justice System. Peel's Metropolitan Police Act of 1829 is often seen as a seminal act in the formation of the modern penal system. The state's 'legitimate force' registered the strength of its 'legal–rational authority' (as Weber puts it). The historians of the 'new police' (Emsley 1996a; Phillips 1983) have shown that there is a range of interpretation of their significance. For the traditional school, the police were a legitimate response to the growth of urban unrest and the criminal tendencies of the masses during an era of revolutionary economic and industrial change. There was also the danger of political revolution after the end of the Napoleonic Wars in 1815. These are the views of Whiggish, conservative historians who celebrate the institutions of state control as evidence for the growth of 'civilised society' and the calming of the passions of the masses. Representative of this view is the work of Charles Reith (1938, 1943) and Leon Radzinowicz (1968), who lionised Peel as the man who had brought efficiency and control to an outdated system reliant on part-time parish constables and aged watchmen. Such an interpretation is also linked to triumphalist views of the police as the guarantor of the British Constitution and its ability to guarantee freedom and democracy. Revisionist work such as that by Robert Storch (1975) suggests a different story. Here the police are seen as the representatives of economic elites who are determined to control the masses in the interests of the existing power relations. Storch quoted contemporary working-class views of the new police as a 'plague of blue locusts' determined to enforce new laws which restricted not only the political radicalism of the masses but also their cultural and sporting 'excesses' in the interests of the preservation of a subservient labour force. E. P. Thompson (1985) has written persuasively of assaults by elites on the 'moral economy' of the English crowd. This meant that the authorities were determined to remove the right of demonstration, which had been a tradition in working-class communities when grievances (in Thompson's research it was outrage at high grain prices) were considered important enough for public display. Hobsbawm (1964) refers to the expression of working-class industrial grievances using 'collective bargaining by riot'. The police, in effect, were an ideal instrument of class hegemony, acting as 'domestic missionaries' as they tightened supervision of the unruly. This view has been endorsed by Marxists, who have seen the police as no more than the agents of a coercive, bourgeois state. However, ideas of 'hegemony' and social control are by no means unproblematic. There is no real evidence of a coherent, identifiable elite class acting to extend police control over town and village in their own class interests. Indeed, there was hostility to the police as 'Continental despotism' among the middle and professional classes. In many provincial areas, widespread resistance to the 'new police' meant that a force was not established until decades after Peel's metropolitan experiment. Neither is there unequivocal evidence of consistent and united working-class opposition to the police as 'blue locusts'. Again, this is not without debate; while Emsley does accept that violent clashes between policemen and working-class communities occurred with frequency, he also points out that

> it would be wrong to conceive of the relationship between the working class and the police in the second half of the 19th century as entirely one of mutual hostility. Many members of the working class also sought respectability and desired orderliness and decorum. It is probable that . . . the appearance of the police on the streets increasingly led members of the working class to believe that they too had the right to freedom from the annoyance of crime and public disorder.
>
> (1996a, p. 80)

QUESTION BREAK

Why would members of the working classes fear the 'new police' as a 'plague of blue locusts'?

How convincing are the views of orthodox historians of crime and justice who see the 'new police' as no more than a justifiable response to the rise of illegality in a society increasingly out of control?

Summarise the main different schools of thought on the creation of the 'new police'.

The twentieth century witnessed the growing centralisation of the administration of the police force as local watch committees and police authorities found themselves by-passed as the technical and financial demands of policing escalated. The advent of the motor car and the steady rise in crime after the Second World War were just two factors which enforced rationalisation and central control. The Desborough Committee of 1919 was a significant step towards rationalisation, and the process was strengthened by the demands of the wartime emergency from 1939 to 1945 and perceptions of threats to social order in the post-war period represented by growing trade union militancy and urban unrest.

For the sociologist Max Weber, the nineteenth century was a period in which the modern state developed, and he pointed particularly to the role of bureaucracy as evidence for the emergence of modern state apparatuses and the extension of legitimised state powers. Social control, and its agencies in the police and criminal justice system, has been the subject of a series of important studies by historians and criminologists (see, for example Cohen and Scull 1985; Ignatieff 1978). While acknowledging that simplistic notions of a crude 'class hegemony' or polarity of classes do little to further understanding of the complexity of nineteenth-century society, they defend the concept of social control as an important element driving public penal policy.

The work of Gareth Stedman Jones has reinforced the social control model. His *Outcast London* shows how the authorities created a range of responses to what was perceived by the 1880s as a flood tide of dangerous classes, a social residuum before which civilised society faced destruction. This is a recurrent theme in a period which, as discussed above, witnessed the triumph of the coercive and retributive ideal. As Stedman Jones explains:

> The social crisis of London in the mid-1880s engendered a major reorientation of middle class attitudes towards the casual poor. In conjunction with the growing anxiety about the decline of Britain's industrial supremacy, apprehensions about the depopulation of the countryside and uncertainty about the future political role of the working classes, fear of the casual residuum played a significant part in the intellectual assault against laissez faire . . . in the 1880s.
>
> [. . .]
>
> The counterpart to the wooing of the respectable working class . . . was the espousal of a more coercive interventionist policy towards the 'residuum'. The residuum was far too great a threat to be left to natural forces and the poor law. . . . At a time when the residuum might overrun London, this policy of laissez faire was dangerous.
>
> (Stedman Jones 1984, pp. 296–297, 303)

A central feature of a modern state is a centrally administered criminal justice system, uniformly organised on bureaucratic lines, endorsing a social and political consensus (as agreed by those social groups sharing power) on the nature of criminality and appropriate state-endorsed penal sanctions. It is in Victorian Britain especially that these characteristics were developed. Before we discuss the changes in the administration of justice, there is an issue which has provoked some debate. If the extension of state power is a feature of the period, how is it that the ideology of *laissez-faire* and the minimalist model of state intervention could be regarded as compatible with this extension of the modern state? The answer lies in the philosophy of individual culpability which governed the operation of the disciplinary agencies. The Poor Law Amendment Act of 1834 (the 'new' poor law) and the Prisons Act of 1865 (the most important Act determining prisons policy in the nineteenth century) provide good examples of official sanction given to the principle of 'less eligibility'. Workhouses and prisons were to be institutions where the regime was to be made more enduringly harsh than the conditions experienced by the lowest labourer outside. In prisons, the dominant penal option, the regime was dominated by the control of time, silent routines, solitary confinement, and meticulous controls over diet, medical treatment, clothing and movement. Repetitive work having no ostensible value or outcome was a requirement. The treadmill and the endless 'oakum picking' (separating the strands in large pieces of old, thick rope) were to impress upon the prisoner the value of obedience and the value of a disciplined and rigorous use of time. Each inmate was to be treated with the same rigorous uniformity. Such a measure of control over body and mind, frequently endorsed by the prison chaplain using the exhortations of the Christian religion, was nevertheless regarded as a means of correcting the inmates' capacity to rationalise the value of criminal conduct. It is interesting to note that transportation to the colonies had declined in the early nineteenth century as policymakers were concerned, among other things, that the removal of felons to such faraway places reduced the possibility of control and uniform manipulation of each individual offender. The focus was on the 'micro-control' of the individual, who was to be treated the same as everybody else. Penality was certainly not individualised (i.e. the particular needs of the individual recognised), but the 'disciplinary gaze' (as Foucault put it) of the institutions of control established a process of 'individuation' as each prisoner was wrapped in the total embrace of the penal institution.

The mid-nineteenth-century state made no commitment to provide comprehensive, universal social support or provide for the rehabilitation of prisoners. The philosophy was summed up in an important government investigation of the prison system in 1863 when the Carnarvon Commission stressed the value of deterrence over any ideas of rehabilitation or reformation of the prisoner. It was this philosophy which was to dominate penal policy until the end of the century. As Carnarvon put it:

> The large majority of criminals were low and brutish, 'mainly swayed by self-gratification and animal appetite'. It followed that such brutes must be managed physically: 'the enforcement of continuous labour, which the true criminal abhors, and an uninviting diet which is unquestionably the odious penalty in his eyes'. Self-gratifying instincts should be foiled by withholding all indulgences and diversions such as secular books, slates [i.e. writing materials], hammocks and the like.
> (comments of the Earl of Carnarvon, quoted in Muncie 1996, p. 186)

The Prison Act of 1877 secured the control of the prison service in the hands of central government and finally removed the vestiges of local autonomy in the penal practice. Hence, it was an important recognition of the powers of the emergent, modern state apparatus. Also in 1877, the new Prison Commissioner was Edmund Du Cane, and this appointment firmly removed the rehabilitative ideal from British prison policy. Penal policy remained the perfect complement to ideas of economic liberalism, free trade and the minimalist free state so idealised by followers of *laissez-faire* principles. The criminal was seen as an individual freely deciding to adopt criminality as a way of life. The prison was in place to reprocess the individual, to re-establish his (prisoners were predominantly male) contract with society. Crime was a product of an individual pathology and not something to be seen as having a social or economic aetiology. This is very much like the neo-liberal sentiments expressed in government circles during the Thatcher administrations of the 1980s and which are still a central part of 'right realism' or 'rational choice theory' in the criminology of today.

The strength of the retributive school was also explained by popular reaction to a series of moral panics. There were concerns about the behaviour of veterans recently returned from the Crimean War, and in 1862 the garrotting of an MP in London brought immediate legislation in the form of the 'Garrotter's Act' of 1863, which brought back flogging and introduced tougher sentences for robbery. The *Cornhill Magazine* wrote of a great 'public dread [that] has almost become a panic', and some historians have used such evidence to accept without question that a substantial increase in crime occurred which justified such a legislative response. Tobias, for example, wrote that 'The streets of London were dangerous places, day and night . . . and many people carried arms. . . . Though London was the main centre of the criminal class, it was by no means the only one' (1967, pp. 139–140).

QUESTION BREAK

Read the following extracts and consider how they can help to understand the development of the prison and/or penality in the nineteenth century. Try to relate them to the theoretical perspectives considered in the previous section.

Extract 1: Wormwood Scrubs, 24 September 1860

Shaving Prisoners. Ordered: That no prisoner should be allowed to shave himself. He must be shaved by an officer, or, by another prisoner in the presence of the officer. With regard to prisoners for trial or under remand GREAT CARE must be taken by the officer that the appearance of the prisoner be not altered by such shaving.

E. J. Jonas. Governor.

Extract 2: The misconduct book, Pentonville Prison, 24 June 1863

Name: Edward Hughes
Offences for which reported: Receiving a Communication in Chapel [i.e. talking in the prison chapel]
Continually laughing and talking at exercise after being cautioned, and calling the officer a liar on leaving the Governor's office
Having thread in his possession
Persistent talking in his cell

Remarks [i.e. Punishment]: Exercise in Round Yard and 6 days on bread and water.
Dark Cell/Close Confinement [i.e. solitary punishment cell] and forfeit badges [i.e. privileges]. All remission lost. To be sent to Dartmoor.

Extract 3: Licence papers, 19 October 1853

Name:---------------William Young
Licence:--------------No. 23
Complexion:----------Fresh
Hair:------------------Light
Eyes:------------------Grey
Height:----------------5 feet $2\frac{1}{2}$ inches
Scars, Cuts, Moles
   And Marks on Body
   and Limbs---------Round Full Face, Feet Flat
Description-----------Moderately Stout
Received at Wakefield 2nd May 1850
Removed from Wakefield 13th March 1851
Received at Portland Prison from Wakefield 14th March 1851
Received at York Hulk from Portland 20th May 1852
Removed to Portsmouth Prison 13th May 1853 from Stirling Castle hulk
Portsmouth Prison 13th May 1853
Licenced [sic] 19th October 1853

Extract 4: Examples of sentencing

(i) 5th September 1855: Edmund Dowding charged with stealing dried cut grass worth 2 pence. Punishment 10 days hard labour in the County House of Correction (Wiltshire).

(ii) 2nd January 1845: At Maidstone Quarter Sessions, Thomas Groves charged with stealing clothes. Punishment 7 years.

(iii) 27th June 1831: Joseph Clayton alias Cary charged with stealing an ass sentenced in Nottingham to 7 years. 'Character bad. Been convicted before. Connexions indifferent.'

(iv) 26th January 1874: Ellen Berrett, aged 13 years, charged at Trowbridge with stealing a pig's foot from a bakehouse. Sentence 14 days hard labour in the Common Gaol and 2 years in a Reformatory School.

(v) 25th January 1873: James Leadbetter ('Aged 11 years, 4 ft. $1\frac{3}{4}$ inches tall, brown hair and eyes, single and without occupation. Scar on forehead and on right shoulder') charged with stealing celery and convicted. Sentence: imprisonment for 4 days with hard labour. Previously convicted for stealing pears and given 7 days hard labour.

Extract 5: The Reverend Sydney Smith, c. 1840

We should banish all the looms in Preston jail and substitute nothing but the tread-wheel, or the capstan, or some species of labour where the labourer could not see the results of his toil, – where it was monotonous, irksome, and as dull as possible, – pulling and pushing, instead of reading and writing, – no share of the profits – not a single shilling. There should be no tea and sugar . . . nothing but beating hemp and pulling oakum and pounding bricks, – no work but what was tedious, [and] unusual.

Extract 6: Contemporary views of the London working class as threat, *c.* 1867

No-one who lived in the suburbs could help feeling that they were in circumstances of considerable peril. Thomas Beggs.

What could a force of 8,000 or 9,000 police be against the 150,000 roughs and ruffians, whom, on some sufficient exciting occasion, the Metropolis might see arrayed against law and order? The Reverend Henry Solley.

Sources: Extracts 1–4 are taken from Hawkings (1992). Extract 5 is from U. R. Q. Henriques (1979, p. 169). Extract 6 is from G. Stedman Jones (1984, pp. 242–243).

Twentieth-century developments

By 1895 the fears of a social crisis had reached boiling point, and the regime of deterrence and harsh sentencing imposed by Du Cane was being seriously questioned. There was concern that the disciplinary approach was not working and the 'dangerous classes' remained a serious source of anxiety. The middle classes especially felt that the state had not removed the threats to social stability represented by the 'casual poor' and 'criminal classes'. A change of philosophy was registered by the 1895 Gladstone Committee on Prisons, which endorsed a more rehabilitative system that would seek to treat prisoners as individuals in need of some support. Deterrence was not completely abandoned, but it was to be complemented by treatment and a degree of consideration for the individual. This was a radical move away from the tenets of *laissez-faire* and the traditional belief that offenders should be classified as rational beings who deserved to be subject to a strict, attritional control regime in prison. These changes were also the result of far-reaching developments in the economy and society of Britain. Uncertainty and concern followed the realisation that UK economic growth was lagging and that rising foreign competition, principally from Germany and the United States, was endangering traditional export markets upon which depended the core of the country's industrial structure and employment. The long-term decline in profits during the 'Great Depression' (1873–1896) and the growth of unions for the unskilled that adopted militant and socialist tactics seemed to threaten social stability. Large-scale industry and the appearance of monopolies and cartels meant the end of the classical free market based on free trade and competition. The shocking extent of poverty and the appalling living conditions in Britain's cities revealed by the social investigations of Booth and Rowntree at the end of the nineteenth century (they showed that over 30 per cent of urban dwellers existed beneath the lowest of poverty lines) added to the sense of impending disaster. In such circumstances there had to be an attempt to both understand and treat the social crisis. Incidentally, the inner city as a site of criminality and 'deviant', transient communities received particular focus in the researches of the Chicago School of Sociology from 1892. Under its pioneer director, Robert Park, the School singled out the centres of cities (research was carried out in Chicago itself) as run-down 'zones of transition' and a source of criminality. Such was the first experiment in 'environmental criminology'.

The exposure of such urban degradation led to an increasing acceptance that the state should extend its competence and intervene more directly to avoid social problems. More directly, social reform was also the product of the realisation by politicians that any retention of political power required extensions to social policy in order to assuage the demands of a growing electorate that could be attracted by socialism and the new political parties and groups on the left. Additionally, there were continued concerns over 'racial degeneration'. Social policy, including criminal justice, was strongly influenced by the new, now discredited, science of eugenics. This meant that legislators felt it necessary to 'improve the quality of the race' by more careful state intervention in the interest of health, welfare and, as far as criminal offenders were concerned, rehabilitation. Lloyd George, the politician identified with 'New Liberalism' and the introduction of National Insurance, felt that 'you can't run an A1 empire with a C3 population'. Of the recruits for the British Army about to fight the Boer War in 1900, one in three were rejected as medically unfit. This was at a time when the army, in the absence of conscription, was not over-fussy about its recruits' physical capabilities. The investigation was significantly called 'The Report of the Committee on Physical Deterioration' (1904). In an age of increasing international tension and economic competition, 'national efficiency' was an important watchword.

There was particular concern over the failure of the prison to solve the problems of criminality. The prison itself had become a source of the problem of recidivism. Novice offenders could emerge from prison as hardened criminals who had benefited from contact with experienced career inmates. The issue had been commented on earlier, in 1880, by Sir William Harcourt when Home Secretary. His letter to the Queen, which must be the earliest reference to what was to become labelling theory, concerned a group of boys (one described as a 'small, delicate boy who can neither read nor write') and girls between 10 and 13 originally imprisoned for innocuous offences such as 'damaging grass by running about in the fields' or 'bathing in the canal'. Harcourt wrote:

> Protracted imprisonment in such cases has an injurious effect both upon the physical and moral nature of children of tender years. The child who has been guilty of only some . . . thoughtless prank which does not partake of the real character of crime finds himself committed with adult criminals guilty of heinous offences to the common gaol. After a week or a fortnight's imprisonment he comes out of prison tainted in character amongst his former companions, with a mark of opprobrium [scorn] set upon him, and he soon lapses into the criminal class with whom he has been identified.
>
> (quoted in Hawkings 1992, p. 34)

There seemed to be a compelling coming together of forces which demanded a complete refounding of policies of punishment. Thus at the end of the nineteenth century there was a redirection of penal practice. Such a transformation in policy was assisted by changes in the intellectual climate as positivism began to dominate social thought and research. Important new theorists in the late nineteenth century established a positivist paradigm that was to have great influence. Writers such as Lombroso, Ferri and Garofalo showed that crime was not the product of individual choice but determined by forces within the offender and in society that were beyond the control of individual offenders. Durkheim had made similar breakthroughs in his classical study of suicide. Placing such actions in a sociological and scientific context meant that such problems were capable of resolution once they had been scientifically identified, weighed and analysed. Lombroso (1876) classified offenders according to physical characteristics (links here with the old 'science' of phrenology) and tried to show that certain human beings were 'throwbacks' to earlier, and less mature and sophisticated, human types and thus were 'born criminals'. His science was therefore based on what were called atavistic tendencies in humans. Such ideas are no longer accepted, yet Lombroso can be called the father of modern criminology, and the founder of the most important developments in British penal practice in the twentieth century because of his concern to establish the understanding of criminality on scientific grounds. The policy implications were not at first clear. Lombroso's ideas of biological determinism and the eugenist focus on the dangers of atavism led to calls for the cauterising and isolation of criminals as a racial 'infection'. This would mean that the primary, and only, aim of punishment should be the removal of offenders from society and the 'gene pool'. Prisoners would be stock-piled and quarantined. However, in Britain the result of the positivist revolution was not to reduce the range of treatment but quite the opposite: it led away from the punitive to the emphasis on rehabilitation. It was here that the growth of alarm about the failures of the prison and the impact of the Gladstone Report had their effect.

Instead of treating all offenders alike, the penal system now introduced discrimination, and special categories of prisoners were given separate treatment. An early example was the removal from general prisons of juvenile offenders. The Borstal schools were made part of the state apparatus in 1908 and the Industrial Schools, which acted as reformatories for juveniles, were also incorporated in a centralised system that attempted to remove the vulnerable from the general prison and meet their particular needs. Thus education became an important part of the rehabilitative process before the First World War. Probation was accepted as a further sentencing option (the Probation of Offenders Act 1907) which was to be made more sensitive to the needs of the individual offender, and underpinned by the notion of rehabilitation. Similar reforms before 1914 led to the removal of the mentally ill into special hospitals such as Broadmoor and Rampton. The first prison specifically for women had been Brixton (opened in 1853), but the incarceration of women in large, mainstream prisons was discouraged by the beginning of the twentieth century. This has led one historian, Lucia Zedner (1998), to suggest that the 'decriminalisation of women' was occurring. However, Zedner does agree that the movement of women into specialist institutions did not reduce their vulnerability to the controls imposed on them by a society dominated by male power brokers who accepted contemporary notions of female instability and dependence.

Penal policy in the post-First World War period saw the development of such 'new liberal' and progressive sentiments, and the treadmill became a thing of the past. Many writers such as Rawlings (1999) and Muncie (1996) have rightly warned that classical theories of deterrence and punishment were not completely forgotten and that many institutions did not necessarily take the new philosophies of punishment to heart. In large public enterprises, policy could be dictated from the top but implemented in terms of deep-rooted local and traditional practice. Du Cane's successor as chairman of the Prison Commission, Sir Evelyn Ruggles-Brise, worked until 1921 to implement the progressive policy, but he ensured it was balanced by the retention of older, classical ideas of pro-portionality (i.e. making the punishment fit the crime) which had roots back to Beccaria. Penal strategies also retained their punitive element with the introduction of indetermin-ate sentences for offenders, which were based on the capacity of the prisoner to respond effectively to treatment. However, the issue here was the individual prisoner, not the offence.

Social reformers were unhappy with what they felt to be the limited impact of the Gladstone Report and the work of Ruggles-Brise, which, for radicals such as the Webbs, R. H. Tawney and Fenner Brockway, had not gone far enough. Alexander Paterson, a reforming member of the Prison Commission after the retirement of Ruggles-Brise, led prison policy between the wars and worked to establish more liberal and rehabilitative regimes. The 'separate system' was finally abandoned in favour of prisoner association, and specialists, such as psychologists, probation officers, health and welfare specialists, were introduced, to provide a framework of support for prisoners. As a result, the prison was no longer as dominant in the criminal justice system as had been the case in the last 75 years of the nineteenth century. A whole raft of penal and non-penal experts had been brought in on the strength of the positivist revolution. Sentencing policy had been overhauled to reduce the severity of imprisonment (for example, the concept of the minimum security or 'open' prison was established) in order to provide such support for prison inmates. The time in prison was now to be constructively used by the prisoner, and the focus was moved to training, education and psychological strategies that would improve the chances of offenders in making a successful return to the outside world.

Of course, there are many interpretations of the changes Paterson and others brought in. Whig historians, we have seen, would view such changes as a tribute to the strengthening humanitarian impulses of the age as the barbarities of the past were overcome by the more sophisticated and civilised procedures of the more informed modern era. This looks like an attractive model, but unfortunately it is not good history. Apart from making the arrogant assumption that the present is always superior to the past, it does not really understand the nature of historical change. Change is the sub-ject of contradictory forces, and simplistic linear views of unimpeded progress do severe damage to any exercise in understanding the past. Alternative approaches would see the rehabilitative ideal as no more than the evolution of a disciplinary society strengthened and disguised by its liberal façade. Both Foucault and Marxist commentators have such a view, with the 'carceral society' and/or bourgeois control and manipulation of the masses seen as compelling features of modern society and reform and rehabilitation dismissed as cosmetic.

After 1945, there was a reinforcement of progressive agendas in many areas of social policy. The Beveridge Report of 1942 led to the Labour government's social democratic 'welfare state', ready to use its resources to resolve social problems in the interest of all. These had their counterpart in the reforms of the criminal justice system. The Criminal

Justice Act of 1948 finally abolished imprisonment with hard labour, extended the successful Borstal experiment and gave young offenders a further opportunity to avoid imprisonment when attendance centres were set up. In fact, such centres were sites of retributive justice and what was later to be called the 'short, sharp shock'. However, by the mid-1960s the progressive era inaugurated by the Gladstone Report in 1895 was coming to an end. The 1960s brought the decriminalisation of homosexuality, divorce and abortion law reform, the abolition of capital punishment and attempts to further distance young offenders from conventional prison sentences through the extension of care facilities. However, there were signs that the progressivism did not enjoy unqualified acceptance, as laws against drug taking were strengthened and immigration was increasingly the subject of restriction.

Classical theories of penalty based on notions of deterrence and rehabilitation were set for a renaissance because, despite the millions of pounds spent on welfare reform and the widespread belief that the economy was improving living standards, the crime statistics for the post-war period climbed and climbed. As the 1960s closed, it became clear that once more, society was threatened by economic problems, a decline in British power and authority in the world, and increasing social unrest at home. Classical theories of deterrence were always beneath the surface, and they now seemed justified, as the research into criminality seemed to show the inability of progressive policies to reduce crime. The welfare state had not secured social democracy and 'freedom': instead, its right-wing enemies saw it as producing a dependency culture funded by excessive public spending which in turn failed to address problems of rising crime. There were moral panics in the 1970s about black criminals and street muggings, race riots, 'wildcat' strikes, drugs and prison unrest, and in the 1980s what seemed to be unprecedented outbursts of civil disorder in Britain's cities. The scene was set for a lurch to the right as the Thatcher and Major administrations of 1979–1997 followed a populist course, reimposing traditional understandings of crime and the state's right to retributive justice. Thatcher famously summed up this attitude by stating, 'A crime is a crime is a crime', and references to the harsh treatment of 'criminals' became a regular manifesto reference. Successive Conservative Home Secretaries claimed that prison was effective (Michael Howard in 1993 declared, 'Prison works!') and the numbers incarcerated climbed annually. Calls for the return of capital punishment and longer prison sentences were annual events at Conservative Party conferences and were notably endorsed by Home Secretary David Waddington in 1990. Here was a 'crisis of penology' as criminologists seemed at a loss to explain rising crime, and progressive agendas were overtaken by populist rhetoric. Important sociologists and criminologists such as Jock Young were, by 1986, lamenting the 'failure of criminology' as they noted the rise of right-wing, conservative penal agendas in Britain and the United States which had resulted from the campaigns for punitive justice successfully carried out by Margaret Thatcher and President Ronald Reagan. Young felt that 'The demise of positivism and social democratic ways of reforming crime has been rapid, [ensuring] a silent revolution' (1996, p. 442).

Certainly, in the 1990s regular Criminal Justice Acts (1991, 1993, 1994 and 1997) dismantled enlightened policy as prison terms were lengthened and non-custodial sentences (tagging, community service) were either increasingly neglected or underfunded. A large programme of prison building was started. The Labour Party attracted electoral support as it too showed its adoption of the retributive ideal with the slogan 'Tough on crime and tough on the causes of crime'. Edmund Du Cane would have been pleased. From 1945 to 1965 the prison population doubled, and overcrowding became a serious issue and was one cause of serious prison rioting. Since then the prison population has risen enormously (see pp. 192–194). It seemed that by the end of the twentieth century conservative, populist policies of retributive justice had become irresistible to all parties.

QUESTION BREAK

Why do you think the rehabilitative ideal failed to survive in the post-war period?

Examine the reasons for the 'unprecedented' rise in the prison population in the last years of the twentieth century.

Identify the similarities and contrasts evident between the repressive regimes of the pre-1895 era and the more punitive criminal justice system of the late twentieth century.

Gender

State-centred studies of the changing administration, philosophy and ideology of punishment tend to ignore the ways in which different groups of the population are affected by the criminal justice system, and in particular can lead to the neglect of the important issues of gender and ethnicity. A central premise of the British criminal justice system, and one that has been maintained for centuries, is that women represent a special pathological case. Female 'deviance' had been the reason for the vicious attacks on women in sixteenth- and seventeenth-century England accused of witchcraft. Ecclesiastical courts and state legislators particularly identified women who refused to respect contemporary norms of social behaviour. For Keith Thomas, in his famous study of witchcraft, the real discourse (or underlying notion) of such legal forms was to attack the 'witch' for her nonconformist behaviour in highly structured rural communities where eccentricity was considered unacceptable. He writes:

> She [the witch] was the extreme example of the malignant or non-conforming person against whom the local community had always taken punitive action in the interests of social harmony. . . .

> The old woman who had taken recourse to malignant threats in her extremity was therefore liable to pay a high price for the consolation they afforded her. . . . Quite apart from the risk of prosecution the suspected witch might be ostracised [shunned] by her neighbours [and she] . . . was also liable to informal acts of violence. The 94 year-old Agnes Fenn alleged in 1604 that after she was accused of witchcraft, Sir Thomas Gosse had punched, pricked and struck her, threatened her with firebrands and gunpowder, and finally stabbed her in the face with a knife.
>
> (1978, pp. 632–633)

What Thomas does not consider is that the use of violence and legal sanctions against women classed as witches was the product of a patriarchal society's demonisation of women. Witchcraft provided church, parish and state with the ideal opportunity to legitimise such male bastions of power and use women as an 'alien other' against which patriarchy could strengthen and prevail. When disaster occurred, 'Women's bodies were the instruments for exorcising political and social evils, establishing the power of institutions, and for the symbolic marking of boundaries of appropriate female behaviour' (Dobash *et al.* 1986, p. 18). Discourses, or unquestioned assumptions about what was 'right and proper', held that women were subordinate creatures whose roles were prescribed by their ability to produce the next generation and act in the domestic sphere as wives, cooks, cleaners and mothers. Women who attempted to reject these roles, or whose behaviour was eccentric and nonconformist, were targeted as dangerous and in need of further control and restraint. Accusations of sorcery and witchcraft were ideal ways to enforce the discourse of male superiority.

Assumptions of female dependence and inferiority have become institutionalised within the criminal justice system. Examples over the past three hundred years can illustrate this. The treatment of women by the courts from the seventeenth century betrayed the impact of such a mindset. Women were often held in houses of correction which were required to instil in them habits of dutiful subservience to their parents or husbands. Women caught stepping out beyond their 'domestic' role were dealt with sharply. They were assumed to be either insane or potential prostitutes. Female thieves, murderers and beggars could expect harsh sentences, and it was common for such women to be hanged, transported and incarcerated for long periods. The exception was where the offence was in some way excusable as a desperate attempt by a woman to maintain her given station in life.

WOMEN CRIMINALS IN THE EIGHTEENTH CENTURY

Case 1
Anne Flynn, convicted of robbery in 1750. She had stolen a shoulder of mutton but the court was affected by her defence that her husband was desperately ill and her two infant children starving. The court recognised she had already been confined for two weeks and fined her one shilling. The jury decided to pay the fine!

Case 2
Mary Young (or 'Jenny Diver') was charged with pickpocketing and hanged in 1740. Mary had been a thief for years and had twice escaped execution when transported. The nickname 'Jenny Diver' was slang for prostitute. Most women indicted were assumed to be prostitutes as well.

Case 3
Hannah Webley, convicted in 1794 for the murder of her infant son. She was hanged. She was unmarried and aged 16 years. The judge said:

> Hannah Webley, you have been convicted of a most cruel and unnatural murder. So far was you led on by fear of a discovery of your shame, as first to curse and then deprive an

helpless infant of life: by this wicked act your own life is forfeited.... You must now suffer a severe punishment for your crime ... [which] dreadful as it is will be an instructive lesson to the female part of creation, and convince them that those who swerve from the paths of virtue will be tempted to the commission of the worst of crimes. I also hope that your punishment will be a lesson to those young men who artfully endeavour to seduce young women from the paths of virtue.

> Sources: The cases are taken from the Newgate Calendars and reprinted in Moore (2000, pp. 112, 101–102 and 56–58 respectively)

In cases 2 and 3, the accused woman had 'swerved from the paths of virtue' and had become targeted as particularly dangerous, therefore. In case 1 the woman was attempting to look after her family, and this was seen as an attempt to continue to conform to the prescribed role of the female as home-maker, and leniency was the result. Interestingly, poor Hannah Webley's death was to act as a lesson for men who were responsible for the damage to that essential guarantee of society's stability: women securely committed to the 'paths of virtue'.

Some historians have shown how the courts began to be reluctant to convict women for infanticide. It was a characteristic female offence, and research has shown that at Surrey Assizes one such offence was tried every eighteen months in the eighteenth century. However, juries were not so ready to convict. The reason is unclear, unless a heightened sympathy for such women as the 'weaker sex' is the explanation. Modern sentencing of women is certainly affected by such stereotypical ideas of women as naturally caring beings, unlike the strong, aggressive male. Unfortunately for Hannah Webley, no such notions affected her treatment by the courts.

The execution of women in the twentieth century in Britain has been the subject of some interesting research by Annette Ballinger (2000), who studied the execution of fifteen women for murder in Britain in the first half of the twentieth century. It is clear from her work that if the reluctance to execute women for infanticide persists into the modern era, by contrast women guilty of murdering an adult are more likely to be hanged than are men who have committed a similar offence. The reason is that such women demonstrate an unsuitability for the 'motherly', caring image that men demanded. As Ballinger notes:

> The mere fact that a woman has broken the law ensures that she will be regarded as someone who has failed to fulfil gender role expectations, and if this is overlaid by a refusal to demonstrate her commitment to conventional female roles in her personal life, especially in the areas around sexuality, respectability, domesticity and motherhood, she can expect to find herself at the receiving end of the full force of ... 'judicial misogyny' [i.e. hatred of women] [Women murderers] fell victim to cultural misogyny in general and judicial misogyny in particular.
>
> (2000, p. 3)

Outside of murder and judicial execution, public, physical punishment of women classed as 'scolds', 'slanderers' or responsible for the cuckolding of their husbands (i.e. adultery) included the stocks, the ducking (or 'cucking') stool and ritual communal shaming. Men subjected to nagging and shrewish or disobedient wives, or those dominated in any way by their spouses, could take comfort in local custom, often reinforced at law, which would reimpose the male sanction. The wearing of a bridle or mask in the seventeenth century was the lot of women certified as beyond the proper control of their husbands.

The disappearance of such public rituals and the penal revolution of the late eighteenth and early nineteenth centuries, which moved punishment away from public scrutiny, have been discussed earlier in the book in terms of the models applied by Foucault, Ignatieff and Garland. But much of this work on this period has ignored the implications for women swept into the new 'carceral society'. The emerging ideas of 'power–knowledge' and control of the body began when punishment was withdrawn from the public gaze, but there were also profound implications for women. These new institutions of control acted as agencies for the strengthening of patriarchal discourses and they were opportunities for tightening control of women in industrial society. The imprisonment of women was transformed, as separate prisons were set up in which the supposedly unique character of the female could be treated. In such institutions, women could experience the most degrading conditions and exploitation of all kinds. The standard work on the imprisonment of women (Dobash *et al*. 1986) stresses revisionist accounts of women's treatment in jails. Such accounts reject 'Whiggish' or humanitarian interpretations which focus on the work of reformers such as Elizabeth Fry and their responsibility for the supposed improvement in the conditions of imprisonment for women in the nineteenth century. Fry's work at Newgate and elsewhere, from 1816 to the 1830s, was important but limited in its effect. It continued the stigmatisation of women and the application of male assumptions of female pliability and submissiveness.

Historians such as Rafter (1983) have found that apart from sexual exploitation and abuse, the female inmate faced appalling neglect in poor, insanitary conditions, and was invariably put to work cooking, washing and cleaning. This was the accepted view of her proper role in life and one to which she had to be reconditioned. The aim was to enforce the stereotypical gendered division of labour and produce the conforming female. Any ideas of rehabilitation, even those discussed after the revolution in punishment strategies signalled by the Gladstone Report of 1895, remained theoretical. However, nineteenth-century reform did provide for the separate confinement of women. After months of solitary confinement followed by domestic work in the prison, women were often placed in secure refuges and reformatories after they had served their sentences. The regulation of women in prison does seem to have been more rigorous than that experienced by men. Women were subjected to the humiliation of constant surveillance and supervision and a work regime that reinforced their gendered destiny as dependent members of society. Such prison regimes were reinforced by strict disciplinary systems, punishment practices using reduced diets ('B & W', meaning bread and water), handcuffs and other restraints, solitary confinement in darkened cells, and the exhortations of prison chaplains who shared without question the belief in male superiority.

Research by modern feminist historians has revised thinking about the control of women in penal institutions dominated by the male discourse. They have found that the marginalisation of women is neither confined to the past nor restricted to the two areas of discrimination often chosen for study: the state prison and the family. Intermediate between the two, a whole range of 'intermediate' or 'semi-penal' and 'semi-formal' institutions were established which extended the female carceral system. The nineteenth and twentieth centuries witnessed an increasing institutionalisation of women in this way. Such 'halfway houses' have been examined by Barton (2001), who found that many private organisations worked to replicate official anti-female ideologies, and were able to continue to strengthen acceptance of women's 'abnormal' behaviour as a 'deviance' in need of containment. Many charitable and religious foundations ran houses for 'fallen women', female 'inebriates' and 'lunatics' in what was a thriving 'voluntary sector'.

QUESTION BREAK: CONTAINING WOMEN

Foucault stressed that institutions of discipline rested on the unwitting internalisation or acceptance by inmates of discourses of obedience, subservience and dependence. They accepted labelling as insecure and maladjusted. Although he was not writing about women, Foucault's analysis shines through the extract below from Barton's work on a range of halfway houses such as the 'Lock Hospitals' for sexually deviant women and prostitutes, Magdalene Homes for girls with venereal disease and houses for 'delinquent' girls and 'mad' women. Read the extract and consider the questions that follow it:

> Women had to be consenting, compliant and co-operative in order for these establishments to function effectively, as being non-statutory they had no power to confine women against their will. However . . . women were frequently pressured into giving their consent for a period of residence through a network of influence which included family, friends, reformers, charity workers, police, court officials, clergy and prison staff. . . . Women would agree to be admitted to these institutions, and consequently conform to their regimes, because the alternatives presented to them were so appalling. Young women labelled as 'immoral' might be willing to submit to a period of semi-penal confinement as they would be made well aware that if they were to become pregnant they stood a fair chance of being forcibly admitted, as were many unmarried mothers, to a lunatic asylum as a long term inmate.
>
> (Barton 2001, p. 117)

Questions

Why was it important that such women be removed from society?

Why do you think young unmarried women would be sent to a 'lunatic asylum'?

Why did dominant male thinking require that particular efforts were made to get prostitutes into such places?

Two categories of female 'deviancy' can be discussed to illustrate the continuation of the patriarchal assumptions of the criminal justice system: the prostitute and the suffragette. Prostitution was often the recourse of women who found it impossible to earn money to survive, and many working-class women were forced into it during times of depression. Victorian sensibilities were predictably outraged and saw the prostitute as a danger to moral standards, the family and the quality of the race. 'Fallen women' were incapable of taking their place as wives and mothers, and were thus targeted as asocial elements best removed from society. The Contagious Diseases Acts (CDAs) of 1864 and 1866 were used indiscriminately in public against women who were suspected, often on the flimsiest of grounds, of being prostitutes. Josephine Butler worked courageously in the 1880s for the abolition of the CDAs, which notoriously classed all women as potential prostitutes and gave them little redress when a case was brought against them by the, obviously male, police. Once again, women were stigmatised by men who made decisions about what was, and what was not, acceptable female behaviour. Simply put, women were a source of infection and to be legally contained. Male sexual licence, however, was accepted as a natural expression of a man's make-up. Such 'double standards' complemented the exploitation of women, which was reinforced by the criminal justice system. Significantly, and ironically, after the repeal of the Acts, many of Butler's supporters worked to support movements for moral purity and to deprive prostitutes of their children, and supported the repression of prostitution through vigorous by-laws administered by local authorities that shared many of the assumptions of the CDAs. Historians of Victorian prostitution show how strong traditional ideas of female separateness were:

> This attack on patriarchy and male vice [i.e. on the CDAs] involved no positive assertion of female sexuality. It was still couched within the terms of a 'separate spheres' ideology and assumed that women were essentially moral, 'spiritual' creatures who needed to be protected from the essentially animalistic, 'carnal' men.
>
> (Walkowitz 1982, p. 256)

The prostitute and the erring mother threatened that bastion of Victorian social stability and respectability, the patriarchal institution of the family. Female transgression was also feared as a potential threat to the quality of the race, and women who refused the gendered stereotypical roles as subservient domestic dependants within the family were considered both 'mad' and 'bad'. It must be said that working-class women as prostitutes continued to be considered the danger. Butler's reform movement was avowedly middle class and it did little to improve the position of working-class women stigmatised within the legal system as prostitutes in particular or as 'wayward women' in general. Women who failed to conform may not have been classed as witches by the end of the nineteenth century, but they were increasingly the subject of medical discourses that classified them as insane. The hysterical woman was a standard character in Victorian fiction, and the incarceration of women on such grounds increased as the psychiatric profession established its professional presence. Asylums were, like prisons, institutions where 'female maladies' and 'lunacies' could be affirmed and controlled as an exercise in patriarchy.

Suffragettes were spectacular victims of the late-nineteenth-century criminal justice system as Acts were passed confining such 'dangerous women' who affronted men with their demands for the suffrage. Mrs Pankhurst's Women's Social and Political Union (WSPU) used violent tactics to bring the issue to the public. These included setting fire to pillar boxes, breaking the windows of West End clubs, the dynamiting of a cabinet minister's country house and violent interruption of political meetings in and outside the Commons. Such violence again was an affront to the received view of the 'proper' place and behaviour of the female, and the full force of the law led to the suffragettes in prison on hunger strike being force-fed using steel 'gags' that wrenched open the mouth in order that tubes could be inserted down the prisoner's throat, causing extensive injury. The prisoners then had liquid food poured into them. There were cases of prisoners dying following such assault. The following is a description of this treatment meted out to suffragette prisoner Constance Lytton at Walton Gaol in Liverpool in 1910.

> The pain of it was intense and at last I must have given way for he [the prison doctor] got the gag between my teeth, when he proceeded to turn much more than necessary until my jaws were fastened wide apart, far more than they would go naturally. Then he put down my throat a tube which seemed to me to be much too wide and was something like 4 feet in length. The irritation of the tube was excessive. I choked the moment it touched my throat until it had got down. Then the food was poured in quickly; it made me sick a few seconds after it was down and the action of the sickness made my body and legs double up, but the wardresses instantly pressed back my head and the doctor leant on my knees. The horror of it was more than I can describe. I was sick over the doctor and the wardresses, and it seemed a long time before they took the tube out. As the doctor left he gave me a slap on the cheek.
>
> (Lytton 1988 (1914), p. 269)

The so-called 'Cat and Mouse Act' was passed in 1913 so that suffragettes on hunger strike in prison could be released if they were seriously ill so that they could be rearrested after their recovery to complete sentence. Contemporary medical opinion saw such women as mentally unbalanced because of the nature of their menstrual cycle and exceptional physiology. In short, it was thought that such 'unladylike' behaviour could only be put down to the fact that because they did not conform to the stereotypical image of the meek and dependent, 'caring' female, they must be mad and treated accordingly.

The twentieth century saw the disappearance of reformatories and 'halfway houses', and the female prison population fell steadily. Thirty-three thousand women had been in prison in Britain in 1913, nearly half for drunkenness, but by 1960 there were only 2,000 (see p. 206). Women's wings in prisons across the country were closed, and hostels, which had proved expensive to run, had a questionable ability to rehabilitate their inmates. Similarly, in this more liberal-progressive period, the sentencing of women to prison was not regarded as appropriate and alternatives to custody (suspended sentences, fines) were created. Where imprisonment was recommended, women were now sent to specialist prisons such as Holloway Prison in London. It was not until the post-1960 period, when female criminality appeared to be on the increase, that 'specialist treatment' in newly designed prisons (Holloway was largely rebuilt) was recommended for female inmates. Significantly, given the history of the treatment and classification of women in the criminal justice system over the centuries, it was now believed that women who offended needed medical and psychiatric treatment as well as exceptional support and guidance before being readmitted to society. So, the discourse of the 'errant' female as pathological has proved impossible to remove even after three hundred years of criminal justice. As Zedner has commented,

Holloway has developed much more like a 'conventional prison' than its originators intended. Yet its specialist facilities for mentally disturbed prisoners are a testament to the continuing view of criminal women as mentally ill or inadequate. The view that a proportion of the female prison population was mentally retarded now seems to have spread to envelop the female prison population as a whole.

(1998, p. 321)

Ethnicity

Perhaps even stronger is the fear, contempt and hostility aroused by members of ethnic minority communities targeted by the forces of criminal justice. Our focus is primarily, but not exclusively, on black communities, yet similar views have been expressed about Irish immigrants, Jewish communities, Russians, Poles and German 'fifth columnists' in the past, and there are moral panics today about asylum seekers. Of course, racist discourses are of ancient lineage, but in the seventeenth and eighteenth centuries the British legal system was required to establish its position on the question of the place of the black community. The country deepened its involvement with the slave trade, and the economics of slave taking and the growth of commerce with West Africa, the West Indies and North America had led, by 1760, to questions on the legality of this trade. Abolition of the British trade came in 1833, but it was preceded by a vigorous debate about the justification for treating the 'negro' as a human being. For those involved in the trade, this commodification of racism was an unexceptional part of everyday business. Racialised discourses were prevalent and have survived in strength to the modern day. They have influenced how black people have been treated in the criminal justice system over the centuries. The trade had been endorsed by numerous Acts of Parliament, and black slaves were classed as cargoes. As such, they were property, and the legal system was presented with many problems that covered not only the status of slaves but also their right to hold property and to gain freedom. The most famous example was the *Somerset* case of 1772, which, after Lord Mansfield's judgment, granted slaves a defence against illegal, indefinite imprisonment and abolished a master's right to remove slaves from England against their will. However, an attack on slavery in England was not an attempt to remove it in the colonies, and there was little legal redress for those unfortunate enough to travel the 'middle passage' on Liverpool slave ships. The criminal justice system was oblivious to the barbarities and murders which were commonplace on the trip across the Atlantic. Walvin gives the example of the Liverpool slaver *Zong* on which 132 Africans were murdered in 1781. The only legal outcome of this outrage was an application by the ship owners for insurance compensation for their loss of cargo.

The issue of the black presence in Britain was given urgency after the loss of the American colonies, when large numbers of freed black slaves, and those still enslaved to British loyalists, travelled to Britain and established a black community. The size of the black presence is a matter of debate, but the rise in the numbers of blacks among the poor and beggar classes in London meant that fears of a threatening 'dangerous class' were deepened as they took on a racialised perspective. Black people were subjected to casual violence, arbitrary arrest and imprisonment; they were typically classified as primitives compared to the civilised and enlightened white Englishmen. Elites reinforced their feeling of superiority over the masses with racialised views of the animalistic blacks, who were beneath classification as humans. They were in fact mere anthropological curiosities. New social, political and legal structures reinforced such views. If criminality was seen as an inevitable characteristic of Britain's working-class residuum of paupers and vagabonds, black people were permanently associated with alien and dangerous forces. 'Alien' and immigrant communities were always assumed to have higher rates of criminality than 'English' people.

QUESTION BREAK: 'UN-ENGLISHNESS'

The identification of law with national interests, and of criminality with un-English qualities, dates from this process of state formation and has a long history which remains relevant to the analysis of 'race' and crime today.

> Anxiety about the criminal predisposition and activities of the immigrant population inspired demands for the introduction of immigration controls in the first years [of the twentieth century]. When the issue of alien criminality was debated in Parliament [in 1902], the settlement of Russians, Rumanians and Poles in the East End of London was described by Tory members ... in military metaphors no less potent than those chosen by Enoch Powell [a prominent Conservative former minister who expressed racist views in the 1960s]. ... He concluded: 'I should have thought we had enough criminals of our own. ...'
>
> (Gilroy 1987, pp. 92–93)

Questions

What were the 'un-English' characteristics which supposedly confirmed 'alien criminality'?

Why might such views becoming prevalent at a time when the British Empire was at its peak?

It is clear that race has had a distinct impact on the operation of the criminal justice system. Research by Hood (1992) and extended examination of policing in the twentieth century and after have indicated that racial minorities are subjected to discriminatory treatment. The great increase in the black communities since the Second World War particularly has extended ideas of racialised inequality, and this has been reinforced by stereotypical images of such communities as hotbeds of crime. When considering the current context, it is important to remember that the criminalisation of ethnic minorities has been a long-standing feature of the criminal justice system. Post-war racism was not unique; rather, it was the continuation of discriminatory practices that were tolerated almost without question in the early twentieth century. By that time, simplistic views of a racial hierarchy had been given credibility by the pseudo-science of eugenics, and the legal system perpetuated racist discourses to the extent that the police operated a casual and institutionalised racism that passed without public comment. Studies of the policing of the British Empire (such as Anderson and Killingray 1991) reveal, for example, the unquestioned assumption of racial superiority which ensured that only white, British men were considered officer material and no black policemen would dare to attempt to arrest a white man. Black criminality, however, was taken for granted, and there was more severe punishment for the 'inferior race'. Colonial administrators had operated racist criminal justice across the Empire for decades, and their return to Britain strengthened such views among governing elites. Race riots had occurred in Britain after the First World War in seaports such as Liverpool, Glasgow, east London, Cardiff and Tyneside where West Indian seamen were concentrated. The lodgings of black seamen and their families were ransacked and some were killed in the disturbances. Police forces and the courts were not conspicuous in their defence of such communities. It is safe to say that so-called alien races in Britain were considered part of the residuum, or what Marxists call the lumpenproletariat, with little chance of anything other than dismissal as a racialised and criminalised other.

Of course, the British state did not publicly legitimise racist principles and the government did not endorse the exclusion of identified, racialised communities. This was not the case in inter-war Germany. In 1935 the Nazis passed the Nuremberg Laws, which made a racist public policy legal – anti-Semitism was conventional. In effect, Jews were driven from the community, losing their political and personal rights. A country's criminal justice system can be seen as representative of its dominant ideologies and discourses. This has been demonstrated in the discussions in this chapter of a range of issues which included the attitudes to the 'dangerous classes' of Victorian England and the gendered threat of uncontrolled women. Criminal justice administration is important, too, to the preservation of racist discourses as official policy.

In Britain after 1945, the rapid increase in immigration did fuel fears of racial degeneration and criminality. Stories of black criminality contained lurid images of sexual perversion, pimping and the 'racial contamination' of the white race. That black pimps were assumed to be earning vast sums living off the earnings of white prostitutes further generated the moral panic. In the late 1950s, after race riots in Notting Hill (London) and Nottingham had attracted huge publicity, the catalogue of crime attributed to black criminals was extended to include drug trafficking and brothel keeping. The demonisation of the black criminal was to reach hysterical proportions with the discovery in the 1970s of a mugging crisis that associated violent street robbery with black criminality. Stuart Hall *et al.* (1978) produced the definitive study of this moral panic and showed it to be the product of police manoeuvres designed to increase the resources delivered to a particular force. The invention of the crime wave was to deepen suspicion of blacks. This is similar to the revelations of Howard Becker, in his *Outsiders* (1963), that the criminalisation of marijuana use in the United States between the wars was produced by the need for the FBI Narcotics Bureau to justify its existence and attract greater Federal funding. Becker sees 'rule creators' as 'moral entrepreneurs' strengthening their own careers at the expense of those thus victimised by the extension of the criminal law. The mugging crisis is a good English example. Here the victims were the demonised, racialised 'alien' black community. It led to the great increase in the incidence of police 'stop and search', which meant that in some areas black people were ten times more likely to be stopped by the police on suspicion than white people.

Police focus on black people – through 'stop and search', for example – picked up more criminality, naturally, than in other cases not so strictly policed. Thus the stereotypes of black, or 'alien', criminality which had been central to the perception of racial difference since the era of the slave trade were continued within a criminal justice system which has in modern times been considered institutionally racist. The acute awareness of these problems admitted by law enforcement professionals in modern-day Britain has brought to light long-standing racist practices which will take time to remove.

Further reading

Dobash, R. P., Dobash, R. E. and Gutteridge, S. (1986) *The Imprisonment of Women*, Oxford: Blackwell. Chapters 1–5 are particularly recommended as an historical study of the punishment of women which emphasises the imposition of patriarchal assumptions of female criminality and the implications for punishment strategies. The book has a comparative theme and analyses developments in Britain and the United States through the past two centuries.

Emsley, C. (1996) *Crime and Society in England, 1750–1900*, 2nd edn, Harlow: Longman. A most useful analysis of the period that includes chapters on the origins and development of the police, class perceptions of criminality, issues of gender and the changes in punishment.

Hay, D., Linebaugh, P., Rule, J. G., Thompson, E. P. and Winslow, C. (1977) *Albion's Fatal Tree: Crime and Society in the 18th Century*, Harmondsworth: Penguin. A classic historical analysis of the use of the criminal law as an ideological weapon. It focuses on the manipulation of the 'Bloody Code' by 'an astute ruling class in their own interests'. Hay's essay 'Property, Authority and the Criminal Law' is particularly recommended as a study of eighteenth-century capital punishment.

Morris, N. and Rothman, D. J. (1998) *The Oxford History of the Prison: The Practice of Punishment in Western Society*, Oxford: Oxford University Press. This provides a comprehensive coverage of the history of incarceration from ancient times to the modern day. Examples are drawn from Britain, continental Europe and the United States.

Sharpe, J. A. (1999) *Crime in Early Modern England, 1550–1750*, 2nd edn, Harlow: Longman. An excellent, wide-ranging analysis of crime, criminality and punishment in the early modern period. Especially useful are chapters 3 and 4 on measuring and controlling crime. Chapter 5 is a valuable study of offenders which includes a useful section on gender. Other areas covered include popular attitudes to criminality and elite perceptions of crime and threat.

4 Victimology

Introduction

It goes without saying that any criminal justice system will be preoccupied with the behaviour, the punishment and the rehabilitation of the criminal. The behaviour of the criminal has been the particular focus of criminology, although work in this area over-laps with a number of academic disciplines, including sociology and psychology. As regards the punishment of offenders, the different aims of and justifications for punishment, whether they be essentially retributive or reformative, have sparked continued philosophical debate. However, this academic obsession with the criminal has been at the expense of detailed consideration of the victim. Indeed, the victim often seems to be added to criminological theorising and debate merely out of politeness or political correctness. The consequences of this omission are important. The lack of academic interest has left the victim in the dark – a situation that has led to a good deal of public policy making not being informed by the needs, wants and status of the victim within the criminal justice system.

This neglect has been recognised in recent years, so much so that the status of the victim within the criminal justice system and within the academic discipline of criminology has become a controversial and important issue, especially in the wake of the 'Victim's Charter'. Published in 1990 under a Conservative government and revised in 1996, the Victim's Charter is a recognition of victims' rights as consumers of the criminal justice system. The Charter is under revision once again in 2003, with particular consideration being given to whether victims' rights should be formally enshrined in law.

The purpose of this chapter is to trace the origins and the emergence of victimology as an academic discipline and to discuss how this has contributed to the status of the victim as a significant actor in the criminal justice process. In order to do this, it is necessary to critically analyse the theoretical and conceptual frameworks that have developed as a consequence of the different 'types' of victims and their very different treatment within the criminal justice system. It is equally important to identify and define those who are victims of crime and to understand those social factors which may render them 'victim prone' or contribute to their victim status.

The chapter starts with a brief consideration of the range of victims of criminal behaviour before looking at the emergence of victimology as a distinct discipline and at the major theoretical positions within it. The rest of the chapter then focuses on examples of victims of private and public crime – in particular, victims of domestic violence and of corporate crime.

Who are the victims?

The trend in victimology has been to divide victims of crime into two crude camps: the victims of 'conventional' crime and victims of 'corporate crime'. Conventional crime may be defined as 'street' or 'public' crimes. As such victims are easily identifiable, the extent of victimisation is relatively easy to quantify. Corporate crime, by contrast, can be defined as crimes committed within a legitimate formal organisation as a result of either deliberate decision making or negligence. Corporate crime is by nature diffuse, therefore it is difficult to identify the extent of corporate victimisation. It is no wonder that the corporate victim is often rendered 'invisible'.

The purpose of the following discussion is to outline the difficulty of these divisions and to demonstrate that victims of crime cannot be categorised so easily. How, for example, can the above definitions cater for victims of child abuse, domestic violence or state-sanctioned violence?

Historically, the term 'victim' originally referred to the sacrifice of a person or animal in the name of religion. Of course, today the term refers to those who have experienced loss, hardship or injury due to any cause. In relation to the study of crime the cause is a criminal act.

Victims can be categorised as primary or secondary. Primary victims are those who experience the act or its consequences at first hand, for instance a child who is the victim of a hit and run driver. Secondary victims are those who suffer the effects but are not immediately involved, for instance the relatives of that child. To define the victims of crime is not an easy task; and it would be helpful here to outline very briefly some of the major examples of victims of crime to highlight this difficulty.

Victims of violence

It has been argued that victims of violence can be defined as victims of 'conventional' crime. However, there are problems with this category. The official construction of violent crime fails to acknowledge *other* forms of violent crime. For example, Stanko argues that 'the hegemonic image [is] that "real" violence and crime is something that occurs on the street, in public, and is committed by strangers' (1990, p. 94). According to Home Office criminal statistics, violent crime can be categorised as 'crime against the person, sexual offences and robbery' (Colman and Moyniham 1996).

Missing from official categorisation is state-sponsored or state-sanctioned violence, which according to McLaughlin (1996) includes the atrocities of military dictatorships and totalitarian regimes, such as the Nazi Holocaust against the Jews and political dissidents, mass political killings in Timor and Uganda, apartheid in South Africa and ethnic cleansing in Bosnia. Scraton *et al.* (1991) have also noted that it can include situations, 'where liberal democratic states employ unreasonable force, act negligently, and tolerate miscarriages of justice'. This therefore allows the inclusion of events such as the investigation into the murder of Stephen Lawrence in 1993 and the police handling of the Hillsborough tragedy in 1989. Scraton *et al.* (1991) state of the Hillsborough case:

> There is no simplistic jump here which suggests that the senior officers' actions were comparable to the tortures in Pinochet's Chile or South Africa's apartheid regime, but the political-ideological processes of explanation and denial, their associated techniques of neutralisation and disqualification, are strikingly consistent.

The Lawrence case and the Hillsborough case have highlighted the plight of victims of the criminal justice system, and there have been numerous high-profile cases of victims of miscarriages of justice over the past twenty years, including the Birmingham Six (who were released in 1991), the Guildford Four (1989), the Bridgewater Three (1997) and the case of Stefan Kiszko (1992). Taylor (1999) has outlined the responsibilities the state should have towards these cases. He argues that

> the state's responsibility in relation to wrongful conviction should not, and does not, end with the quashing of such a conviction. But on the other hand such recompense does not arrive quickly and neither can it compensate for the horrors that have been endured by defendants and their families.

Other victims of violence include victims of domestic violence and victims of child abuse – victims who have until recently remained largely within the private arena. However, feminist arguments have highlighted the patriarchal attitude that sees women and children as the property and responsibility of the man, and have argued that domestic violence and child abuse is no longer a private worry but a public issue (to use Charles Wright Mills's (1970) famous distinction).

Victims of child abuse

Child abuse has been described as any form of adult behaviour which (intentionally or otherwise) causes harm to a child. Kempe and Kempe (1981) identify four possible types of abuse: physical violence, physical and emotional neglect, emotional abuse (such as being continually terrorised, berated or neglected) and sexual abuse. Child abuse is an area that for a long time was ignored, if not tolerated, in our society. However, today charitable organisations such as the NSPCC and government projects such as Childline have highlighted the need for the protection of children. High-profile cases such as those of Myra Hindley and Ian Brady in the 1960s, Fred and Rosemary West in the 1980s and the murder of Victoria Climbie in 2000 are a reminder to society of the threat of child abuse. And the successful prosecution of celebrity figures such as Jonathan King and

Gary Glitter is a reminder that child abusers do exist, exist in all walks of life, and are punished regardless of their status.

Victims of domestic violence

Domestic violence is not the exclusive domain of female victims, although nine out of ten recorded incidents are of domestic violence upon women. Victims of domestic violence can suffer from a number of types of abuse, including physical violence, psychological, emotional and verbal abuse, social abuse (enforced isolation), economic abuse (total control of finances) and sexual abuse (rape and coercion into sexual acts).

Victims of corporate crime

Corporate victimisation is complex, as it is often indirect and diffuse, therefore there is difficulty in identifying victims. Victims are generally described as workers, consumers and the general public. Victimisation ranges from corporate manslaughter to fraud, pollution, medical blunders and health and safety issues. Recent high-profile cases include the collapse of the US company Enron and of Worldcom, which led to massive losses for shareholders.

This brief introduction to some of the main examples of victims of crime (and victims of domestic violence and of corporate crime will be examined in greater detail later in the chapter) indicates that the amount and extent of victimisation relate to a number of variables. As the examples given demonstrate, victimisation may relate to age, class, race, gender, area of residence. These factors often work in combination with one another. One form of victimisation may be compounded by another, which means that some individuals or groups may be more vulnerable to victimisation. For example, ethnic minority groups are over-represented in lower socio-economic groups, which may affect their area of residence, forcing them to live in high-crime areas, which leaves them more vulnerable. This is also compounded by the fact that they are susceptible to institutional racism and racially motivated crime.

QUESTION BREAK: VICTIMS OF RACE CRIME

The following extract looks at victims of race crime and also demonstrates that we need to look beyond conventional explanations and ideas to demonstrate the extent of the impact of crime on victims.

Race attacks are almost 10 times more likely to happen in rural areas, according to an exclusive survey for The Observer, which also shows that more than two thirds of people think the police are as racist as ever.

Two years after the publication of Sir William Macpherson's report into the Stephen Lawrence murder inquiry, our findings show that one in 12 of the ethnic minority population in

Northumbria have reported a racist incident since February 1999, compared with one in 200 in the West Midlands.

Using official Home Office figures on racist incidents in each constabulary and plotting them against the size of the local ethnic minority population, a startling racial audit shows a country where safety lies in numbers.

The most dangerous areas for ethnic minorities are also those where there are the smallest communities. Northumbria tops the list, but is closely followed by Devon and Cornwall and south Wales, where racial crimes affect one in 15 and one in 16 respectively. Other race crime hotspots are Norfolk, Avon and Somerset, Durham and Cumbria. Between them, the top 10 worst constabularies in England and Wales for racist incidents are home to just 5 per cent of the total ethnic minority population.

By contrast it is the urban centres – London, Greater Manchester, West Yorkshire and Leicestershire – which appear to be the safest. Racist incidents affected just one in 200 of the ethnic minority population in the West Midlands, according to statistics.

- ICM Research interviewed a random selection of 1,206 adults aged 18–plus from 25–30 January 2001 across the country.

(From J. Rayner, 'Risk of Race Attacks Highest outside Britain's Big Cities, Survey Reveals', *Observer*, 18 February 2001)

Questions

According to the article, what variables might contribute to racial victimisation?

Why do you think people belonging to ethnic minority groups may suffer more racial victimisation in rural areas?

The emergence of victimology

Victimology as a separate academic discipline has sought to highlight the plight of the victim. Although it is generally still studied as a sub-discipline within the realm of criminology, in the past half-century or so there has been an increasing interest in establishing victimology as a distinct discipline in its own right. The intention of this brief overview of the history of and background to victimology is to trace its development from its emergence in the 1940s through to the present day. This historical review and analysis will also take account of the changing theoretical debates within victimology.

However, before we consider the different victimological perspectives, it is important to set the emergence of victimology in its historical, social and political context and to do this by addressing the issue of how (and why) the victim has become the focus of much (greater) intellectual inquiry.

The devastation of two world wars played an important part in encouraging an acceptance of the notion of the victim. The effect of the Second World War was especially noticeable during the 1950s, when the growing emphasis on social rights was an important element in the establishment of the welfare state. It was a short step from the notion of social rights of citizens to include the right of victims. Victims of (conventional) crime, victims of racial discrimination and victims of war all helped to propel the concept of the victim into academic circles and political policy. The post-war settlement was a time of consensus and reparation which fostered a climate that allowed victims to begin to organise themselves in pressure groups and demand some recognition and status within the criminal justice system. The importance of Margaret Fry in this process cannot be overestimated. She played a key role in the creation of the Criminal Injuries Compensation Scheme, which emphasised the contractual nature of post-war Britain. Although the scheme did not materialise until after her death in 1964, her ideas made a significant impact upon criminal justice debate and policy. In referring to her role, Rock points out that

> In her last formulation of the problem; compensation would represent a collective insurance provided by society. All tax payers would be regarded as subscribers. All tax payers were at risk of becoming victims. Since the state forbade citizens arming themselves it should assume responsibility for its failure to provide protection.
>
> (1990, p. 66)

Fry highlighted the injustice of a criminal justice system that emphasised the criminal and displaced the victim. Most importantly, she championed the politicisation of the crime victim (Miers 1978), which led to the beginnings of the victim movement and helped to set the agenda for the next decade.

The 1960s saw the establishment of a victims' movement that was especially active in the United States. However, this movement did not develop a united front but was fractured by a range of interested parties each with their own group interests, motives and perspectives. Feminists, black rights activists, consumer victims and victims of war (and in the United States, particularly the Vietnamese War) all claimed the title of victim and each saw the criminal justice system as prioritising the needs of the criminal. The demand for restitution and compensation became increasingly difficult to ignore. The demise of the rehabilitative method in the 1970s and the rise of a neo-classical ideology that advocated just deserts gave the victim movement a legitimate, political voice. As Smith stated, 'It was not until the conflict between the rehabilitative ideal and the resurgence of classicalism in the 1970s that public indignation over the forgotten victim began to appear' (1985).

The 1970s saw the efforts of earlier campaigners come to fruition. Concern for the neglected victim led to the establishment of a number of voluntary organisations and social policy changes within British and US law. Victim Support was founded in Bristol in 1974 and has grown to play an important role within the criminal justice system. In 1999 Victim Support received £12 million from the government to fund the 400 Victim Support groups that cover the country, with the full-time Victim Support coordinators deploying some 16,000 volunteers.

By the 1970s the feminist movement had matured and had played its part in the formulation of equal rights campaigns and policy, culminating in the Equal Pay and the Sex Discrimination Acts of 1975. Moreover, the feminist movement allowed and encouraged radical feminists to set up women-only organisations, which have flourished not only in Britain but also in the United States, such as Women Against Violence Against Women (WAVAW), the National Coalition Against Sexual Assault (NCASA) and the National Organization of Women (NOW). The success of NOW is significant, as the organisation participated in the drafting of the Violence Against Women Act (VAWA II), which was first introduced to Congress in 1998 and which expanded the protections first won in the 1994 Violence Against Women Act. This new, dynamic feminist movement promoted the official recognition not only of crime against women and children such as rape, domestic violence, sexual abuse and child abuse, but also of those crimes produced by patriarchal institutions and a sexist society, such as discrimination, poverty and prostitution.

The influence of the feminist movement began to be felt within British social policy in the 1970s and was largely influenced by two women's groups: the National Organisation for Women (NOW) and Women's Political Causes (WPC). In 1972 the first women's refuge opened in Chiswick, London and the first rape crisis centre in London in 1974 (Mawby and Walklate 1994). In the late 1980s Victim Support also acknowledged the rights of women by establishing the Victim Support Working Party on domestic violence. Today, recent government policy against domestic violence and child abuse has been established by the prominent campaign Zero Tolerance. However, despite the influence of the feminist movement, women's status as victims still tends to be marginalised – a factor that will be discussed in more detail later in the chapter (pp. 111–113) when considering critical victimology.

In a different vein, right-wing political and economic ideology of the 1980s radically changed the status of the victim. Consumerism permeated the institutions of Britain, and the criminal justice system was no exception. Jefferson and Shapland (1990) have gone as far as to argue that 'The idea of consumers of the criminal justice system is one of the more important initiatives of the 1980s. Agencies for the first time are being conjoined to care about lay people who are using their services'.

Developments in business culture in the 1980s, including the growing importance attached to the market and market forces, also encouraged new theoretical debates among academics concerning the question of the corporate criminal. This in turn highlighted the invisibility of many of societies' victims and allowed a much broader-based discussion. Prominent cases such as the Maxwell case involving pensions fund fraud and the widespread fraud in the US savings and loans (S&L) industry in 1989 raised in the public's mind the rights of the consumer. The publicising of the corporate criminal also allowed the voice of the corporate victim to be heard within politics, the media and criminological debate.

Dramatic economic changes that affected the structure of society also affected the nature of corporate crime. As the traditional industrial base shrank, so the service/financial industry began to grow, and the relationship between corporate crime and the state altered: 'While manufacturing crimes tend to advance corporate profits and thus follow the logic of capital, financial fraud undermines that logic, jeopardizing the stability of the financial system and/or institutional survival' (Calavita and Pontell 1994).

In this context, it becomes more important for the state to prosecute corporate criminals, which in turn highlights the plight of victims, especially in fraud cases. The work of the victim surveys in the 1980s (such as the British Crime Survey) also highlighted the amount of pain that was wrought by crime – both conventional and corporate.

More recently, the position of the victim has become much more central to government policy and has led to a gradual transformation of the criminal justice system. The Labour Party's electoral manifesto in 1997 pledged to place the victim centre stage; and the formulation of the second Victim's Charter drawn up by a Conservative Home Secretary and maintained by the Labour government has had a considerable effect on the treatment of victims in the criminal justice system. There is now an expectation (enforceable by law) that court officials be sympathetic towards the victim's ordeal, especially in rape and sexual offences trials. Again the Victim's Charter can be seen as an ideological document that underpins the notion of consumerism. As Paul Rock puts it, 'the first Victim's Charter talked of the rights, the second of 1996 of standards of service' (1999).

The establishment of policies around human rights has enabled the victim to be heard. On both a global and a local level, human rights has become a philosophical issue that has dominated much of the 1980s and 1990s. Cohen states:

> Whatever the concept of human rights means, it has become a dominant narrative. Arguably, with the so-called death of the old meta-narratives of Marxism, liberalism and the Cold War, human rights will become the normative political language of the future.
>
> (1996, p. 491)

The 1990s also saw the maturing of the Green movement, which has been influential in creating new pressure groups and successfully lobbying and arguing for laws and control. This further widened perceptions of the range of corporate crime and therefore corporate victimisation. The regulation of corporate crime is a direct response to the suffering of victims who have had to live with and deal with the effects of environmental pollution. Ecological movements worldwide have drawn attention to the problems; and it is no longer a question of saving socialism or capitalism but rather that the whole of humanity is existing on a threatened planet. To that extent, then, ecological groups have emphasised the victim as being humanity itself and have considerably broadened the concept of the victim.

An awareness of the large numbers of victims of race and sex discrimination has also grown out of the era of human rights. One particular landmark case was that of Stephen Lawrence, who was murdered on 22 April 1993. This case highlighted the plight of victims of racial violence in society and, according to the subsequent Macpherson Report (1999), the extent of institutional racism within the Metropolitan Police Force.

The first years of the new millennium have to some extent consolidated the position of the victim. In 2001 the opportunity for victims to have their statements read out in court was introduced. And in March 2002 the Labour government unveiled plans to provide victims of crime with a Bill of Rights, to appoint a commissioner for victims and to establish a government advisory panel which would consist of victims of crime and their relatives. David Blunkett, the Home Secretary, stated:

Victims of crime are still too often treated with indifference or with disrespect. I am not having that. These are the very people the criminal justice system should protect and defend, the very people who should be cared for and considered at every stage and by every element of the justice process.

(*The Independent*, 22 March 2002)

However, the success of victims of crime in establishing their rights through the Victim's Charter has been limited. The Charter, for example, does not take account of victims of 'workplace crimes' – something that the TUC has taken issue with in recent years:

[T]he TUC believes that if the Victim's Charter was extended to cover workplace injury and illness, it would signal the importance of such crimes (which are all too often seen as mere technical breaches of regulations, or only accidental, leading to injury or illness).

(Trades Union Congress, *Rights for Victims of Workplace Crime*, 26 May 2001)

All these 'new' victims represent different periods in history and provide victimology with new areas to research. As a consequence, new perspectives have emerged which have broadened the theoretical debates around the status of the victim in contemporary society. The theoretical debates within victimology, beginning with its academic genesis in the 1940s and the focus on positivist principles, now face a challenge from radical and critical victimology. In a post-modern era, traditional epistemologies within victimology are subject to criticism. In highlighting the increasingly recognised and important role of the victim, Howarth and Rock argue that:

Additions to the roster of victims of crime can have a very real usefulness to criminology. They can illuminate the complexity of crime, the abundance of the groups it affects and creates, the multiple consequences that it inflicts, the diversity of the responses that it elicits, and the concomitant intricacy and scale of the social structures it generates. Crime has diffuse and proliferating repercussions which are now only beginning to be (mis)understood.

(2000, p. 59)

QUESTION BREAK: CHANGES IN VICTIMISATION

In this section we have highlighted how different times and eras have led to the emergence of new and different groups of victims.

Questions

What groups of victims became particularly recognised in each of the following decades: the 1960s; the 1970s; the 1980s; and the 1990s?

Why did these 'victims' emerge at those particular times?

What sort of 'future victims' might emerge over the next few years?

Theories and methods of research in victimology

The intention of this section is to set out and examine the major theoretical perspectives within victimology and the methodologies that underpin them.

The term 'victimology' was first coined by Frederick Wertham (1949), who called for a 'science of victimology'. However, as regards theorising about victimology, it can be argued that Mendelsohn and von Hentig are widely recognised as the 'founding fathers' of the sub-discipline. Both have been profoundly influential in establishing victimology as an academic discipline, but in very different ways. Von Hentig's work is closely linked to criminology in that its concern and focus is with the victims of crime – so victimology is analysed as a part of criminology. In contrast, Mendelsohn's victimological theorising is very much bound up in the philosophy of human rights – and victimology is seen as, essentially, an independent discipline. As Mendelsohn himself states,

> We must point out a fundamental difference between the points of view of Professor von Hentig and Professor Ellenberg on the one hand and of ourselves on the other hand. The former consider the study of the victim as a chapter of criminology, whereas we consider it as a separate science, which because of its structure and its aim should be independent.
>
> (1963, p. 241)

This division, and Mendelsohn's views in particular, help explain why victimology has been able to incorporate those who are best described as 'unconventional victims' – a particular area that has been crucial to the development of both radical and critical victimology.

However, despite these differences, both theorists are proponents of what has become widely known as positivist or conventional victimology. The key characteristics of positivist victimology can be described as 'the identification of factors which contribute to a non random pattern of victimisation, a focus on interpersonal crimes of violence, and a concern to identify victims who may have contributed to their own victimisation' (Miers 1989). Miers, therefore, draws upon a number of influences which underpin positivist victimology, including a concern with the patterns and regularities of victimisation and the development and application of the key concepts of 'victim precipitation', 'victim proneness' and lifestyle.

Arguably the first systematic study of the victims of crime was von Hentig's book *The Criminal and his Victim*, published in 1948 (of course, the use of the male term was even more the norm in the 1940s). The importance of this study cannot be overestimated. It transformed criminology from a one-sided study of the offender. Indeed, Fattah (1986) went so far as to argue that 'Since criminal behaviour is dynamic, it can only be explained through a dynamic approach, where the delinquent, the act and the victim are inseparable elements of a total situation which conditions the dialectic of the anti-social conduct'. Von Hentig proposed a dynamic approach which discussed how the offender and the victim were involved in an interaction, thereby challenging the concept of the victim as passive. *The Criminal and his Victim* includes a chapter dealing with victims entitled 'The Contribution of the Victim to the Genesis of the Crime' in which the concept of victim proneness – the notion that some individuals might be more susceptible to victimisation than others – is discussed. In order to operationalise this concept, von Hentig developed his now famous typology of victim proneness. It is worth listing it in full: the young; the old; the female; the mentally defective; immigrants; members of minorities; dull normals; the depressed; the acquisitive; the wanton; the lonesome and heartbroken; the tormentor; and the fighting victim. People in each of these categories were said to be victim-prone owing to their social and/or psychological state. In other words, these are characteristics which may have precipitated the offence through which they were victimised.

QUESTION BREAK: CATEGORISING VICTIMS

While we may question von Hentig's use of certain typologies – such as the dull, normal or the lonesome – it is worth considering whether these categories tell us anything about our own personal risk of victimisation.

Questions

How many of the typologies do you fit into?

How and why would they make you more victim-prone in today's society?

Mendelsohn (1963) on the other hand developed a sixfold typology of victims which reflected their culpability: in other words, the extent to which the victim was responsible for her or his victimisation. According to Mendelsohn, certain victims of crime were more or less culpable – an obvious example of greater culpability being the aggressor who through the fault of his own actions is killed. While both of these approaches tend to overemphasise notions of blame and vulnerability, they nevertheless provided the impetus for further research within the discipline of victimology. Furthermore, the idea of the blameworthy victim was to form the basis for theories of victim precipitation.

Wolfgang (1958) subjected von Hentig's ideas to empirical testing in his study of criminal homicide in Philadelphia. As a consequence, he developed the term 'victim precipitation', which refers to situations in which the victim is a direct precipitator of the offence. He argued that

> The term victim precipitation is applied to those homicides in which the victim is a direct, positive precipitator in the crime. The role of the victim is characterised by his having been the first in the particular homicide drama to use physical force directed against his (usually) slayer. The victim precipitated cases are those in which the victim was the first to show any use of a deadly weapon to strike a blow in altercation – in short the first to commence an interplay or resort to physical violence.

The risk of being a victim

In recent years the notion of a risk society has become very much in vogue in academic thinking (Beck 1992). However, over twenty years ago, positive victimologists were using similar ideas for understanding the risk or chance of being a victim. It has been argued that a much more realistic approach would be to try to understand victimisation in terms of risk. This can be related to the concept of lifestyle, which was introduced to victimology by Hindelang, Gottfredson and Garofalo in 1978 and takes us beyond the individual victimising event, instead emphasising the constraints and impact of structure on the individual. In other words, variables such as occupation, status, daily routine and leisure outside the home can compound one another, giving rise to increased chances of victimisation. In relation to occupation, for example, it has been documented that hospital workers are at increasing risk of attack during their working hours from violent, often drunk, patients.

This theory has been adapted by Laub (1990) in developing 'routine activities theory', which attempts to predict the risk of victimisation according to lifestyle, behaviour and demographic characteristics. The risk of becoming a victim of crime varies as a function of demographic characteristics, such as gender, age, race or socio-economic class. It is a fact that men, and particularly young men aged between 18 and 24, have a higher risk of assault than women (with the exception of sexual assault and domestic violence), yet they also have higher rates of assaultive behaviour than any other group. These characteristics are further complicated by the fact that residential location and exposure to potential assailants vary as a function of lifestyle. For example, if a person's lifestyle or routine activity places that person in considerable contact with young men, then it would follow that his or her risk of victimization is high.

As a result, the concept has also been praised for shifting the focus away from victim blaming and emphasising instead the importance of the individual's daily routine.

Positivist methods and victimology

In considering positivist victimology it is important to keep in mind that it relies on positivist methodology – research based upon the logic and methods of scientific inquiry. In its embryonic stage this viewpoint led to the development of typologies (in the work of both von Hentig and Mendelsohn, for example) and, more recently, large victimisation surveys which claim to have identified 'victim-prone' personalities and victim precipitation – the argument that some victims actually cause their victimisation.

For some time, information about crime was gathered from official police records. In response to the criticism that crime statistics recorded by the police are an inadequate tool and do not measure the 'dark figure' of crime or the experiences of victims, positivist victimology developed the victim survey. The victim survey was first developed in the United States in the 1960s as a consequence of a 'war on crime' initiative. The first

British victimisation survey was published by Sparks *et al.* as *Surveying Victims* in 1977. The British Crime Survey was produced by the Home Office in 1981 and the results were published by Hough and Mayhew (1983), whose findings referred to the likelihood of victimisation – for instance, that

> A statistically average person aged 16 or over can expect a robbery once every 5 centuries (not attempted), an assault resulting in injury (even slight) once every century, the family car to be stolen or taken by joy riders once every 60 years, a burglary in the home every 40 years.

The methodology used to develop the British Crime Survey has allowed the differences in risk, in terms of, for example, age, sex, race, to be highlighted. The survey also raises victims' issues and provides evidence of levels of crime, public attitudes to crime and fear of crime. It includes crimes which are not reported to the police and has become an important alternative to police records. It provides evidence of how victims are treated by the police and what they want in the way of police attention (Mayhew *et al.* 1989). However, there are various weaknesses in the methodology which create a number of limitations. Such limitations include *non-response*, whereby some groups are omitted or under-represented. These include those in institutions, the homeless, young people (especially victims of child abuse) and victims of corporate crime. *Response bias* is also a problem, as respondents may not give accurate answers to questions: they may have difficulty recalling the incident, or in some cases may fabricate information. There is also the problem of forward and backward telescoping, with people mistaking the length of time since an event occurred (Mirlees-Black *et al.* 1996). And the range and extent of offences such as domestic violence and sexual offences are likely to be poorly measured because of their delicate nature.

However, it is important to acknowledge that in spite of these legitimate criticisms, the victim survey has developed from positivist victimology and has helped to place criminal victimisation firmly on the political agenda – perhaps most notably through the British Crime Surveys, which have been produced annually since 2001 and which are seen as an authoritative source of data by criminal justice agencies, the media and academics.

QUESTION BREAK: CRIME SURVEYS

The British Crime Survey 2001/2002 interviewed 40,000 people over the age of 16. It asked adults in private households about their experience of victimisation in the last 12 months.

Questions

What victims might be excluded from the British Crime Survey?

Explain how the survey can be improved in order to take account of these victims.

How could the data from the chart (Figure 4.1) help the police to improve their service?

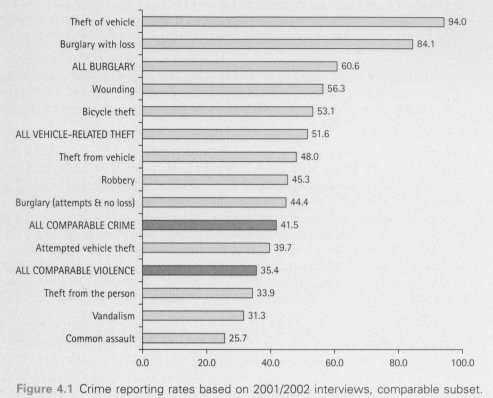

Figure 4.1 Crime reporting rates based on 2001/2002 interviews, comparable subset. Source: British Crime Survey 2002

Critique of positivism

As well as there being difficulties with positivist methods, positivist ideas have led to a great deal of debate and have been strongly criticised, not least because of their attempts to cite the victim's role as a causal effect in his or her victimisation. The use of the notion of victim precipitation and its connotations of victim blaming is highly controversial, but still remains a prominent feature in the formulation of explanations and reasons for crime which are employed by various agencies within the criminal justice system. However, a major limitation of the concepts of victim precipitation, culpability and proneness is that they are heavily focused on the individual 'victimisation event'. As a consequence of this, victimology as a discipline has received strong criticism. Clark and Lewis (1977), for example, argued that 'In the social sciences, victim blaming is becoming an increasingly popular rationalisation for criminal and deviant behaviour . . . over the past few years, victim blaming has become institutionalised within the academic world under the guise of victimology'. This scathing attack on victimology and in particular on positivist victimology echoes the sentiments of feminist criminologists in particular. According to feminists, victimology became a weapon of ideology used to further the view of a patriarchal society and legitimise physical and sexual dominance of the male over the female. As Clark and Lewis put it:

> The male researcher finds his escape in victimology. He seeks the problem's cause in the behaviour of its victim, and goes on to persuade himself and the public at large that by changing that behaviour the problem can be controlled. In this way the study of victimology becomes the art of victim blaming.

The controversial nature of victim precipitation has been highlighted in relation to rape, and in this context has received a great deal of media attention over the past twenty or so years. In some of the most publicised cases, there has been a clearly negative portrayal of women who have been raped and a tendency for their ordeals to be trivialised, with a consequent 'blaming of the victim'.

In particular, feminists have rejected the operationalisation of the concept of victim precipitation provided by Amir, who used the concept to investigate patterns of forcible rape. Amir studied 646 reports of forcible rape in Philadelphia and concluded that 19 per cent of the rapes were precipitated by the victim. According to Zedner, Amir's definition of the concept of victim precipitation in relation to rape (Amir 1971, p. 262) could be defined as follows:

> The victim actually, or so it was interpreted by the offender, agreed to sexual relations but retracted . . . or did not resist strongly enough when the suggestion was made by the offender. The term also applies to cases in which the victim enters vulnerable situations charged sexually.
>
> (Zedner 1992)

The scientific basis of positivism relies upon that which can be objectively observed and measured, therefore positivist victimology has a tendency to focus on the public rather than the private. Dichotomies like public/private have always been criticised by feminists because of their invocation of a scientific objective rational reality, which ignores natural, subjective and emotional accounts of victimisation. Until recently this had allowed certain crimes (in particular those that occur behind closed doors, such as rape and domestic violence) to be under-reported and therefore rendered invisible.

More fundamental to the feminist position, however, is the use of traditional epistemologies which, they argue, have promoted a view of sociological (and general) knowledge as androcentric. Therefore the methods, theory and patriarchal academic modes of production (Stanley 1990) used to study victims are seen as illegitimate, as they are based upon partial knowledge. Indeed, many would argue that the theories and methods of sociology derive from the visions of the social world that men have. This line of criticism will be returned to below when we examine critical victimology.

Radical victimology

In response to some of the criticism lodged against positive victimology, the radical victimological perspective emerged in the late 1960s and 1970s. As mentioned, radical victimology can be traced back to the work of Mendelsohn and his argument for a victimology of human rights that allows for exploration of the role of the state in defining who 'legitimate' victims are and, more importantly, how the criminal justice system is implicated in the 'construction' of victims and criminals. As a consequence, radical victimology acknowledges, in particular, those victims who have been rendered invisible.

These victims have been best described by Quinney (1972) as 'victims of police force, the victims of war, the victims of the correctional system, the victims of state violence, the victims of oppression of any sort'. It is evident, then, that the effect of the victim movements of the 1970s and 1980s have been instrumental in placing radical victimology on the theoretical agenda within victimology. In essence, radical victimology questions and criticises the tendency of positive victimology to concentrate upon conventional victims rather than 'unconventional' victims. Radical victimology's holistic approach towards the victim allows issues relating particularly to women, such as rape and domestic violence, to enter the public arena. Moreover, the emphasis on the role of the state in the production of victims gives the corporate/white-collar victim a legitimate status. The concern to expose human misery and the role that the capitalist state has in the distribution of this misery has been outlined in the work of Box, particularly in his study *Power, Crime and Mystification* (1983), in which the identification and extent of victims of corporate crime is graphically documented.

What might be termed conventional radical victimology has, then, helped to expose the limited structural basis of victimisation and therefore the problems facing the poor and the powerless. However, it did not contribute in any meaningful way to empirical research. And, as implied above, although positivist victimology generated much invaluable data, its research was based upon conventional constructions of crime and therefore neglected sexual and racially motivated crime and victims of corporate crime.

It is within radical left realist victimology that the issue of reliable and valid research has become paramount. Theoretically, radical left realism has developed from the left realist perspective within criminology, typically associated with the work of Lea and Young (1993). It therefore acknowledges the role of the state in what Young has called the 'square of crime' (Young 1997) and argues that in order to fully understand crime in all its dimensions, all four corners of this 'square' – offenders, victims, the community/public and the state – and the interrelationships between them have to be fully investigated.

In relation to methodology, radical left realists have argued for more locally based victim surveys which show the geographically and socially focused distribution of criminal victimisation; furthermore, local crime surveys tend to be explanatory rather than descriptive (as with positivist examples such as the British Crime Survey). Variables such as age, gender, ethnicity are taken into account during the sampling process and, as a consequence, local surveys have challenged the view that crime is a rare occurrence, have helped to uncover the social characteristics of the victim and have highlighted the problem of intra-racial, intra-class and gender issues around crime. Valuable data have emerged from such surveys – Jones *et al*. (1986), for instance, uncovered high levels of racially and sexually motivated crime through the Islington Crime Survey. Other local crime surveys include those carried out in Edinburgh and Merseyside (Kinsey 1984; Anderson *et al.* 1990). Also, victim surveys have included questions on commercial and health and safety at work offences, which has allowed victims of corporate/white-collar crime to be given a voice (Pearce 1990). Local authorities and crime prevention organisations have adopted the local victim survey in order to assist in the development of policy. As Young has argued, in order to make the plight of the victim real, it is essential to develop 'an accurate victimology understanding problems as people experience them' (1986, pp. 23–24).

Local surveys have helped to dispel the view that crime affects few people and have highlighted those people faced with specific difficulties and at particular risk (of domestic violence or racism, for example). However, as with positivist victimology, the radical left realist approach relies on victimisation surveys and therefore focuses on patterns and regularities rather than trying to understand the underlying mechanisms which contribute to the victimisation process. A critique that has been lodged against the methods of radical theorists is that local crime surveys assume a harnessing of the democratic process – in other words, they assume that the community participates in the decision-making process and its members understand their rights as a citizen and the obligation of the state. In similar vein to radical victimology, the critical theorists (who are discussed in the following sub-section) would also ask whether people are aware of their social reality and whether it is safe to assume that the state is neutral in its response to crime and victimisation.

Critical victimology

Partly as a response to the shortcomings of other victimological perspectives and partly to build on the insights of feminism and left realist approaches, a new, 'critical' victimological approach has emerged in recent years. As with radical victimology, with which it overlaps in a number of ways, it is based on an essentially interpretivist, 'micro' approach to theorising about social issues – in the context of victimology, to theorising about victims of crime. Critical victimology looks to include the 'hidden' victims of crime in its analysis and to consider and highlight the role of the state in perpetuating inequalities in the 'production of victims'.

This more interpretive approach to victimology can be illustrated by the emphasis given to labelling and, as Miers (1990) suggests, the focus on 'who has the power to apply the label'. It is well established that labelling and the interpretivist perspective of interactionism provide a massive input to (and led to a change of direction in) the sociology of deviance in the 1960s and 1970s. Equally, though, this perspective attracted a good deal of criticism from critical criminologists of the period. In a similar vein, the emphasis on the 'label' in critical victimology has been seen as doing little to help us understand the structural formations that underpin our definitions and interpretations of the victim.

The early critical victimological approach has been criticised and developed by Walklate (1989, 1990) among others. In particular, she has advocated a critical victimology that takes seriously the need for the (sub)discipline to be based on empirical, objective research and to take close account of the structural context in which it is operating, but at the same time to do this without losing the real insights and strengths that can be offered by an interpretive understanding.

A key issue here seems to be the need to define what is the 'real'; and to examine the processes which help provide an understanding of everyday reality. This issue is high-lighted partly to take account of the fact that it is quite possible for victims not to know about their victimisation and, therefore, the causes of it. It is for this reason that critical victimology advocates the need to examine the processes which 'go on behind our backs' in the context of defining victims. Mawby and Walklate (1994) make the point that this emphasis on hidden processes has also been a major concern of feminist work (and its attempt to ensure that women – and in this case women victims – are recognised as occupying both the public and the private domains).

Critical victimology problematises the relationship between the citizen and the state: it does not see the state as neutral; rather, the state's mechanisms contribute to those victims we see and those we don't see. It is therefore not objective but self-interested and self-motivated. This, according to critical victimology, raises problems in relation to race, gender and class and how they are articulated in policy terms.

Idealistically, the notion of the citizen as consumer maintains the citizen and state as neutral entities. However, the inextricable link between citizenship and consumerism gives the impression that citizens' social rights are being catered for, yet

> The rights of citizenship are a reality only for those who have belief in their authen-
> ticity and the skills needed to exercise them. Indeed, if rights are to exist in a real
> sense, it is essential that those entitled to social services know what their rights are
> and that they are able to lay claim to them.
>
> (Barbalet 1993, p. 54)

In a similar manner, if that state in question is a patriarchal one, the question arises of whether we are all awarded the same rights, as the notion of the 'citizen/consumer' would have us believe. Mackinnon states that 'The liberal state coercively and author-itatively constitutes the social order in the interests of men as a gender through its legitimating norms, forms, relation to society, and substantive policies' (1989).

The reduction in the role of the state during the Thatcher era, in response to what was seen as a dependency culture and the notion of the nanny state, created what has been termed possessive individualism. This has also affected the idea of victimisation. As Young puts it, 'Everyone is a victim, then everyone has a part to play in the struggle against crime. More strongly everyone has a duty: it is part of the offices of the citizen to minimise the risk of becoming a victim' (1996, p. 56).

Critical victimology, then, can be seen as a theoretical perspective that examines the wider social context – in modern industrial societies, this context has tended to focus on the ways in which capitalism and patriarchy influence the ways in which victims are perceived and responded to. In doing this it emphasises the key role of the state and of the law but at the same time acknowledges the importance of the micro level of analysis – in other words, of agency as well as structure.

This theoretical approach to or refinement of critical victimology, developed by Mawby and Walkate (1994) among others, draws upon Giddens's (1984) theory of structuration in highlighting the importance of both macro- and micro-analysis – of structure and agency, as Giddens terms it. Stucturation as emphasised throughout critical victimology allows the victim a voice. Critical victimology highlights the importance of people's ability to fight for themselves against their structural constraints, and quite often with surprising results. Examples of successful 'voices' include Greenpeace, the Hillsborough campaign (especially in boycotting the *Sun* newspaper in Liverpool), Rock against Racism and anti-capitalist protests against the World Trade Organization, as well as centres that have been established to support victims of domestic violence.

Critical victimology has developed partly as a response to the methodological flaws within positivist and radical victimology. It does not deny the worth of the criminal victimisation survey, but stresses the importance of considering historical, social and political processes. At an empirical level, critical victimology argues that comparative and longitudinal studies need to be employed, although there is no uniformity into its methods. That said, it could be argued that critical victimology is an approach that has attempted to incorporate a critical understanding of the role of the law and the state in the victimisation process as well as recognising the important role of human actors in influencing the conditions under which they exist. It has also been informed by the work of feminism and has brought feminist thinking into the mainstream of victimology.

Victims of private crime

As discussed earlier, positivist victimology has been the most prominent theoretical mode of study of victims and has concentrated on victims of 'public' or 'conventional' crime. As a consequence, victims of private and or 'unconventional' crime have until relatively recently been rendered largely invisible within academia. Such victims may include victims of domestic violence, victims of child abuse and victims of corporate crime. This public/private dichotomy has always been found problematic by feminist writers, and it is for this reason that critical and to some extent radical victimology are of paramount importance in placing the victims of private crime (for example, domestic violence and child abuse) on the social and, more crucially, political agenda. We will now look at domestic violence as a specific and major example of private crime.

Victims of 'private' crime: domestic violence

Violence in the home has become recognised as a major issue and concern, and society is now more aware than at any other time in history of the nature and extent of such victimisation. The civil rights movements of the 1960s and 1970s (especially those relating to women and children) highlighted oppression and violence within the home. As a consequence, violence in the home has been legally and politically recognised, which has successfully led to *some* awareness within the criminal justice system (with the instigation of domestic violence and child protection units and protective laws) and the voluntary sector (which has provided refuges and self-help groups) of the extent of the problem.

This increased focus on violence within the home (which can range from sexual to physical to mental abuse) gives the impression that this is a new phenomenon that contemporary society has to deal with. However, feminist theory in particular has highlighted that this problem was 'institutionalised' during the Victorian era; in other words, given credence through the norms and values which governed everyday life and legalised through the criminal justice system. This was an era when the phrase 'An Englishman's home is his castle' meant just that. The father/husband was the ultimate ruler and could legally chastise his wife and children in any manner he saw fit. This, however, is not to deny the involvement of women within violence in the home.

There is currently no legal definition of domestic violence, as it is not seen as a specific offence, but covers a range of criminal behaviours. However, Her Majesty's Inspectorate of Constabulary introduced a new definition in April 1999 for the purpose of returns of reports and in order to aid the gathering of statistics. The definition used by the police service is as follows: 'the term domestic violence shall be understood to mean any violence between current or former partners in an intimate relationship, wherever and whenever the violence occurs. The violence may include physical, sexual, emotional or financial abuse' (www.homeoffice.gov.uk).

This definition has to some extent alleviated the concerns of many feminist researchers who argued that definitions of domestic violence used by agencies of the state (the police, the courts, etc.) were much too narrow, either not dealing with the forms that violence was likely to take or projecting domestic violence as a heterosexual problem, omitting those victims who suffer domestic violence within same-sex relationships. However, for many the term 'domestic violence' is in itself problematic. Most violence in the home is perpetrated by men towards women – the term 'domestic violence' hides the gender of the perpetrator (Morley and Mullender 1994). Similarly, the term 'violence' has been criticised for being too narrow. The term should be broadened to include verbal abuse, intimidation, physical harassment, homicide, sexual assault and rape.

Domestic violence may, then, be defined as the actual or threatened physical, economic, psychological, verbal, sexual or social abuse of an individual by someone with whom they have had or are having an intimate relationship. There are many ways in which each criterion may manifest itself, and this will to some extent depend on the victim's (the survivor's) social status and support network. So domestic violence can be actual or threatened abuse, which allows for an understanding of the victim's fear and intimidation, often cited as the most upsetting ordeal a victim will go through, worse than the eventual attack or row.

This definition implies that domestic violence is not necessarily restricted to physical abuse; it can include anything from punching and kicking, to sleep deprivation and even murder. It is also sexual: any sexual act against the woman's (and in the vast majority of cases it is a female who is the victim) wishes, which can be anything from rape to forced prostitution. Economic abuse is an often overlooked but important area as it is often the main reason why women stay in violent relationships. Regardless of the fact that there are more women within the workplace than ever before, many women are still financially reliant upon their husband/partner. Economic abuse may take the form of the perpetrator making the victim beg for money or withholding money, even in some cases for basics such as food and sanitary towels.

Psychological or emotional abuse is often the cruellest form of abuse as it breaks down the victim's defence strategies and destroys the image they have of their 'self'. This can be achieved through constant criticism: they are 'ugly', they are a 'bad' person, no one else would want or love them. Social abuse is closely linked to psychological abuse in that it also breaks down self-esteem. It is often the case that social abuse involves behaviour that is based on an approach of divide and conquer, thereby removing the victim from any support systems that he or she may have. The victim may be isolated from friends, forbidden to see family members and allowed out only at specific times.

QUESTION BREAK

Think of other examples of abuse/domestic violence that have not been discussed here. Try to think of examples of the different forms – including psychological, emotional and social abuse.

Explaining domestic violence

Although it is not the purpose of this section to investigate in any great depth the causes of domestic violence, it is worth briefly outlining the major perspectives that have developed over the past thirty or so years. Biological and psychological explanations are related to the extent that they argue that such violence is a result of specific, individual factors. The medical world, for instance, has focused on human DNA in order to explain a range of behaviour, including homosexuality, mental illness and violence. It has been argued that violence can be attributed to having an extra Y chromosome. Socio-biologists have even argued that violence within the home has the function of helping the 'fittest to survive' (Draper and Burgess 1989). The psychological approach also aims to understand domestic violence through individual factors such as personality traits, mental illness and internal defence mechanisms. For instance, Snell et al. (1964) claimed that it was a wife's masochistic personality that caused her to be abused by her husband and, by implication, that victims of domestic violence actually enjoyed experiencing pain and thus wanted to be abused. Erin Pizzey (1974) argued that male perpetrators were psychologically maladjusted and had often grown up in abusive families themselves – a process that encouraged a 'cycle of violence'. These ideas have been criticised because of their assumption that victims are culpable in part for their victimisation and that all women who are abused within a relationship are in some way 'crazy'; and that men who abuse are psychologically maladjusted and come from violent homes. Strauss (1980), for example, found that men who abused their partners did not have an uncommonly high rate of psychological disturbance. More importantly, these theories ignore issues around power and raise the question of why, if perpetrators of domestic violence are psychologically maladjusted, do they not beat their bosses, friends and fathers rather than wait until they are in the privacy of their own homes before engaging in violence?

From a sociological perspective, domestic violence is investigated in relation to structure, and feminist approaches have tried to shift this focus from victim as individually culpable to an analysis of the socially constructed political, economic and cultural contexts within which violence against women flourishes. Domestic violence (especially against women) is explained in relation to gender, in particular the subordination of women by men in society (patriarchy). Gender relations are characterised by power, and in relation to domestic violence, men dominate women through abuse whether it be physical, psychological, social or economic. Domestic violence is seen as understandable within a historical socio-political context that relates to family life and marriage (Dobash and Dobash 1998). Feminists argue that these institutions have been dominated by men through the years and that this has been allowed by a patriarchal society. The social construction of masculinity and violence allows men to produce and maintain their authority over women and children. Within Victorian society, for example, the criminal justice system sanctioned men's rights to control women and children through abusive means if necessary.

In a similar vein, sex-role theory argues that sex-role socialisation can explain why violence in general and more particularly within the family is perpetrated by men. Throughout primary and secondary socialisation, girls are socialised into the victim status: they are taught through play and observation that they are to be passive and yield to the control of men. Similarly, boys are taught that they should display strength and control. Sexual childhood socialisation (or 'sex scripts', as Strong and DeVault (1995) put it) also teaches children the required behaviour within relationships: boys are taught to be the sexual aggressor and girls to be submissive. Moreover, the socialisation of girls and women in society forces them into accepting patriarchal values, which leaves them open and vulnerable to abuse.

So the earlier theories of domestic violence, in particular biological and psychological ones, emphasised the role of the individual, whether the perpetrator or victim. By contrast, sociological theories, notably feminism, have looked beyond the individual and analysed the social and political structures which have allowed domestic violence to continue. One of the most significant of these structures has been the criminal justice system.

Victims of domestic violence and the criminal justice system

The criminal justice system is not an institution in isolation; many areas of life may affect its response to certain phenomena. In particular, contemporary dominant discourses (e.g. patriarchy), political movements, government policy, pressure groups, public opinion, and the media have all (whether we like it or not) affected the response of the criminal justice system. As an example, we will consider how the police respond to victims of domestic violence.

As stated earlier, the victims' movement of the 1970s highlighted issues of social rights, and domestic violence became a prominent area – no longer a private issue, the victims of which suffered in silence. Since this politicisation of domestic violence, the government has recognised that this form of violence deserves state protection, intervention and the status of 'real' crime, yet the criminal justice system has responded slowly and at times inconsistently to this status.

Up until 1975 the police service's role in relation to domestic violence had been negligible. The attitude had been to avoid arrest and prosecution, and to observe the notion that such behaviour was a private affair between spouses and that intervention (except in relation to particularly violent episodes) was to be discouraged. In 1975 the first public policy on domestic violence outlined the serious nature of this type of crime and detailed the role that the police should play in relation to arrest. Following this report, various government acts and recommendations were put into place which aided the police in performing their role, including the Domestic Violence Act 1976, the Domestic Violence and Magistrates Act 1978 and the Matrimonial Homes Act 1983. Further, Home Office Circulars of 1986 (no. 69) and 1990 (no. 60) urged the police to improve services to victims and to treat domestic violence in the same way as any other serious crime, and encouraged forces to keep accurate statistical records.

Despite the new rules, regulations and initiatives (the high-profile Zero Tolerance campaign being an example), the public still seem to be reluctant to involve the police in domestic violence incidents. Twenty-nine per cent of those who took part in a BBC survey stated that they would be reluctant to involve the police in an incident of this sort (*BBC News*, 11 February 2003). Conversely, the police are often still reluctant to intervene, despite governmental and public pressure.

So what reasons are there for the lack of public faith in the police and for the apparent police apathy towards incidents of domestic violence?

Public faith in the police is often drawn from experience – either direct or indirect. In relation to domestic violence, the police are often criticised for their apathetic reaction to it. Studies have shown that victims often feel that response to their situation has been inadequate. Grace (1995), for example, found that police failed to deal with incidents of domestic violence seriously or sensitively. The feeling was that domestic incidents are low on the list of priorities for an overburdened police service and that time could be better spent looking for 'real' criminals rather than wasting time on another 'domestic'. Victims also feel that the police cannot offer effective support once the incident has been reported (Hoyle 1999). Drawing on victims' experiences, many feminist theorists have highlighted the misuse of discretionary powers available to the police when dealing with incidents of domestic violence. Decision making is influenced by the police culture, which can be patriarchal by nature, therefore individual judgements may often be based upon stereotypes and bias (Edwards 1989).

However, people's perception of the police does not always match the reality, and it is clear that dealing with domestic violence is often problematic for the police. Police work is subject to the organisation's bureaucratic structure, and the police decision-making process is reached via a number of considerations. Obviously, evidence is of the utmost importance when trying to bring a domestic violence case to court and needs to be substantial enough for the Crown Prosecution Service (CPS) to consider prosecution. Hoyle (1999) explains this phenomenon as being partly due to the importance afforded to the 'victim's preferences'. Although a victim is not allowed to withdraw charges (this is within the remit of the police and the CPS), the victim often withdraws her or his statement for a number of reasons, both personal and practical. Also, despite the efforts by the police to set up domestic violence units and recruit domestic violence officers, such officers regularly complain that they feel marginalised and that their area of work receives low priority and status.

Recently there has been a new effort made by the Metropolitan Police to deal with domestic violence incidents more effectively. The 'golden hour' is a new initiative that lays emphasis on the importance of gathering evidence from the scene of a domestic dispute within an hour in order to gain the best chance of conviction of the offender. Community Safety Units have also been put in place to advise all victims of hate crime (including domestic violence).

Victims of domestic violence have various ways in which to access the criminal justice system. There are at the moment a number of laws that serve to protect victims of domestic violence. The Protection from Harassment Law (the 'stalkers' law') is unique in the fact that this is the first law to protect from behaviour that is not specifically criminal. The Harassment Act 1997 criminalises the psychological nature of domestic violence. The Youth Justice and Criminal Evidence Act 1999 has also put in place measures to provide protection for victims and witnesses, including victims of domestic violence. Harriet Harman, Solicitor General and MP, has called for the Law Commission (the independent body which advises the government on law changes) to review policy with regard to domestic violence victims. Some of the changes that Harman is calling for are anonymity for victims and a new law preventing harassment by abusive partners.

After the initial police report and arrest, the next stage that the victim of domestic violence must endure is the court process. The majority of domestic violence cases, and crime cases in general, are tried at the magistrates' courts, so it is crucial that the attitudes of magistrates towards domestic violence are free from bias. The implementation of the Victim's Charter outlined that victims at court must be treated sympathetically, leading to the Magistrates Association calling for an examination of magistrates' approaches to domestic violence cases.

Despite this reflective mood, Gilchrist and Blisset (2002) uncovered evidence that there remains differential treatment and punishment towards crimes involving public and private violence. Their results found that 32 per cent of those accused of assault within the home were given a custodial sentence, compared to 37 per cent of those accused of assaulting a stranger. Moreover, explanations for the perpetrator's conduct were discussed more openly and deemed more 'important' in domestic violence cases than in stranger assaults. As Gilchrist and Blisset put it, 'This type of discussion mirrored the language and explanation commonly heard in domestic violence perpetrator programmes: excusing the man, minimizing the assault and blaming the victim for the perpetrator's behaviour' (2002, p. 360).

It would seem that despite the structural measures taken to protect victims of domestic violence and punish the perpetrators, there is always danger of individual bias from a particular magistrate or judge – and this is an area that it is very difficult to monitor effectively and deal with.

QUESTION BREAK: UNCOVERING DOMESTIC ABUSE

Read the following extract and answer the questions that follow.

ICM interviewed a random sample of 1020 adults aged 18+, face to face in January 2003. Interviews were conducted across the country and the data has been weighted to the profile of all adults.

One in four adults in Britain has experienced domestic violence, a poll for the BBC suggests. In the survey of more than 1,000 people, a quarter said they had been involved in violence, either as the victim or perpetrator.

The research by pollsters ICM covered all the relationships from short term to marriage. More than a quarter of the women who were questioned (27%) said they had been physically abused. The corresponding figure for men was 21%. Of those who had been involved in domestic violence 37% of women had reported an incident to the police, compared with 19% of men.

More than a third of the sample said they knew someone who had experienced domestic violence but women were much more likely than men to tell a friend or go to the police.

Yet the issue of whether the police should intervene in domestic violence remains contentious. Nearly three out of 10 people surveyed said they thought the police should always be called. But twice as many feel they should not be routinely involved. Seven out of ten people said they thought the police were more likely to give priority to dealing with an incident between people in the street than a disturbance between a man and a woman in their own home. Almost half the respondents thought that it was up to the people concerned to sort it out behind closed doors. Only 29% thought that the police should always be called in such cases.

The extent of domestic violence has always been difficult to measure because many people are reluctant to talk about their own experiences. This survey confirms that it is still a major problem that affects people of all ages and social classes, right across the country.

(*BBC News*, 11 February 2003)

Questions

The survey revealed that a majority of people still feel reluctant to involve the police in cases of domestic violence. How could you account for this attitude?

The survey suggests that 'the extent of domestic violence [is] difficult to measure'. Explain the reasons why people might be unwilling to divulge information about their experiences of domestic violence.

Corporate crime and its victims

The plight of victims of corporate crime rarely features in discussions of criminology or victimology. Here we will attempt to identify the diverse nature of corporate victims, illustrated by case studies involving employees, consumers and general citizens. The discussion devotes some space to the physical and emotional effects upon the victims and then considers some of the problems affecting the legal treatment and status of the victims of corporate crime within a capitalist society.

The writer generally associated with placing the corporate crime on the criminological agenda is Edwin Sutherland. Sutherland's book *White Collar Crime* (1949) is arguably the first text that gives credence to the fact that corporate crime creates many victims. His study demonstrated that corporate crime was widespread and virtually endemic within contemporary national and transnational corporations. Sutherland dealt with the economic impact of corporate crime in a comprehensive manner. His contribution in relation to corporate victimisation rests upon his analysis of the difficulties in recognising and giving status to the corporate victim. He argued that this stems from the fact that many corporate offences are less readily definable as crime than are other types of offence, in part because of the rippling effect of corporate crime, which may involve only a small loss to individual victims but enormous gain to the perpetrators. For that reason, there tends to be a lack of deep public resentment towards corporate crime, as there seems to be no identifiable victim.

Corporate crime is often seen as part of the broader concept of white-collar crime, and is defined by Croall (1992) as 'the abuse of a legitimate occupational role which is regulated by the law'. This includes occupational crimes committed by employers and corporate crime in which business or corporations exploit consumers and workers. Our interest here is to draw attention to the way in which the corporate organisation promotes certain types of activity or inactivity resulting in victimisation rather than to consider the way in which individuals negotiate their own activities within an organisational framework.

Using radical criminology, Box argued that most crimes are committed by powerful multinational corporations, the government and the police. He argued therefore that we must reconceptualise the definition of serious crime. Box acknowledges the real suffering of what he terms 'conventional victims', but feels that it is imperative that criminology look at the victims of corporate crime.

> Murder, rape, robbery and assault . . . Maybe they are only *a* crime problem and not *the* crime problem. Maybe what is stuffed into our consciousness as the crime problem is in fact an illusion, a trick to deflect our attention away from the other, even more serious crimes and victimising behaviours, which objectively cause the bulk of avoidable death, injury and deprivation.
>
> (Box 1983, p. 3)

Consequently, Box provides an illuminating commentary on 'intention' versus 'indifference' (to harmful consequences), thereby comparing the status of the corporate victim with that of the conventional victim. Moreover, Box's concept of 'avoidable harm' should be carefully considered when analysing the status of the corporate victim in relation to current legislation pertaining to the corporation.

Since Box's classic study, the plight of the corporate victim has captured the attention of a number of theorists (e.g. Pearce and Tombs 1998; Croall 1992; Levi 1992).

However, it would seem that there has been less systematic exploration of victims of corporate crime than of victims of 'conventional' crime, which has led to a tendency within victimology and criminology to emphasise the victims of 'conventional crime'. Two reasons contribute to this lack of attention: the problems of measuring victims of corporate crime and the way in which the corporate victim is rendered invisible.

Until recently, corporate crime has been viewed as a 'victimless' crime, with those who suffer from it being seen rather as victims of disasters or accidents, not really as victims of criminal activity. Indeed, Fattah states:

> Despite the scope of white collar crime and despite the fact that its depredations far exceed those of conventional crime it is totally left out of victim campaigns. Moreover, other socially harmful actions such as pollution of the environment, the production of hazardous substances, the manufacture and sale of unsafe products, and so on, cause more death, injury and harm than all the violent crime combined.
>
> (1986, p. 5)

Whereas the liberation movements created an academic breeding ground for victimology which challenged the legitimacy of the legal system and directed attention to the crimes of the powerful, in legal and social terms the victim is still largely invisible. This problem occurs as a result of lack of 'victim awareness': within the criminal justice system there are no established legal concepts or definitions that take account of the victims of corporate crime. Similarly, there is a lack of any substantial empirical evidence (through a lack of effective measurement) to raise awareness of the growing number of such victims.

There are difficulties involved in offering any accurate measurement of corporate victimisation. For the impact of crime to be measured, the victims first of all must define and recognise the behaviour or activity affecting them as criminal. This is especially difficult in relation to corporate crime. Corporate victims are not always aware that a crime has been committed or that the behaviour or activity affecting them holds any criminal consequences. This is what Geis (1967) has called 'victim responsiveness'. He argues, 'It is particularly notable, first of all, that people do not react vigorously, deep with outrage to most forms of white collar crime' (Geis uses the term 'white-collar crime' in a similar sense to corporate crime.) In similar vein, Levi states (in relation to fraud), 'Fraud then is an unusual type of crime because the fraudster gets the victim to part with his money voluntarily albeit under false assumptions about the transaction' (1987, p. 24).

Walklate (1989) has argued that the notion of 'victim responsiveness' is related to the victim's state of mind, and this appears to include an unwillingness to report incidents to the relevant regulatory bodies. This may be due to the fact that victims feel foolish for being taken advantage of or that they do not know what the relevant bodies are and the extent to which corporate victimisation exists.

The neglect of corporate crime by both criminologists and victimologists is not due to a lack of interest within the area but more to the fact that there are many difficulties to be overcome in researching this area. Collating and comparing statistical information in relation to corporate victimisation proves difficult owing to the sheer number of agencies and departments involved in regulating corporations. In relation to fraud, for example, Levi points out:

> Consumer frauds (including restrictive trade practices) may be dealt with by the Trading Standards offices or by the Office of Fair Trading: bankruptcy, liquidation, banking, and investment frauds are within the remit of the Department of Trade and Industry; and tax frauds are dealt with by the Inland Revenue or the Customs and Excise departments.
>
> (1987, p. 24)

Moreover, data from official agencies can only reveal prosecutions and not sanctions or settlements that may be reached; obviously this reveals only a partial picture concerning the victims of business activities. Therefore, given the difficulties of using official sources to construct a measure of corporate crime, there are even more difficulties in using these sources as indicators of levels of corporate victimisation.

Criminal victimisation surveys are also of little use in measuring victims of corporate crime. Hough and Mayhew (1983) point out that 'They can only discover crimes which have clearly identifiable people as victims, they cannot easily count crimes against organisations (such as fraud, shoplifting or fare evasion).' Therefore, criminal victim surveys rest upon clearly identifiable people as victims, which causes a problem in regard to corporate crime, especially when considering concepts of 'victim responsiveness'.

Identifying the victims of corporate crime

Whether as consumers, workers, investors, passengers, residents or employees, most people will become victims of corporate crime. Here we will concentrate on victims of corporate crime in relation to workers, consumers and the citizen, and to illustrate the seriousness of corporate victimisation will refer to Stuart Hills's concept of 'corporate violence':

> actual harm and risk of harm inflicted on consumers, workers, and the general public as a result of general decisions by corporate executives or managers, from corporate negligence, the quest for profits at any cost, and the wilful violations of health and safety and environmental laws.
>
> (1987, p. 7)

Hills aims to heighten awareness of the respectable businesspeople who impersonally maim and kill for profit. The solution to corporate victimisation, according to Hills, is to develop a broad-based democratic political movement that may bring about structural changes.

Consumers

The growth of the consumer society has brought many practices which adversely effect us as consumers. Consumers as victims of corporate violence are not a new phenomenon. Dowie (1977) documents the case of the Ford Pinto and its dangerous petrol tank. On discovering that the Ford Pinto had a design fault with its tank, it was decided by Ford's board of directors that it would be more economical to pay out insurance upon any future deaths or injuries rather than recall the Pinto and redesign the tank. Dowie claims that between 500 and 900 burn deaths resulted from the ensuing explosions.

Fifty years on, it is still just as difficult to gain convictions for corporate manslaughter cases involving transport. Successful manslaughter cases are difficult to bring, and high-profile attempts at prosecution often fail (for example, the 1997 Southall rail crash and the 1987 Zeebrugge ferry disaster, which killed 192 people). Another (in)famous case related to the Dalkon Shield contraceptive, which killed several women, left many childless and caused enormous suffering to countless others (Perry and Dawson 1985).

Such cases have occurred over the decades, and the cases of consumers as victims have become ever more complex. Consumers throughout the Third World can be the victims of corporate violence through exploitation by multinational corporations. For example, Nestlé has been accused of promoting a product (milk formula) that resulted in the death of hundreds of thousands of babies in Third World countries. It has been argued that through promotional campaigns the company claimed that its product was more nutritious and healthier than breast milk. The result was that mothers were encouraged to pay extortionate prices for a product that they could not afford nor had need of.

As medical knowledge and the use of drugs has expanded over the past twenty years, so the consumer's safety within the medical world has become an issue. John Braithwaite, now a Trades Practices Commissioner, provided a devastating expose of the pharmaceutical industry in his study *Corporate Crime in the Pharmaceutical Industry* (1984). International bribery and corruption, fraud, negligence in the testing of drugs, and criminal negligence in the unsafe manufacture of drugs demonstrated that the pharmaceutical industry had an appalling record of lawbreaking. Evidence of such malpractice was also evident in the thalidomide case – a drug which after years of extensive animal testing was marketed as a perfectly safe tranquilliser for pregnant mothers. The end result was that more than 10,000 grossly deformed babies were born. During the trial of the manufacturers in the 1970s, numerous court witnesses, who were all animal experimenters, said under oath that the results of animal experiments are never valid for human beings. However, the incredible reaction to the thalidomide tragedy by the pharmaceutical lobby was that it was an exception and that it emphasised the need for more animal testing, not less.

As technology advances and more high-tech gadgets invade the market, consumers of these manufactured goods are at risk of becoming victims of a new type of corporate crime. The Department of Trade and Industry has highlightd the danger of unscrupulous firms who are using computers, mobile phones and fax machines to market their product. Ambiguous promotional messages are being sent via e-mail and text messages, and to answer these messages may cost the consumer a premium-rate call. For most of us, mobile phones and computers have become essential and part of everyday life, and also a new way in which we can be victimised.

QUESTION BREAK: CONSUMERS AND HI-TECH SCAMS

Growing numbers of consumers, particularly young people, are becoming the victims of swindles via email, text messaging and fax, the Department of Trade and Industry (DTI) said today.

Unscrupulous firms often use bogus prize draws and special offers to entice recipients to reply, it said, and as the popularity of text messaging grows among children, this group is likely to be heavily targeted.

Millions of promotional text messages are now being sent every week, and phone owners can currently do little to avoid receiving them, according to premium rate regulator Icstis (Independent Committee for the Supervision of Standards of Telephone Information Services).

In one case dealt with by Icstis, mobile phone owners received the message 'I fancy you.' It then invited the person to call a premium rate number without making clear the call charges. In another scam, hotel and restaurant owners were asked to fax copies of their brochures and menus to a potential client. The fax number turned out to be a premium rate line....

Some consumers told Icstis that they have received the message up to 40 times in one day alone. Others say their children, as young as 11, are repeatedly receiving the message.

Today's DTI warning is designed to coincide with the launch of National Consumer Week. Consumer minister Melanie Johnson said: 'Every day, people throughout the UK open their mail, turn on their computers or switch on their mobile phones to learn that they've won "an exciting prize" in a draw, lottery or some other promotion. While much of the marketing conducted in this way is legitimate, unfortunately it also includes examples which are misleading or untrue. All too often those people taken in by scams make the mistake of being too trusting and lose money as a result.'

Icstis advises consumers that all premium rate services should begin with the numbers 090. Premium rate text messages where the recipient is asked to reply usually contain a four or five digit number.

A European directive which came into force in the UK in August was designed to combat unwanted emails sent by companies – commonly known as 'spams'. Messages should make it clear in the title what they are so recipients can delete them straight away if they wish.

(*Guardian*, 12 November 2002)

Questions

What other similar consumer scams can you think of?

How might the victims feel?

What groups in society do you think are most likely to be victims of 'high-tech scams'?

Workers

Employees have long been exploited within the workplace in relation to low pay, long hours and unsafe conditions. In Britain a large number of deaths and injury within the workplace result from the failure to comply with safety regulations. Reports carried out by the Health and Safety Executive in the 1980s indicated that in at least two-thirds of fatal accidents, managers had violated the Health and Safety at Work Act (Tombs 1990). Workers not only are affected by safety regulations but can die as a result of diseases contracted at work, most notably from asbestos poisoning (mesothelioma) but also from lung disease and occupationally related cancers.

The Health and Safety Executive (www.hse.gov.uk/statistics) revealed some disturbing figures in April 2003:

- Two hundred and forty-nine workers were killed in incidents at work.
- An estimated 10,000 people died due to occupational illnesses – 4,000 due to asbestos alone.
- The cost of health and safety failures in Britain is over £18 billion each year.

As the industrial base of the nation has shrunk and modern service work increased, so the nature of corporate violence against employees has changed also. This may lead to health and safety issues being less visible; for example, it has been proven that CRTs (computer monitors) can seriously affect the health and safety of employees. Exposure to radiation in chemical plants and dangerous materials in laboratories and hospitals also illustrates the point that victims of corporate crime are often those employees who are in low-level, low-paid, non-unionised jobs and are the victims of poverty that corporations create in their pursuit of maximising profit. A recent example of this involves the sports retail giant Nike. In November 1997 in a document that had been leaked to Corporate Watch (the watchdog on the Internet), it was alleged that Nike was running Vietnamese sweatshops where workers (the majority of whom were women) were low paid and mistreated, working in appalling conditions. It was only through media attention that Nike eventually pledged to end child labour, follow the occupational health and safety standards, and allow non-governmental organisations (NGOs) to participate in the monitoring of its Asian factories (Corporate Watch Web site 1998).

The real impact of crime within the workplace is rarely considered. Medical costs in the event of injury, counselling in the event of mental abuse and higher prices of products due to theft affect a number of people. Gill (1999) states:

> If staff are affected by the crime they may need counselling and time off; if they leave there are additional recruitment and training costs in addition to the impact this may have on the image of the company from staff, customers or the community at large.

The citizen

To be a victim of corporate crime one need not be either an employee or a consumer. Fraud such as tax evasion and large-scale embezzlement can affect the finances of every one of us as taxes are increased to compensate the Treasury. New technology, especially the Internet, is generating what has become known as 'cybercrime'. Wall (1999) has identified four areas of such activity: cyber-trespass (hacking), cyber-thefts (fraud, appropriation of intellectual property), cyber-obscenities (pornography, sex trade) and cyber-violence (stalking, hate speech). He has also highlighted the problem of defining who are the victims of cyber-crime – owing to the fact that victims can be individuals or social groups and the harms done may range from actual to perceived: 'In cases such as cyberstalking or theft of cybercash, the victimisation is very much directed towards the individual. However in other cases the victimisation is more indirect as with cases of cyberpiracy cyberspying/terrorism' (1999).

Citizens are also threatened by noxious emissions from factories, by chemicals in water supplies and by pollution of beaches and rivers. The victims of such pollution have gained a higher profile recently as a result of the heightened awareness of pollution through EU regulation. Richard Mills, the secretary of the National Society for Clean Air, has recently stated that 'even on a conservate estimate, air pollution is killing 10 times more people than road incidents every year' (*Guardian*, 5 December 2002). The Environment Agency has for many years argued that the penalties for companies that pollute should be increased considerably to avoid such companies regarding pollution and the possible court action as an acceptable 'business risk'. Furthermore, an increasing number of diseases such as cancer and asthma are being associated with corporations that pollute the atmosphere through factory emissions (*Independent*, 1 June 1998).

Although both men and women can, of course, be victims as consumers, workers and citizens, it is still the case that a neglected area of victims of corporate crime is that of women as victims. The invisibility of these women victims in current criminological research is attributed to the paternalism within society and the focus on causal rather than structural explanations of criminality. Examples of the corporate victimisation of women include women working in sweatshops, men-only occupations, the pharmaceutical industry and work-related diseases. Gerber and Weeks (1992) argue that feminist theories sensitive to the gendered nature of human existence are required to analyse female corporate victimisation adequately.

Unlike many issues related to women's health, the recent controversy of silicone breast implants did create a great deal of public interest. Rybrant and Kramer (1995) use the feminine gaze to place the silicone implant dispute within the larger theoretical framework of corporate violence. Their case study of the historical development of this debate illustrates: duplicity in the chemical industry; the power of special interest groups; the importance, and the complicity, of governmental regulatory agencies; and the vital impact of cultural perceptions of beauty on women. Obviously the last of these also affects the treatment that women receive in the criminal justice system. In litigation surrounding the Dalkon Shield contraceptive case, women were blamed for being promiscuous, and similarly, women who received silicone breast implants for cosmetic as opposed to medical reasons have been awarded lower damages (Finlay 1996).

The physical and emotional effects of corporate crime

The physical effects of corporate crime are self-evident: disease, illness, deformity, accidents and death can and do occur as a result of corporate malpractice. The emotional aspects of corporate crime are less visible and as a consequence have received very little academic attention. This is especially true of victims of financial fraud, although such victims share many of the same devastating outcomes as their counterparts who have suffered serious violent crime. Indeed, certain white-collar crime victims may suffer more emotional distress. Wells (1989) argues that some of the effects include guilt, shame, disbelief, anger, depression, sense of betrayal and loss of trust. These emotional repercussions are often misunderstood by law enforcement, criminal justice and victim service providers, as well as the community at large; indeed, the victim is often doubly victimised by this dynamic. As Walsh and Schram have described,

> People who have lost money to white collar criminals (like swindlers and con artists) often encounter scepticism, suspicion and contempt when they seek help. This negative treatment leaves them feeling guilty and ashamed. The double standards used in handling white collar offenders and their victims (except rape victims) has been attributed to the status of the accused perpetrators, the difficulty in establishing criminal intent in such cases and the belief that imprisonment is not the cure for this kind of stealing.
>
> (1980, p. 33)

Another factor is the largely ambivalent attitude towards, and negative images of, these victims held by the public and by the criminal justice officials. A number of aphorisms are used to blame these victims: 'fraud only befalls those of questionable character' or 'an honest man can't be cheated'. The stereotypical response to cheated parties is that they have disregarded the basic rules of sensible conduct regarding financial matters. Their stupidity, carelessness or complacency undermines their credibility and makes others reluctant to activate the machinery of the criminal justice system on their behalf so as to formally punish those who harmed them, and to validate their claims to be treated as authentic victims, worthy of support rather than as mere dupes, losers or suckers who were outsmarted (Karman 1990).

Victims of financial crime often describe a tremendous violation of their personal integrity, using phrases such as 'It was like being raped' and 'I have lost all of my sense of trust.' Because the psychological wounds are not perceived in the same way as wounds to the body, nor as generally understood as the emotional scars of a sexual assault, the effects on victims of corporate crime are often, and inappropriately, minimised. Wells notes that victims of corporate crime, unlike the victims of violent physical crime, have 'wounds' that 'are not always easy to see and most often internal rather than external' (1989, pp. 26–27). However, he goes on to support the notion that victims of corporate crime have a similar sense of violation and often require 'psychological first aid'.

Victims of corporate crime and the criminal justice system

Thus corporate victims suffer physically and emotionally. Despite this, the criminal justice system does not have the necessary mechanisms in place to support or protect corporate victims. This type of victimisation is often described as 'an accident' or 'a disaster', which minimises the serious nature of such crimes.

Crimes committed by corporations for the most part do not fall under the jurisdiction of the police; they are the remit of regulatory bodies. The fact that this type of crime is regulated rather than policed tends to create the impression that the victims' case is less urgent than in those cases that involve 'conventional' crime. Monetary support for those agencies that deal with corporate crime tends to be very low compared to other criminal justice agencies. For example, in 1995/1996, £10.3 billion was spent on the criminal justice system, with 60 per cent of this on the police. Expenditure on the Health and Safety Executive in 1996/1997 was £213 million, involving only 4,077 staff (Health and Safety Commission 1997).

Unlike victims of more conventional crime, victims of corporate crime are excluded from the Victim's Charter. The charter, which was enacted in 1990 and revised in 1996, is 'a statement of service standards for victims of crime'. However, the exclusion of corporate crime means that victims are exempt from the safeguards that the charter may provide. The Trades Union Congress has been particularly outspoken and critical of the charter and has pressed for it to be extended to cover the victims of workplace crimes. Moreover, the charter points to Victim Support as an agency that can be contacted to help victims with their ordeal. However, this organisation does not deal with corporate victims – leaving the victims of corporate crime in a vulnerable situation.

Legislative reform in relation to victims of corporate crime has been promised by the government in the form of a new statute on 'corporate killing', but has still to materialise. At present, the criminal justice system does have on its books the statute of corporate manslaughter. This means that powerful individuals within corporations can be charged and punished for this type of offence. This law has been criticised for being unfair and ineffective. In particular, directors or managers, not companies, are held responsible; schools, police forces and other unincorporated organisations cannot be prosecuted; and third, Crown immunity means that Crown and government organisations are above the law and therefore exempt from accountability. This law, and in particular the idea of Crown immunity, can be criticised for being biased and working upon the premise of outdated concepts which allow government agencies to commit criminal offences.

In 1996 the Law Commission recommended the introduction of a new offence of 'corporate killing', and the Labour government committed itself to the change in 1997. However, the new law has not been enacted as of yet, although its importance cannot be overstated. The Centre for Corporate Accountability has argued that this enactment is important, as:

• The offence applies not only to companies but all employing organisations, including Crown bodies and to British companies that operate abroad.
• The offence is investigated by a properly trained team of investigators, comprising both the police and inspectors from the Health and Safety Executive and is prosecuted by the Crown Prosecution Service (or Procurator Fiscal in Scotland).
• The offence enables company directors to be prosecuted for 'aiding and abetting' the company in committing the offence of 'corporate killing'.
• British companies that commit the offence abroad can be prosecuted in British courts.

Clearly, this new offence will help victims of corporate offences gain some credibility within the justice system. However, as Hills argues,

> Until there is great public understanding of the relationship between the corporate decision making and human suffering – indeed until there is a sense of public sensibility that provokes moral outrage at this corporate indifference, the far reaching structural reforms that could make a major and lasting difference are unlikely to occur.

(1987, p. 202)

QUESTION BREAK: CORPORATE KILLING OR MANSLAUGHTER?

What would be the advantages of a statute that recognised 'corporate killing' rather than 'corporate manslaughter'?

How difficult would it be to enforce such a law?

Read the comment from Hills above. Why is it so important for the status of the corporate victim that there is public moral outrage against corporate crime?

Victims of fraud do have limited success in the criminal justice system. The Serious Fraud Office (SFO), for example, was created by the Criminal Justice Act in 1987 to investigate major fraud. Under Rosalind Wright and, more recently, Robert Wardle, the SFO has enjoyed an 80 per cent conviction rate for the past six years. However, during the early and mid-1990s a number of high-profile cases collapsed or failed, earning the office the title 'seriously flawed office'. The chronology of failed cases includes the following:

- the collapse of the 'Guinness case' against Lord Spense and Roger Seelig (£10 million fraud charge) in 1992;
- the sentence of Roger Levitt to 180 hours' community service for a £358 million fraud charge in 1993;
- the 1994 acquittal of George Walker (head of Brent Walker) of £164 million fraud charges;
- in 1996, the clearing of Kevin and Ian Maxwell of fraud charges following the loss of £440 million in pension funds.

This section has explored the relatively hidden nature of corporate victimisation. Far from being a 'victimless' crime, it is now evident that all of us will at some stage become a victim of corporate crime, whether within our public or our private lives. Despite this, the victims of corporate crime have remained relatively invisible. This is due in part to the diffuse nature of this kind of victimisation, but the main contributing factors are inadequate legal sanctions and ineffective law enforcement. It is evident that corporate victimisation is not a priority in the criminal justice system.

> **QUESTION BREAK**
>
> Positivist victimologists measure risk of victimisation in terms of individual social characteristics or lifestyle (see pp. 106–109).
>
> **Questions**
> How does (a) gender; (b) age; (c) economic situation/occupation; (d) geographical location affect the likelihood of becoming a victim of each of the following corporate crimes: cyber-crime; health and safety lawbreaking; medical blunders; pollution?

Further reading

Croall, H. (1992) *Understanding White Collar Crime*, Milton Keynes: Open University Press. A clear introduction for the student of white-collar and corporate crime, this text highlights the victims of corporate/white-collar crime. It also gives a detailed account of how white-collar criminals are treated within the criminal justice system.

Hoyle, C. (1999) *Negotiating Domestic Violence*, Oxford: Clarendon. This is a study of police response to domestic violence based on interviews and observation. It examines police culture and its effect on police structures, training and practice and outlines the very difficult position of the victim of domestic violence.

Mawby, R. and Walklate, S. (1994) *Critical Victimology*, London: Sage. This is a useful text as it details the rise of victimology and gives a detailed and critical account of theoretical debates.

Punch, M. (1996) *Dirty Business: Exploring Corporate Misconduct. Analysis and Cases*, London: Sage. This book explores corporate misconduct in some detail. Part 1 reviews the literature on corporate deviance (with case studies); part 2 explores cases of corporate crime in some depth; and part 3 draws on the literature review and case studies to offer some conclusions.

Useful Web sites include:

The home page of the Home Office for the UK – www.homeoffice.gov.uk (and specifically the Victims of Crime Index)

Centre for Corporate Accountability – www.corporateaccountability.org

The International Victimology Website – www.victimology.nl

Part II

The criminal justice system

5 Police and policing

A brief history of policing

In this section the main issues that we will be addressing are the reasons for the emergence of modern policing at the beginning of the nineteenth century and how policing has developed since then.

In his detailed political and social history of the English police, Emsley (1996a) argued that since the middle of the nineteenth century there has been a growing centralisation of the police in England; and that this cannot be explained in terms of some sort of conspiracy but is rather due to a number of particular pressures that have moved policing in this direction. First, there has been what Emsley describes as 'a rationalizing of the police in the interest of what has been seen as economy and efficiency', a process that has involved legislation to reduce the differences between different police forces and a limiting of the authority of police committees of local government. Second, during periods of national emergency, closer contact between local police forces and central government was established – in periods of war and widespread strike activity, for instance. And while such measures may have been intended only as temporary centralising measures, they set precedents. Third, as the police became seen as professionals in handling crime and public order, so government ministers and civil servants began to communicate directly with the experts and to bypass amateur local police committees. This growth of professionalisation led senior police officers to discuss and decide policy with one another – again marginalising local committees.

Emsley suggests that this sort of centralisation of policing in England was strengthened by the fact that the British constitutional structure has been pretty stable for over two centuries – there have been no serious challenges to its legitimacy and it has had no need to be reformulated as a result of defeat in war.

Early institutions of law enforcement

Although the modern form of policing is generally seen to have emerged in the nineteenth century, the history of law enforcement stretches back many centuries. In medieval times, high constables of the hundreds and petty constables of the manors were well-established positions. The latter were parish constables of a sort, and were usually men appointed from within the community. One of their tasks was to report to the local courts about 'felons, miscreants and nuisances'. Although locally appointed, they did acquire royal authority and were given responsibility for maintaining the king's peace in their district.

Another early agent of local law enforcement was the watchman – a position which was made obligatory by legislation in 1285, with all towns and boroughs having to provide a number of watches. London, for example, was divided into twenty-four wards, each of which had to have a watch of six men supervised by an alderman. By the seventeenth century, justices of the peace were expected to ensure that night watches were kept in their towns from sunset to sunrise.

Justices of the peace were constitutionally superior to constables and watchmen in the law-enforcement pecking order of medieval England. This position originated from Richard I's reign (1195), and the first justices of the peace were also the social superiors of constables – indeed, they were often lords of manors. They presided at the courts to which petty constables brought cases. Justices of the peace were appointed by the Crown, through the offices of the Lord Chancellor – with patronage playing a big part in the appointments. The office of justice of the peace was well established by the late sixteenth century, and the holders became key figures of local government. The workload of justices of the peace varied, often according to the particular individual's inclination. They did not have to attend quarter sessions, for instance, and some were more dedicated than others.

The emergence of the modern police force

The period of the later eighteenth and early nineteenth centuries saw a radical trans-formation in Western societies. It was a period of rapid industrialisation and of the growing influence of capitalism. The shift from traditional occupations and lifestyles to the new practices of the industrial factory system saw massive migrations of rural populations to the centres of industrial production and the rise of a new urban, indus-trial class. This period also saw the great ideological revolutions in France (1789) and America (1775–1783), which encouraged a questioning of traditional forms of authority. Such changes were accompanied by a concern about increases in crime and disorder. The concerns which promoted a development and extension of the early institutions of law enforcement were driven to a large extent by fear of property crime from the better-off sections of society. These developments were evidenced in the improvements in the watches in London and elsewhere. Small regular patrols of watchmen were organised for the streets of London, and by 1824 there were twenty-four men divided equally into day and night patrols. As well as in the City of London, similar patrols were set up in the districts outside the City, such as Westminster. As early as the 1790s, an armed patrol of about seventy men had been established at Bow Street to watch the main roads into the centre of London, and by 1828 there was a Horse Patrol, a Night

Foot Patrol and a Day Foot Patrol. In 1785 the then Prime Minister, William Pitt the Younger, had proposed the establishment of a centrally controlled police for the entire metropolis, which had led to the London and Westminster Police Bill and the setting up of nine police divisions.

These brief examples illustrate the beginning of organised, modern policing. Such developments led almost naturally to Sir Robert Peel, as Home Secretary in 1822, introducing legislation for the creation of the Metropolitan Police. Initially this legislation was kept to London, as he seemed to feel that the creating of a large, centralised police force for all England was not appropriate.

The Metropolitan Police of London

Prevention of crime was seen as the first duty of the new Metropolitan Police constables – and beat patrols (a sort of natural follow-on from parochial watchmen) were designed with that in mind. Although efforts were made to ensure the police did not look like soldiers, a good deal of early criticism focused on the military nature and style of the new police. In addition, there was also some concern about the costs of the new police, who were to be paid out of local rates – as had been the case with the watches.

In spite of some early criticism, within a decade or so the Metropolitan Police came to be seen by London's property owners as a fairly effective preventive force. By the 1830s Metropolitan policemen began to appear elsewhere in the country at the request of local authorities – for instance, supervising race meetings or acting as stewards at public disturbances (such as anti-poor law demonstrations). Sir Robert Peel's Metropolitan Police acted as a model for provincial police reformers during the 1830s and 1840s, with a Royal Commission being set up in 1836 to inquire into the best means of setting up a rural constabulary.

Essentially, then, the new forms of policing of the late eighteenth and early nineteenth centuries grew out of the growing concerns about the consequences of an increasingly industrialised and urbanised society. As indicated, a major driving force behind these changes was Sir Robert Peel. However, it is important to bear in mind that police reform (as with other major social changes and reforms) is invariably a slow process involving experiment, debate and compromise; and the debates and experiments over policing continued through the nineteenth century and beyond.

So why did the modern police force emerge at this time – at the beginning of the nineteenth century? Until then the threat to individual liberty had been used as an argument against organised policing. However, the coming of industrial capitalism led to large numbers of impoverished workers – unemployed or poorly employed – moving to the expanding urban centres. This, along with the general population growth, led to a fear of the new industrial proletariat – in short, to a fear of the 'dangerous classes'. This line of argument suggests that it was class interest which accounted for the emergence of the modern police. In addition, it could be argued that the previous, locally based form of policing was uncoordinated and unpredictable whereas modern, public policing was a way of promoting the greater efficiency and order needed for the smooth running of industrial capitalism.

It should be borne in mind that even after establishment of the 'new police', other groups and individuals continued to do 'police tasks'. Private watchmen and gamekeepers were still employed by those who could afford them; and the docks maintained their own police, as did the railways until nationalisation in 1948. More recently, of course, there has been a massive rise in the private security industry.

So from its very inception, the police force has been subject to a sort of creeping centralisation. This was inevitable, in part at least, because of the Home Office influence through the Treasury grant it provided for police forces. It was also encouraged by the tendency for police forces to work together to police major events, such as big industrial disputes or political demonstrations.

QUESTION BREAK: THE EMERGENCE OF A POLICE FORCE

Of two main theoretical explanations for why an organised police force emerged in the early nineteenth century, the first is the argument that sees this development as, essentially, reflecting a progressive view of history. The emergence of the new police was a response to the need for a more efficient organisation to deal with the (perceived) increased crime and disorder at that period (evidenced in the writings of Reith; see Emsley (1996a) and McLaughlin and Muncie (1996)).

The second is the Marxist argument, which focuses on the new police as an element in a broader strategy of control of the labouring classes (see Storch 1976 in McLaughlin and Muncie 1996).

Read the extract that follows and suggest how it relates to those different explanations.

The shift in opinion which enabled [police] reforms began in the late eighteenth century – the key moments being the Gordon Riots in 1780 and, for the rural gentry, the Swing Riots in 1830, although the feeling that there was a pervasive climate of disorder among the labouring classes was, perhaps, more important. Towns like London and the rapidly growing cities of the industrial north represented a new and vibrant engine of wealth, but they seemed out of control. That impression appeared to be confirmed by increasing crime and radicalism, both of which seemed to be spreading into the countryside.

It was not that disorder was new ... rather it was that there was a growing lack of tolerance among the ruling classes born of a sense that old structures of authority, which depended on paternalism and deference, had at last broken down. The ruling classes realized that the connection ... between themselves and the labouring classes had no foundation. The reaction of some was to seek to shore it up, while others assumed that the problem lay in the moral degeneration of the labouring classes and that liberty and property could only be protected from the consequences of this moral decline by intervention from local and central government.

(Rawlings 2002, p. 144)

The early developments in establishing a national policing structure were formalised with the passing of Grey's Bill for police reform in 1856. This led to an Act that made the formation of police forces obligatory for local government at borough and county levels. It also established Inspectors of Constabulary, who were expected to make annual inspection of every force in the country and to present a certificate of efficiency, which was necessary for a particular force to get its Treasury grant. However, and in spite of these moves towards a centralised police force, local police forces still remained unequivocally under local authority control, with there being obvious differences from one local area to the next. For instance, the uniforms and colours of local forces varied – a legacy that has continued to the present day, with different forces using different colours on their cars, for example. However, the dominant style of policing was based on the Metropolitan model, and this became the pillar of the constitutional and legal structure of Victorian England – characterised in the notion of the English 'bobby'.

Although there was some affection for the English 'bobby', the early police officers were also regularly assaulted by members of the public, and in some of the rougher working-class areas police officers had to patrol with cutlasses. Indeed, certain areas were virtually left to themselves, with police numbers being insufficient to provide any effective form of crime control. Early complaints of police corruption and about police brutality in dealing with crowds exacerbated the negative view of the new police held by many. While the police were intentionally kept distinct from the military (with the uniform, for instance, purposely avoiding military colours), it was widely felt that there was a strong link between the police and the armed forces. Indeed, as Rawlings (2002) points out, the denunciation of the police as a military force was common. The colloquial term for the new police, 'Jenny Darbies', was a corruption of the French *gens d'armes*, a symbol for the English of despotism. Concern over the cost of the police was also apparent, with *The Times* suggesting that 'their pay constitutes a very serious tax on the London householder' (*The Times*, 19 August 1830, quoted in Rawlings 2002). Criticisms over the police peaked in November 1830, when Vine Street police station was besieged by thousands of demonstrators. Nor was opposition to the police limited to London. Rural areas saw them as agents for enforcing unpopular government policies. They were regarded by some as a sort of invading army who were liable to destroy local lifestyles, recreation and working practices (Rawlings 2002, p. 143).

Policing at the turn of the twentieth century

As indicated, there was some opposition to the new policing of the Victorian period, with working-class communities not liking what they felt to be police interference in their areas, which probably contributed to the feeling of many working-class people that there was one law for the rich and one for the poor. However, as Emsley points out, this did not mean that 'the relationship between the working class and the police in the second half of the nineteenth century [was] one of mutual hostility' (1996b, p. 80). And certainly a very positive view of the British police was held by 'respectable' society and the 'Establishment' by the turn of the century, with *The Times* in 1904 describing the police as 'a great human mechanism, perhaps the greatest of its kind'. Rawlings refers to contemporary sources in suggesting that

By the early twentieth century, [the police] had become 'the nurse of national morality' and the defence against an invasion of 'vice and crime', while the 'romance of Scotland Yard' involved nothing less than 'the building up . . . of a vast, ingenious machine which has become one of the greatest instruments of civilisation the world has ever seen'.

(2002, pp. 152–153)

As regards the management and control of the new police, there were different kinds of authority. The Metropolitan Police were answerable to the Home Secretary, county police were responsible to local standing committees, and borough police to watch committees. However, the idea that there was a particular and peculiarly British style of policing seemed to have taken a hold, with the beginnings of a corporate identity for the police helping this development – as illustrated by the creation of the Chief Constables Association in 1893.

Another manifestation of the developing corporate identity of the police was police unionisation. Trade unionism was emerging elsewhere, of course, and to begin with, police organisation was on a pretty *ad hoc* basis. The police were not seen as skilled craftsmen, these being the sectors where unionism developed significant strength initially. Police union organisation occurred most notably in urban areas, with the fact that the police in those areas often lived in barracks helping nurture feelings of solidarity. This was particularly the case in London, with agitation over pay, pensions and conditions apparent at the end of the nineteenth century in the Metropolitan Police. Although the attempt to establish a police union in 1890 did not succeed, the idea did not die and received some support and coverage in the journal for police officers, the *Police Review*.

Early police recruitment

Sir Robert Peel's 'vision' was that the Metropolitan police officers should come from the working classes and should be able to rise through the ranks through their own efforts. In contrast, the managers within the Met, the commissioners as they were known, would be 'gentlemen'. A similar approach was adopted by provincial police forces, and most police recruits from the 1840s through to the 1940s were from the working classes, usually with semi- or unskilled backgrounds. Indeed, many joined because they were unemployed, and they often had little idea what the job involved. Large numbers of these initial recruits came to loathe the discipline, the night work and other elements of the job, and there was a very high turnover in the early days.

QUESTION BREAK

Although the majority of early police recruits were from working-class backgrounds, there were obvious differences between policing and most working-class jobs.

Questions
Summarise these differences.

What sort of issues or problems might these differences raise for a working-class police officer?

There were constraints on the early police officers that marked the job out from other working-class occupations. Police officers had to follow a military style of discipline and were subject to a detailed intervention in all aspects of their lives; in particular, there were much closer and more explicit expectations of, and controls over, their private lives. Up until the Second World War, police officers had to ask permission to marry, and prospective wives had their characters investigated to ensure they would be 'suitable' as policemen's wives. During the nineteenth century, police wives were not allowed to be in paid employment and were expected to act rather as auxiliaries to their husbands (taking messages and suchlike).

As regards the recruitment of women police officers, the First World War boosted the demand for women to serve in the police. Initially, women police were employed to patrol women working in large numbers in munitions factories. In an attempt to open up policing to women, some women of 'higher' social class backgrounds with suffragette and feminist leanings enrolled as police officers. However, women officers were not given equal treatment within the police, and while some chief constables kept women on after the war, others were keen to dispense with them, and it was not until 1949 that the Police Federation agreed to accept women as full and equal members.

While the job of the early police officers had its unpleasant side, there were also clear advantages over other working-class occupations. Police officers were provided with good health provision for themselves and their families, there were rent allowances and a pension scheme. The nature of the job in the early days was hard and there was a real danger of assault. This helped a tough, masculine culture to develop, with an emphasis on 'being able to look after oneself in a fight' as an element of this. It also encouraged a strong occupational solidarity. As mentioned, the nature of police accommodation, particularly the police barracks, further encouraged this group solidarity among officers, especially in London. In addition, there was a clear feeling of togetherness that did lead to a pride in the job – a pride and consciousness that was fostered by the *Police Review* journal.

In this brief historical overview we have considered the new emergent police as one body. There were, however, divisions within the organisation, most notably between beat officers and detectives. According to Rawlings,

> The beat constable represented the idea of preventive policing; the detective's existence demonstrated the failure of that project. The beat constable was meant to be in the public eye. . . . The detective, on the other hand, was secretive, his ability to melt into the community was a matter of pride. . . . The separation between the branches became more pronounced as detection came to be represented as dependent on the acquisition of special skills.
>
> (2002, pp. 186–187)

This division became even more pronounced in the twentieth century, with the CID tending to see itself, and act as, an elite and separate organisation.

> **QUESTION BREAK**
>
> To what extent do you think that the nature of the job encouraged the development of a tough, masculine police culture? Or is the job of policing likely to attract people who have those sorts of attitudes?

Policing since the Second World War

Although there is a danger of generalising, the British police were, on the whole, respected and reasonably well regarded in the early years, and through the first half, of the twentieth century. Arguably, this essentially positive view changed in the latter decades of that century. A brief review of some of the background and historical factors that have played a part in the changes of attitudes to, and styles of, policing from the 1960s will help to establish a context from which to consider contemporary policing. Although many of these factors overlap, as a starting point it is helpful to attempt to categorise them in some way. To that end, we will group them under the following headings: changes in police organisation and practice; police–public relations; and general social changes.

Police organisation and practice

A new technology of policing, extolled in particular by Harold Wilson's Labour government of the 1960s, was embraced with enthusiasm by the police and Home Office. The new technology was a key factor in the development of the Unit Beat System of policing. This developed out of experiments in the Lancashire constabulary to cope with the large new town of Kirkby on the outskirts of Liverpool. The use of special patrol cars (rather than 'bobbies on the beat') had begun in 1958 and was popularised in the television series *Z Cars* – set in a town modelled on Kirkby. By 1965, policing in Kirkby had been completely reorganised, with mobile beats with radios replacing all other beats. This soon spread, and by 1968 the Unit Beat System covered two-thirds of the population of England and Wales. These developments distanced the police from the public they were policing, with police officers in cars not being as approachable as the police officer on a foot patrol.

Meanwhile, there were growing concerns, especially in the late 1960s and the 1970s, over police corruption and scandals. In an account written in the 1970s, Cox *et al.* (1977) refer to the 'fall' of Scotland Yard between 1969 and 1972, when many London detectives were jailed and hundreds more left the force in disgrace. These developments undermined the reputation of the British police and led to major inquiries into the Metropolitan Police – in particular, into allegations of widespread corruption among detectives working in the vice world of Soho. Those allegations eventually led to the trial and jailing of the two most senior officers ever brought to justice: ex-Commanders Virgo and Drury. In 1972 Robert Mark was appointed as Commissioner to the Metropolitan Police and set out to cleanse the detective side of the force. He set up a department to investigate complaints against police officers, moved detectives from one department to another and put some back on the beat. In his five years as commissioner, 500 men were dismissed or required to resign. Robert Mark's work in this direction was followed up by his successor, David McNee (who set up Operation Countryman to investigate the robbery squad). Although scandals and corruption were not a new phenomenon, what was a revelation in the 1970s was that it was 'systematic and widespread', with some of Scotland Yard's most senior officers being found guilty and jailed. And this was not just the case within the Met. In 1989, for example, the entire West Midlands Serious Crime Squad was disbanded amid allegations of corruption.

QUESTION BREAK: POLICE CORRUPTION

In spite of the efforts of commissioners such as Robert Mark and David McNee in the 1970s, there are still regular examples of police corruption and malpractice. Read the extract below and consider the questions that follow it.

Yard detectives jailed over drug racket
By Stewart Tendler
Crime Correspondent

Five Scotland Yard detectives were in jail last night after a female supergrass helped to uncover one of the worst cases of police corruption for over thirty years.

The officers, who seized drugs during police raids which were then passed on to criminals to sell on the streets, were last night branded a 'disgrace' by Scotland Yard.

The exploits of the elite drug squad, nicknamed the 'Groovy Gang', ended when Evelyn Fleckney, an underworld drugs queen known as 'chairman of the board', gave evidence against some of the corrupt officers.

(*Guardian*, 5 August 2000)

Questions
What might lead police officers to engage in corrupt practices?

How might police work encourage corruption and malpractice more than other occupations?

Police–public relations

During the 1960s, public attitudes to the police became characterised by a growing dissatisfaction with, and concern over, police behaviour. This concern was fuelled by the policing of public mass demonstrations such as CND marches and, later in the 1960s, rallies and demonstrations over the Vietnam War and apartheid. In these and other instances there was strong criticism of the police for being too heavy-handed; and increased media coverage served to sharpen such criticism.

As well as the policing of civil and political demonstrations, the way the police handled industrial disputes excited similar concern and criticism: for instance, the policing of the 1972 miners' strike, the Grunwick trade union dispute of 1977, the steel strike of 1980 and, most dramatically, the miners' strike of 1984–1985. As regards that last event, in one sense it could be argued that the police 'won' in that coal supplies continued. However, the policing of the strike was very confrontational (most graphically illustrated by the 'battle of Orgreave'), and led to a rift between the police and people whom they could not easily label as 'radicals': 'ordinary' miners and their families. This miners' strike was seen as 'politicising the police', who became seen as 'Thatcher's army'.

The inner-city rioting and disorder of 1980 and 1981 in Brixton, Toxteth, Moss Side and elsewhere, and of the mid-1980s in Handsworth (Birmingham) and Broadwater Farm (London), reflected an increased alienation between the police and sections of the population. In all these events, the police played some initial part, through arresting black youths or raiding public places such as cafés that were predominantly used by black youth, and then were patently unable to prevent the full-scale mayhem and disorder that followed.

Related to this, and an important factor in police–public relations and the crisis of confidence therein, is the issue of race. The disorders referred to above reflected a massive deterioration in police relations with black communities; and race is an issue we will return to in looking at police culture (see pp. 157–159).

Sanders and Young (2000) make the point that successful policing depends on information and cooperation from the community. However, community support for the police cannot be assumed and appears to be diminishing. Sanders and Young highlight findings from the British Crime Surveys that indicate that the proportion of the public who thought the police do a 'very good' or 'fairly good' job declined from 92 per cent in 1984 to 82 per cent in 1994 and the proportion who thought they do a 'very good' job from 43 per cent to 24 per cent.

QUESTION BREAK: POLICING THE MINERS' STRIKE

Read the extract from discussion of the policing of the 1984 miners' strike by Waddington *et al.* and consider the questions at the end of it.

The picketing of Orgreave, May–June 1984
Pickets began arriving at Orgreave very early in the morning [of 29 May]. By about 7 a.m., two large groups had been formed . . . about thirty minutes later, those pickets opposite the gate were charged by police officers – some on horseback, some on foot, and others with dogs. The pickets responded angrily. Some objects, mostly pieces of wooden fencing, were thrown in retaliation. . . .

The pickets were frustrated. They were being effectively prevented from carrying out any form of picketing at all. . . .

The police's immediate response to this situation was to spread a line of riot officers, equipped with white crash helmets and body-length perspex shields, right across their ranks. . . . Some pickets were provoked, others panicked. Many started to throw stones . . . Very soon this pattern, of pickets throwing stones and the police charging in on horseback, became routine. . . .

Analysis
The public image of Orgreave was of an orgy of violence, endorsed by the police view that a hooligan element the worse for drink had taken over. . . . The ingredients of this view are

familiar and seem to figure in most police accounts of public disorder. Violence is attributed to a combination of drink, irresponsible leadership and outside agitators. There seems little evidence of the influence of the latter. . . .

[We suggest that there needs to be] a deeper level of analysis. . . .

Orgreave seems to have been identified by the police as the show-down with the miners, the outcome of which would indicate the future progress of the whole strike.

As for the events at the scene itself, there is still no clear picture. The miners' account is that they were deliberately provoked by the police. . . . For them, throwing stones was largely a defensive measure. . . .

The police explained their own conduct as equally defensive . . . they acted against the pickets only when provoked. . . .

The use of mounted police seemed to have the effect of heightening the crowd's anger. . . . This and other moves do appear to have been premeditated. As subsequently became clear at the trial in Sheffield of fourteen pickets charged with riot at Orgreave – all of whom were acquitted – the police tactics used there mainly followed closely those recommended in the secret manual 'Public Order Tactical Options' drawn up by the Association of Chief Police Officers (ACPO) in the wake of the riots of 1980–1. They included the charging of the crowd with truncheons and the incapacitation of ringleaders. Their effect was wholly provocative, as was the rhythmic beating on shields – recommended by the manual – which greeted the return of the mounted police.

The events of 18 June indicate that the police used the opportunity to vent all the feelings of resentment accumulated over the previous three weeks. . . .

The events at Orgreave were removed from a local context, with its potential for locally negotiated agreements between police and pickets, and inserted into a national arena of irre-concilable conflict. Orgreave was not seen as a local picket during an industrial dispute but a trial of strength in a politically charged struggle. . . . The confrontation between the South Yorkshire police and the area NUM had been transformed into a confrontation between the state and the 'enemy within'.

Summary

In our discussion of Hadfields [where a mass picket occurred during the 1980 steel strike] we noted a number of factors which helped to account for the relatively low level of police–picket violence. These included the definition of the dispute, the liaison between picket organizers and police, the organization of the police, their attitude to minor breaches of the law, and the extent to which police and pickets shared a definition of behavioural norms. On all these criteria Orgreave was different.

(Waddington *et al.* 1989, pp. 84–92)

Questions

What criticisms could you make of the policing of the picketing at Orgreave?

What reasons could you offer for the police's actions?

General social changes

The supposed growing affluence of society in the late 1950s and the 1960s, illustrated by the comments from politicians of the time that the British had 'never had it so good', led to an increase in car ownership and the consequent extension of police work into traffic duties. This increased the potential for antagonistic encounters between citizens and the police ('they should be catching criminals, not bothering law-abiding folk like me' is a widely held attitude). Of course, there has been widespread debate within sociology over the 'meaning' of this increased affluence (in terms of perceptions of class position, for instance), and notions of consumerism and the consumer society have been used to suggest that modern societies are increasingly characterised by and organised around patterns of consumption. The ownership of more consumer goods – in particular, cars with all the attendant legislation surrounding their ownership and use: speeding, parking, taxing, and so on – can lead to more frequent opportunities for encounters with the police.

The style of policing in Northern Ireland has also impacted on attitudes to the police across the United Kingdom. The image of the police there is of a force that is routinely and heavily armed in a way not seen on an everyday basis on the mainland – again helping to further undermine traditional notions of policing.

Although these factors have all played a part in changing the public's attitude to the police and policing in Britain, encouraging a much more critical and negative view among sections of the population, it is important to bear in mind that alongside such criticism there was and is still a great deal of sympathy and support for the police. While post-1960s modern policing has adopted a much tougher approach and style than that associated with the old image of Dixon of Dock Green, the police were still seen as, essentially, upholding the cause of right against wrong: The Sweeney/Jack Regan image popular in the 1970s was of tough, macho officers whose hearts were in the right place but who were prepared to kick out against the bureaucracy that got in the way of catching 'real' criminals.

The statement of common purpose and values that was publicised in 1990 and displayed on notice boards across all London police stations evidences the concern the police had about their image:

> The purpose of the Met is to uphold the law fairly and firmly . . . to protect, help and reassure people in London: and to be seen to do this with integrity, common sense and judgment.

> We must be compassionate, courteous and patient, acting without fear or favour or prejudice to the rights of others. . . .

> We must respond to well-founded criticism with a willingness to change.
> (cited in Morgan and Newburn 1997, p. 77)

The anxieties, revelations and events of the recent past were clearly a driving force behind this sort of mission statement.

As indicated, all these historic, contextualising factors signified (and encouraged) a move away from traditional notions of policing and the image of the local bobby to a sort of state role for police. In the miners' strike of 1984–1985, for example, the Association of Chief Police Officers (ACPO) told all its chief constables in writing that they had the Home Secretary's assurance that resources for policing the miners' strike would not be a problem; in other words, they were given a blank cheque, perhaps further evidence of the 'politicising of the police'.

So where has this left policing today? In the past thirty years or so, two major threads or developments of policing have become apparent. There has been a dual emphasis on crime prevention and crime detection which has pulled the police in quite different directions. On the one hand, there has been an emphasis on targeting serious offenders and on crime detection. This has encouraged a more strong-arm, militaristic approach with greater use of guns, CS gas, surveillance, and so on. On the other hand, crime prevention has been a key motif, with the involvement of community and other public services emphasised. This 'softer' approach has supported greater citizen participation, more police patrols, and developments such as juvenile liaison schemes and neighbour-hood watch.

Faulkner (2001) argues that there is no inherent contradiction between the two styles of policing and that both are needed. Attempts to reduce crime can be made through partnership, community-based methods of policing while the police also enforce the law more vigorously against those who are suspected of breaking it. However, 'soft' policing focusing on preventive work in the community involves different policing skills and different relationships with the community than 'hard' policing and an emphasis on finding and convicting criminals. The application of 'hard' policing can get in the way of successful community policing, particularly if the two approaches or styles of policing are adopted in the same place at the same time. Faulkner points out that it is usually community policing that suffers: 'because the inputs and outputs (though not the outcomes) of "hard" policing are easier to measure than those of "soft" policing, the process may tend to promote "hard" rather than "soft" police methods' (2001, p. 260).

These different approaches to and styles of policing highlight a contrast between *reactive* policing, with all the technology and gadgetry, and *proactive* policing aiming to foster closer police–community partnerships. Below we will consider where this history has taken contemporary policing and how the different styles of policing are accommodated in the modern police service.

The police role today

Waddington (2000) describes policing as 'morally ambiguous'. The police occupy a unique role in society in that they are allowed to exercise coercion over other citizens and to act in ways that would not be tolerated if done by anyone else. As he puts it:

> [P]olice officers may legitimately intrude into the privacy of others: it would be quite abnormal for anyone other than a police officer to approach strangers in a public place and to demand (however politely) that they give an account of themselves.
>
> (2000, p. 156)

This moral ambiguity is perhaps highlighted by the fact that much police work is not about fighting crime (an activity that is generally strongly supported by the public). Certainly, the popular image of police work as being, essentially, about fighting crime does not seem to be the reality. Analysis of calls to the police shows how relatively little time is spent on crime matters compared to matters of 'plight' – such as being locked out of one's home (Waddington 1993). Waddington's research found that only 6 per cent of calls from the public led to arrests, with another 12 per cent leading to crime reports that might be followed up in the future. Indeed, it would seem that any generally held notion that most police involvement with the public occurs when people contact them to report serious criminality is not really the case. The ACPO estimates suggest that typically only 18 per cent of calls for help are about crime and they take about 30 per cent of police time, while the other 70 per cent of police work consists of reassuring the public, giving advice and assistance, regulating problematic personal/interpersonal situations, and dealing with a miscellaneous range of other problems.

As Morgan and Newburn put it when describing 'the police function':

> The police frequently are the only 24-hour service agency available to respond to those in need. The result is that the police handle everything from unexpected childbirths, skid row alcoholics, drug addicts, emergency psychiatric cases, family fights, landlord–tenant disputes, and traffic violations, to occasional incidents of crime.
>
> (1997, p. 79)

QUESTION BREAK

What do you think would be the most common reasons for calling the police?

What response do people expect when they call the police?

Why do people think that calling the police will help?

Aside from the need to get a crime number for insurance purposes, it would appear that the police provide a symbolic and visible representation of the rule of law and present the public with a reassuring appearance of authority. When, for instance, burglary victims report a crime, they do not really expect the burglar to be caught, yet calling the police is an almost automatic thing to do; it helps to re-establish the 'order' of things. And it is not only victims who see the police as symbolically representing order; the presence of police officers in public places provides reassurance. Even if they are not doing anything, the public feel safer – at events such as football matches, for instance.

As Waddington (1993) suggests, this point arguably goes to the heart of policing. It is commonplace to hear comments about 'more bobbies on the beat', and images of golden law-abiding days, without any real evaluation of what those bobbies are actually going to achieve. In fact, there is plenty of evidence which shows that they are unlikely to prevent or detect crime. For example, victim surveys such as the British Crime Survey point out that an average beat control might pass within 100 yards of a burglary every eleven years (and then not necessarily know it was happening!). As well as reassurance, perhaps what is behind the demand for 'bobbies on the beat' is the idea of ordinary police officers who are approachable and non-threatening, who provide the public with the feeling that order is being maintained. And if this is the case, it is pointless to try to measure the success of foot patrols in terms of crime and detection rate, or to be unduly panicked by statistics demonstrating increases in rates of known crimes. This is not to say that the officer on the beat is just an expensive public relations exercise, but that she or he is likely to have little effect in terms of winning the 'war on crime'.

The police's role in maintaining public order

It has been argued that one reason the police cannot really do much about crime is that crime control is not their real function; their main role is to support the authorities through dealing with threats to political order – such as demonstrations, strikes and riots. The emphasis here is on public order policing, which has always been a very sensitive role for the police. If the police use excessive force to suppress popular dissent then they are likely to be seen as a 'state' rather than a 'public' police and will lose public sympathy and, therefore, some legitimacy.

Up until perhaps the 1970s there was a general feeling that maintaining public order would not be a massively controversial aspect of policing in Britain – because Britain was a democracy that allowed for disagreement, because public protests would be orderly, because the police would use minimum force, and so on. However, as has been discussed, there were increasingly bitter conflicts – industrial disputes, urban riots, political demonstrations – in the 1970s and 1980s; and in some of those events the police seemed to lose control of the situation (for instance, the miners' strikes of the early 1970s, the inner-city disorders of 1980 and 1981). These situations led to the police reshaping and rethinking their strategies for maintaining order. Local forces established public order units, with more police officers being trained in the new public order tactics and strategies. Of particular importance for the future of policing, the National Reporting Centre was strengthened and allowed to deploy police from different parts of the country. In the miners' strike of 1984–1985, for instance, police were bussed in from all over the country to counter mass picketing.

An important question to consider here is the extent to which such developments have signalled a move to 'paramilitarisation' of the police. There are two opposing responses to that broad question.

Jefferson (1990) argues that 'paramilitarisation' has indeed taken place, and suggests that this has been an insidious development. New tactics might well start as something exceptional and temporary to deal with particular instances of disorder, but they soon become normal and institutionalised police responses. Ordinary officers who have been mobilised in such riot situations are likely to find it difficult to readjust to normal duty; the 'mindset' of officers becomes locked into such tactics. In addition, new, elite squads are developed and the policing of mass events tends to become seen as a science, with certain groups within the police recognised as the experts in it.

The other side of the 'paramilitary' argument is put forward by Waddington (1991). He argues that we need the police to maintain a democratic social order; the police give us a sense of security in various situations where public order is important such as football matches, rallies, marches, rock festivals. In reality, the police spend a great deal of time informally negotiating with groups and offering advice to avoid confrontation and trouble, and Waddington goes on to make the point that most public order situations do pass off peacefully. Police officers at every level try to avoid confrontation because they know that media images of violence lead to calls for public inquiries and do not help the police in winning support and approval from the wider public.

He also makes the point that there are people and groups in Britain who will hijack public events and 'have a go' at the police, and that society has a duty to provide its police with adequate protection from extremist elements. Essentially, Waddington is arguing that the police are not really responsible for any 'paramilitarisation' in their approach; rather, they have had to react to the situations of violence that they have been faced with.

The police's role in maintaining order brings them into contact with groups of people who are not criminal and who can claim to be acting out of a sense of citizenship – pickets and protesters are usually acting in what they see as a principled manner and on behalf of a wider community. Waddington suggests that protesters and pickets can 'claim to be the moral equals of the police with a degree of success rarely achieved by criminals' (2000, p. 157). He illustrates this point by referring to the confrontations over the export of live animals to Europe in 1995. The animal rights protest at the small Essex port of Brightlingsea gave the police a difficult public order situation. The protesters were made up of a wide cross section of society, and their concern about the export of animals in cramped crates clearly had a moral justification. The exporters demanded that the police protect their right to trade lawfully and to use the Queen's highways to do so. The protesters took the direct action of lying in front of trucks that were carrying calves, and this willingness to suffer discomfort as part of the protest encouraged a great deal of sympathy for them and made the police's actions in trying to remove the protesters more 'morally dubious', as Waddington put it.

MAINTAINING PUBLIC ORDER: A CASE STUDY

The extract that follows could be compared with that on the policing of the miners' strike in 1984–1985 (pp. 142–143) and, as with that extract, it raises issues concerning the police–public relations.

Riot police thwart animal welfare protest
At least 250 police, some wearing riot gear, pulled around 500 people from the main street of the town where residents had successfully halted the first attempt to load lambs on Monday. The scenes came as operators who had planned to fly calves from Swansea to the Continent pulled out after receiving death threats. Protesters had set up a round-the-clock vigil at the airport to prevent the exports. . . .

Assistant chief constable Geoffrey Markham described the operation as a success, with only two arrests and no serious injuries. But he added: 'I would have thought it would have been a frightening experience for young children to see that number of police officers deployed in that fashion.'

He also blamed sheep exporter Roger Mills for the size of the police action. . . . Mr Markham said: 'The exporter Mr Mills informed me that he intended to move his vehicles in Brightlingsea with or without police support. I considered that if he went on his own with those large vehicles, that in the interests of public safety, that would have been an extra-ordinarily fraught situation.' . . .

He added: 'I am sorry that we caused any upset to the people of Brightlingsea because that is the last thing we wanted to do.' He conceded that no more than 60 of the demonstrators were 'hardline outsiders'.

Rock Morgan, Brightlingsea mayor, praised the protesters and criticised the police, saying: 'I saw nothing but a peaceful protest and the level of police response in my opinion was over the top and completely unjustified.'

Clifford Brown, a retired carpenter, said: 'I have never before been in a demonstration and could not believe these police with truncheons and visors looking every bit like storm troopers.'

Heather Dewdney, a 16-year-old childminder, said: 'I was sitting in the road showing no violence when I was dragged across the road on my back. We then saw a man being beaten by a policeman and when I asked for his number he punched me extremely hard between my breasts.' . . .

Maria Wilby, of the pressure group Brightlingsea Against Live Animal Exports, said she was shocked by police tactics and said dozens of people had been injured. 'There were mothers with toddlers here today and some were pulled out by their hair.'

(J. Erlichman, *Guardian*, 19 January 1995, cited in McLoughlin and Muncie 1996)

Questions

Describe the 'moral ambiguity' that the police may have faced in policing the demonstration at Brightlingsea.

As with the Orgreave demonstration (see p. 143), what reasons can you offer for the police actions?

This case illustrates the distinction and contradictions between the police's roles of crime fighting and order maintenance. Public order maintenance, according to Waddington, is the maintenance of 'a particular order', and although the police may be enforcing the law, if that law is seen as unjust then their enforcement is also tainted – illustrating his argument about the 'morally ambiguous' nature of public order policing.

Police culture

The solidarity of the police as an occupational group was highlighted in our brief look at the early history of policing. This solidarity has encouraged the development of a distinct occupational culture within the police. In looking at this police culture, an interesting question to start with is that of whether police officers have a distinctive set of personality characteristics that set them apart from the public.

It could be argued that because of the nature of their work, a police career attracts recruits of a particular psychological disposition. However, a more sociological/cultural approach would stress that it is group socialisation and institutional routines that generate a particular working personality and a strong occupational subculture – what is commonly termed a 'canteen culture'. The whole process of becoming a police officer happens in a very institutionalised manner – with probationers at the bottom of a hierarchical structure and quasi-military bureaucracy that emphasises command, discipline and following orders. Probationers are placed under the guidance of experienced officers from whom they pick up the real world of practical policing: the folklore, the common-sense discourse on crime, and so on. New officers also develop a sense of knowing when something or someone is not right – they learn when to use conciliation and when to use the full force of the law; they learn how to identify and classify offenders and suspects.

That said, police officers do have considerable autonomy, which in practice serves to strengthen the internal police culture. Law enforcement is a complex activity, and officers have to exercise discretion in all sorts of situations. As they translate written law into law in action, they make key decisions all the time. A patrolling officer ignores a large number of offences and potential offences every day (prostitutes soliciting, illegal parking), partly because taking action is time-consuming, which inevitably means that there is less time to deal with other offences. The way in which this discretion is exercised reflects the general occupational culture. New recruits, for instance, will almost inevitably pick up and apply the practices of the more experienced officers whom they are placed with when learning the day-to-day realities of policing.

Although there are bound to be different views and approaches to their work held by officers in any organisation as large as the police, the occupational culture of the police can be described as a 'monoculture' in that it is perpetuated through the way new members are selected, trained, socialised and accepted by their colleagues. This monoculture is characterised in particular by isolation and solidarity. Police officers tend to be isolated from previous friends, the community and even their families. Their work encourages a tendency for them to become suspicious of everyone, and the authority vested in them furthers a sense of isolation. This isolation encourages a 'them–us' worldview, which leads to a strong degree of solidarity between police officers. Indeed, solidarity seems to be a basic police cultural value, and one that is encouraged by a tendency for police officers to socialise together as well as to count on one another for support. As we will touch on later, police solidarity can have both positive and negative effects on policing practice.

The nature of police work requires the police to develop methods for recognising certain types of people as 'typical' criminals; they are likely to have a picture of stereotypic villains. Through acquiring 'conventional wisdom', they know about criminals, how to recognise them and where to locate them – in 'bad' neighbourhoods, for example. As a consequence of this, the police tend to concentrate on street crime such as robbery, burglary and assault, with a consequence that the population on whom they concentrate are liable to feel 'picked on', which leads to a sense of injustice that will in turn affect police–public relations. In addition to this, the nature of police work makes it likely that they will experience some depersonalisation in their work; they may be viewed by members of the public not as people but as uniforms – 'filth' or 'pigs', for instance. In a similar vein, and in order to do their job, police have to depersonalise the public by stereotyping them as 'rough', 'respectable', 'toe-rags', 'slags', and so on.

In terms of what has been done to change elements of police culture which encourage this sort of 'them versus us' attitude, there are difficulties for senior officers. Police officers place great value on group solidarity and will 'close ranks' to keep working routines as they would prefer. This can be frustrating for senior officers, who find themselves not being able to prevent a sort of action-based police culture whereby officers tend to persist in rushing from incident to incident and show less interest in the proactive business of fostering links with the community. This is partly due to the well-documented subcultural emphasis on 'action and excitement'. Emphasis on the exciting and dangerous nature of police work is reflected in the image of policing portrayed by the media and the image probably held by the public in general. In contrast to this image, police patrol work is invariably boring and somewhat aimless. The extract below taken from the Policy Studies Institute (PSI) report into the Metropolitan Police in the 1980s highlights the potential conflict between the image and reality of police work and the way this impacts on police behaviour.

QUESTION BREAK

Read the extract below from the PSI report *The Police in Action*, based on a participant observation study of the Metropolitan Police by David Smith and Jeremy Gray:

A considerable amount of police behaviour can best be understood as a search for some interest, excitement or sensation. An officer on foot will often spend a whole shift without doing any police work, and without talking to anyone except to greet them and provide simple information. . . . Even officers in cars with mainsets can spend several hours without responding to a call and without finding something to do on their own account. Of course, there are times when a car rushes straight from one call to another, but overall these are definitely unusual except in very restricted areas.

The importance of boredom and aimlessness is very much obscured by most popular treatments of police work, whether in fictional or in documentary style. They naturally concentrate on the interesting bits, and, so, of course, do the police themselves. . . .

Most constables would like to have a reasonable number of dramatic or at least interesting crimes to deal with. One PC complained at length to a sergeant that the 'ground' where they both worked had become much quieter; he looked back with nostalgia to the old days when the ground was much 'harder' and 'you could literally be strolling past a pub and a bloke would come staggering out with a knife in his back . . . '

A considerable number of stops are carried out mainly for something to do. When DJS [David Smith, one of the researchers] spent a whole night walking with a probationer who could find nothing at all to do, the probationer eventually waited on a main road where there was virtually no traffic and stopped the first two cars that came by. Both were young men on their way to work, and both said they were frequently stopped by police at about 5 am as they went to work.

(Smith and Gray 1983, pp. 51–55)

Questions

Aside from shift workers, which groups of people do you think are most likely to be stopped and questioned by the police?

How might this affect police relations with such groups?

Solidarity is emphasised in most studies of police culture and practice, and although it is by no means unique to the police – all occupational groups will have it to some degree – it is particularly apparent within the police. While it can encourage the covering up of errors, group solidarity can also be a positive feature when it comes to helping out colleagues. Chan (1996), for example, has highlighted how police culture can be functional for police officers in an occupation that is unpredictable, alienating and can be dangerous. Police solidarity offers reassurance and is not just a result of isolation; there is a need to have colleagues who can be relied on in tight spots. As Reiner puts it, 'Solidarity is knitted from the intense experience of confronting shared dangers and pressures, the need to be able to rely on colleagues in a tight spot, and the bonding from having done so' (1997, p. 1016).

The fact that the police's occupational culture and police working practices place great emphasis on solidarity and mutual support arguably benefits those who are part of that culture. However, as we will now examine, those officers who do not belong to the majority social categories in the police (essentially those who are not male and white) are placed at a distinct disadvantage by this occupational culture.

Sexism, racism and homophobia

In looking at police culture it is useful to focus on some specific elements of it, in particular the extent to which it is sexist and racist. Here we will highlight a few issues and questions that might be explored in relation to these aspects of police culture.

Sexism

One of the most obvious and consistent factors shown by criminal statistics is that very few criminals are women. This does not necessarily mean that women suspects are treated favourably or chivalrously by the police. However, it does seem that women are responded to by the police and the criminal justice system more generally in terms of how closely they correspond to a conventional imagery of 'good women'. As Reiner puts it, women tend to be viewed as either 'whores' or 'wives' (1997).

Table 5.1 Police officer strength[1] by rank and gender, at 31 March 2000

	Males	Females
Chief Constable	44	3
Assistant Chief Constable	137	12
Superintendent	1,164	62
Chief Inspector	1,465	109
Inspector	5,553	388
Sergeant	16,867	1,633
Constable	76,570	17,948
All ranks, total	101,800	20,155

Source: Home Office, *Social Trends* 31, 2001

Note: 1 Full-time equivalents employed in the 43 police force areas in England and Wales. With officers on secondment, the total police strength was 123,593.

As regards women who work in the police, the data on female (and ethnic minority) officers show that there is a great lack of equality in respect both of number of officers and of promotion to top positions within the police (see Table 5.1). Although the proportion of female officers has risen in recent years, women still occupy very few of the most senior posts, and it was not until 1995 that the first woman chief constable was appointed: Pauline Clare as chief constable for the Lancashire police.

While the percentage of women officers is rising, the dominant attitude in the police still amounts to what is essentially a cult of masculinity. Until the 1975 Sex Discrimination Act, discrimination within police forces was open and institutionalised, with different departments for female and male officers. Although this is no longer the case, the police as an institution are still seen by many commentators as essentially and strongly masculine, and there is still plenty of evidence of discrimination against and harassment of women officers. There are various 'common-sense' reasons for the continuing 'macho' culture within the police – male officers feeling that women colleagues do not have the necessary physical strength, that their presence in violent situations would put male officers at risk and that their domestic commitments would come before commitment to their police career.

As indicated by the figures in Table 5.1, women officers have fared badly with regard to promotion to senior positions, A particular *cause célèbre* was the case of Alison Halford, who in 1990 was assistant chief constable in the Merseyside police force and the highest-ranking woman officer at that time. Halford brought a sex discrimination case against the force on the grounds that further promotion for her was being turned down while male officers with less experience and qualifications were being appointed. Her decision to go public led to a very public and bitter dispute with the chief constable and the police authority on Merseyside. She accused senior officers of ingrained hostility to women officers, of patronage to male colleagues and of tapping her telephone in an attempt to undermine her position. In turn, she was suspended and was accused of being promoted beyond her ability for reasons of political correctness, of not being a team player and of irrational behaviour. In 1992, after the police authority was found to have acted unfairly in the opening disciplinary proceedings against her, Alison Halford took an out-of-court settlement and so the case was never dealt with officially.

In terms of the generally sexist nature of police culture, a cult of masculinity would seem to be apparent within the police force. The PSI report into the Metropolitan Police in the 1980s (see p. 151) found that the emphasis on masculinity was particularly strong in the CID. This macho image was associated with drinking, which for CID officers seemed to be an integral part of their working lives. While drinking in pubs, CID officers were often 'on duty' or 'working overtime', and as they had a legitimate reason for being in pubs, it was difficult for them, or anyone else, to regulate the amount of time they spent there. The PSI report goes on to suggest that CID officers who did not drink with colleagues would be seen as a bit odd; as one officer put it, 'In the department, drinking is a way of life.'

Another aspect of the male code is the ability to handle squeamishess. As a young officer dealing with his first death told the PSI researchers,

> Soon after I went on district I had to deal with a fatal accident with an old PC who was a real devil. The bloke had the top of his skull knocked off and his brains were spilling out. I was not too happy about it all. When we got back to the police station, the old devil took me to the canteen and deliberately ordered spaghetti Bolognese and sat there eating it in front of me.

(Smith and Gray 1983, p. 74)

Although the proportion of women police officers is increasing, the dominant attitude in the police seems to have changed relatively little from what the PSI report referred to as a 'cult of masculinity'. This exerts a strong influence on attitudes towards female officers. The PSI report found that, as with other male-dominated groups such as the army, a certain pattern of talk about women and sex is almost expected, with male officers adopting the sort of values and responses that they think are normal within groups of men. However, although the police are male dominated, male officers have to work closely with women as colleagues, and most of the women officers interviewed by the PSI researchers felt that male officers were prejudiced against them, that the importance of physical strength in police work was greatly overemphasised and that they were regularly excluded from some of the more interesting areas of police work. Many women officers seemed to accept, or at least accommodate, these attitudes. One recounted how an inspector at her training school had said to her, 'Why don't you admit it, you're only here to get a husband, aren't you? Why don't you resign and save us a lot of time and money?' She had stayed cool and let it 'run off her back'. Complaints made by women officers about their treatment were supported by the observations of the PSI research, which found many drivers trying to avoid working with women.

More recent research indicates that the macho elements of police culture have by no means disappeared. Carol Martin (1996) examined the day-to-day experiences of women police constables in her research with the Sussex police. The participants in her research were all from one division (of 105 officers) within the Sussex police and she interviewed nine female officers and thirteen male officers with a range of experience and length of service as police officers. A number of the women officers interviewed had worked in the Special Enquiry Unit (SEU), undertaking work that had traditionally been handled by the old Police Women's Section. While the unit dealt with all sexual crimes, by far the greater part of its work consisted of dealing with women and child victims. The SEU was staffed entirely by females with one male, a detective sergeant, as their supervisor. When asked why there was this preponderance of women working in that field, one officer commented:

> 'The work is considered very much "women's work". . . . The status of the work is low because it's women that do it. We don't have detective status and yet we are investigating what we consider, after murder, to be the most serious crimes there are: rape, buggery, serious sexual abuse, serious indecent assault. One supervisor [a man] is a DS though.'

Martin found that the women officers involved with the SEU were very committed to their work but felt that there was no reason why it should be seen as a predominantly female posting. Some did acknowledge that there was a demand from the public for female officers to be available to deal with female and child victims. However, it was clear that several women officers felt that the preponderance of women in the unit contributed to its low status among other officers, in spite of the fact that its work was largely investigative – and such work is normally accorded higher status within the police. As one male officer put it, 'I know some colleagues who would have been interested if there hadn't been the sort of stigma attached to it that it was girls only.'

In looking at how gender impacted on their careers as police officers, Martin's respondents highlighted two major issues: sexism and family responsibilities. As regards the latter, having a career and having children was still seen as problematic:

> 'I believe this is the hardest job to come back to. They treat you as if you've got a disease as soon as you are pregnant, you're immediately off the section and there's no guarantee you will go back to the same division or job.'

While equal opportunities policies might be able to deal with issues of sexual discrimination, women officers in this study certainly felt that indirect discrimination was widespread in that they felt they effectively had to choose between career and family. Women officers who returned after maternity leave found that child-care problems were exacerbated by shift work and that they were virtually confined to nine to five office-based police work (often not the reason they had joined the police in the first place).

All but two of the nine women officers interviewed by Martin had experienced sexual harassment of a physical nature, and all these incidents had occurred when they were either on probation or newly in service. In spite of this startling figure, only one had complained, and the 'aggressor' had received a warning. Two others had responded physically (for example, 'a knee in the groin'), and while this may have ended the particular harassment, it had left those officers resentful. 'Blaming the victim' was felt to be a real issue in this context, and although the women knew of the grievance channels, most felt that an incident would have to be very serious to go through such channels. The other side of sexist treatment was the chivalrous attitudes shown to women officers. While this may have its pleasant side, Martin found a clear feeling that it undermined the position of women officers and compromised their capabilities as police officers through perpetuating a 'weak link' argument in situations of potential danger and violence.

QUESTION BREAK

Suggest ways in which a chivalrous attitude might work against the career prospects of women police officers.

All the officers in this study were aware of the 'canteen culture'; although most denied that it was excessively macho or sexist, there was an agreement by male and female officers that there was an element of coarse language and sexist joking, but it was stressed that 'the girls give as good as they get'. Although harassment has been identified by others as the greatest problem faced by women in the police (Heidensohn 1998), these officers, both male and female, believed that issues around maternity leave and child-care were the key ones that worked against female officers. And although the sexism of the canteen culture was acknowledged, most of the women officers did not appear personally threatened by it, or at least had found strategies for coping with it.

In a comment on women in policing, Heidensohn (1998) points out that while there is a trend for increased recruitment of women to the police, the deployment of those women within the police and the promotion of them remains a contentious area, with the most prestigious and high-profile positions still mainly restricted to males. She suggests that the main barrier to real equality within policing remains the sexist nature of the internal police culture. She does, however, highlight some positive developments and a general acceptance, by senior managers in the police at least, that the skills needed for success in the job are no longer those of the traditional macho officer. The achievements of individual women officers who have risen to senior positions have also had a significant impact. She concludes by commenting that 'It is difficult to argue that old style cop culture still plays a useful role in present day policing. Eradicating it in favour of a more inclusive organizational style would be a worthy aim for the 21st century police.'

Another aspect of the macho elements of internal police culture can be seen in relation to attitudes to sexuality and, specifically, homosexuality. With regard to this, strenuous heterosexuality seems to be the basic order of the day in police culture, and this emphasis on masculinity can increase the likelihood of homophobia. Emsley (1996a) refers to a book written by a homosexual police officer, Daley, in which he talks about how he was victimised because of a lack of interest in women and also because of an interest in books and music. There has been much less debate and research on issues of sexual orientation and policing than with regard to sexism or racism. While data can be found on female and black police officers, the numbers of homosexual or lesbian police officers can only be estimated. In terms of how the police respond to issues of sexual orientation, Walklate (2000) points out that while forward-thinking and liberal-sounding statements can be made, the influence of the strongly heterosexual, macho police occupational culture ensures that the reality of the work experiences of gay and lesbian police officers is similar to that described by Daley. The formation of the Lesbian and Gay Police

Association in 1990 might have been expected to lead to greater confidence among gay and lesbian officers; however, the furore and negative publicity that have surrounded the establishment of this organisation provides a clear example of the deeply rooted negative attitudes to homosexual and lesbian officers (as well as homosexual and lesbian people in general). Brown (1997) argues that in spite of police equal opportunities policies with regard to sexual orientation, there is still a real and distinct gap between policy and what happens 'on the ground'.

Racism

As with female officers, but more so, there are relatively few black police officers. In 1998, only 2 per cent of the police officers in England and Wales were from ethnic minority backgrounds, and the highest-ranking ethnic minority officer was an assistant chief constable in Lancashire (Walklate 2000). Over twenty years ago the Scarman Report (1982) highlighted the need to recruit more ethnic minority police officers and, given the figures above, the recruitment strategies since then do not seem to have been very successful. Walklate suggests that reasons for this include the negative image of policing held by ethnic minority, and especially young black, groups and the fact that ethnic minority officers face difficulties both from their own communities and from within the police force. This lack of black officers does not in itself mean that there is a racist element to police culture, although it may be indicative of the attitudes within the police and of the attitudes held by the black population towards the police. As with gender, discrimination on grounds of race is against the law; however, this does not ensure equal treatment of black police officers. Brown (1997) points out that black officers experience racial prejudices and discrimination from both the public they police and their fellow officers.

Again, the PSI report into the Metropolitan Police (Smith and Gray 1983) is a major source of information here and a useful starting point in looking at the extent of racism in the modern force. One area the report particularly looked at was the relations between police and black people in London (it is interesting to note that in the early 1980s, when the research was conducted, the term 'coloured' was used throughout, a term now considered inappropriate in referring to black people). It found that racist language was used in a casual and almost automatic way within the Met, even over the radios that were picked up by all officers, as well as anyone else listening in. For instance, the researchers heard one inspector say, 'Look, I've a bunch of coons in sight.' Whether the use of racist language means that the people who use it behave in a racist manner, or even hold racist attitudes, is an issue that was considered by Smith and Gray, the report's authors. They cite one young officer telling them:

> 'I know that PCs call them [black people] spooks, niggers and sooties, but deep down the majority of PCs aren't really against them, although there are some who really hate them. . . . I call them niggers myself now but I don't really mean it.'

In their overall conclusions, the PSI report found that there was some racism in the Met but that it did not lead to black people receiving greatly inferior treatment from the police. While this interpretation may be correct, it could be argued that it is difficult if not impossible to prove it. The findings on stopping and arresting suspects provided some evidence that black people (although not Asians) were more likely to be stopped and that the police did tend to link crime and black people and so tended to be more suspicious of black people. Without going into the findings on police–public relations in great detail, the report did highlight a widespread lack of confidence in the police among the London population, and especially among young black Londoners: 62 per cent of young blacks (15–24 years of age) thought the police used threats or unreasonable behaviour.

The PSI research was conducted almost twenty years ago and raises the question as to what extent such findings are still relevant.

In 1995, black teenager Stephen Lawrence was murdered in London by a gang of white youths. The judicial inquiry, led by Sir William Macpherson, into the Metropolitan Police investigation of this murder is a very useful source for considering evidence concerning racism within the police (Macpherson 1999). In particular, the inquiry considered the issue of institutional racism and the extent to which it applied to the police. The inquiry (also) made recommendations for reforms in many areas of policing, including recruitment, the investigation of racially motivated crimes, and the relationship between the police and black and Asian people.

The notion of institutional racism had been considered before Macpherson and indeed was rejected by the Scarman Report into the inner-city disorders of the early 1980s. Scarman was aware that 'unwitting racism', as his report put it, could exist and that some officers no doubt held racist attitudes, but stopped short of describing the Metropolitan Police as institutionally racist. In contrast, in giving evidence to the Macpherson inquiry, a number of chief police officers acknowledged that institutional racism was still widely prevalent within the police. This view was confirmed in the report itself, which accepted that there was institutional racism and defined it as

> the collective failure of an organization to provide an appropriate and professional service to people because of their colour, culture or ethnic origin. It can be seen or detected in processes, attitudes and behaviour which amount to discrimination through unwitting prejudice, ignorance, thoughtlessness, and racist stereotyping which disadvantage ethnic minority people.'
>
> (Macpherson 1999)

In his evidence to the inquiry, the chief constable of Greater Manchester, David Wilmot, accepted that institutional racism existed in his force:

> 'We have a society that has got institutional racism. Greater Manchester Police, therefore, has institutional racism. Some of it is not of the overt type; it's that which has been internalized by individuals and it's our responsibility to try and make sure that it's eradicated.'
>
> (quoted in the *Guardian*, 14 October 1998)

In response to these comments, a survey undertaken by the *Independent* newspaper found that two other chief constables, from Sussex and West Yorkshire, also accepted the existence of institutional racism within their forces, while ten chief constables admitted that their forces had racist officers in their ranks – although they were keen to point out that this did not mean all their officers were racist. As Paul Whitehouse, the chief constable of Sussex, put it, 'Yes, there is institutional racism within Sussex police but that does not mean that Sussex Police is an inherently racist service' (quoted in the *Independent*, 15 October 1998).

As well as the issue of whether the police are institutionally racist, concern about the way in which the police use their powers to stop and search has been an issue of particular concern and controversy. Bowling and Phillips (2002) make the point that it would certainly seem to be the case that young black and Asian men, in particular, see the inequitable use of 'stop and search' as the most obvious example of the police abusing their powers in a racist manner. They then go on to consider explanations other than racism for the differing stop rates of black people. The stopping of young black people may reflect the age and class profile of the black population in Britain. Another explanation is classified by Bowling and Phillips as 'subject availability' and refers to the fact that most stops occur in the afternoon, evening and night and, because of their higher levels of unemployment and school exclusions, black people are more likely to be 'available' for stopping on the streets at those times. This can also be linked to lifestyle factors such as going out more frequently in the evenings.

In concluding their examination of racial discrimination in policing, Bowling and Phillips categorise the range of different explanations under four broad headings which it would be helpful to introduce here. First, there is the 'bad apple' argument, that racial prejudice and discrimination in the police service is apparent in the attitudes and behaviour of a small number of racist police officers. This explanation was favoured by the Scarman Report into the inner-city disorders of the early 1980s and is reflected in the view that the 'solution' is to locate and remove the 'bad apples' and then to prevent any more getting in. Second, the 'reflection of society' argument suggests that as the police service is a cross section of society, it is inevitable that some police officers will hold racist views. This is not to condone such views or discriminatory actions but to see the police service as no exception to wider society, where racial discrimination is endemic. These explanations can be criticised for not taking any account of the way in which prejudices are part of the police organisational culture. The 'canteen culture' explanation sees racism as one of the core elements of police culture (see the discussion on the PSI research on pp. 157–158), along with conservatism, machismo and solidarity with other officers. Linked to the view that racist attitudes are a part of police culture – although, of course, not held by all officers – is the view that there is an inevitable clash of cultures between the white population and ethnic minorities. This clash of cultures is reflected in the stereotypes held about different minority groups and the view common among many white people that 'their' white culture was being rejected; as Bowling and Phillips put it, 'the failure to "accept" Englishness, made ethnic minorities at once threatening and vulnerable to attack'. The final possible explanation, of 'institutional racism', was highlighted in our consideration of the Macpherson Inquiry into the Stephen Lawrence murder.

QUESTION BREAK

Of course, many elements of police culture and working practices are by no means unique to the police and are probably common in many male work organisations. But in the context of policing, people are perhaps bound to wonder what the general public, including those who are female, gay or black, can expect if this is how the police treat their own female, gay and black officers.

Questions

Suggest other occupational subcultures which might demonstrate similarities with the police's 'canteen culture'.

Bearing this in mind, to what extent do you think we should expect 'higher' standards and different cultural norms in the police? To put it another way, should the police be 'better' than the general population or should they be representative, with all that that entails?

Further reading

Bowling, B. and Foster, J. (2002) 'Policing and the Police', in Maguire, M., Morgan, R. and Reiner, R. (eds) *The Oxford Handbook of Criminology*, 3rd edn, Oxford: Oxford University Press. This chapter examines some of the key issues that relate to public policing in the twenty-first century: in particular, issues around police management and governance that we were not able to examine in detail, including how to measure and assess what the police do, police partnerships with other agencies, transnational policing, and police accountability.

Emsley, C. (1996) *The English Police: A Political and Social History*, 2nd edn, Harlow: Longman. This provides a comprehensive coverage of the history of the English police, from the earliest agents and institutions of law enforcement to the increasingly centralised, state-regulated role of the police in the 1990s.

Leishman, F., Loveday, B. and Savage, S. (eds) (2002) *Core Issues in Policing*, 2nd edn, Harlow: Longman. This edited collection includes chapters from academic researchers and practitioners who provide different approaches to examining the context and functions of the police and to considering the future.

Morgan, R. and Newburn, T. (1997) *The Future of Policing*, Oxford: Oxford University Press. A concise examination of the key issues facing policing in modern Britain and the pressures faced by the police in a context of limited public spending and public demand for more and 'better' policing.

Newburn, T. (ed.) (2003) *A Handbook of Policing*, Cullompton, Devon: Willan Publishing. This is a comprehensive text (running to over 900 pages) that provides a detailed overview of policing in Britain. It is divided into four sections: comparative and historical perspectives; the context of policing; doing policing (how the police operate in specific areas such as drugs, terrorism and organised crime); and themes and debates (including chapters on race, gender, ethics and restorative justice).

The following Home Office Web site includes information on police powers, recruitment, training and resourcing: www.homeoffice.gov.uk/crimpol/index.html

The Web site for the Centre for Crime and Justice Studies (www.kcl.ac.uk) provides information on events, research and publications in the criminal justice field. The Centre for Crime and Justice Studies is a charity based at King's College London which aims to inform and educate about all aspects of crime and the criminal justice system.

6 The courts, sentencing and the judiciary

A glance at the newspapers, television schedules or cinema listings on any particular day will demonstrate the fascination – some might say obsession – we have with crime and criminals – with what crimes are committed, with who commits them and with what happens to those criminals who are caught. It is this last aspect that provides the focus for this chapter. Questions such as 'should all murderers get life imprisonment?', 'what should life mean?' and 'should burglars go to prison?' excite widespread interest and debate, evidenced by the front-page headline in *The Times* (20 December 2002) which announced that the 'Lord Chief Justice tells courts not to jail burglars'. Indeed, the media interest in crime and criminals is largely based around what happens to offenders who are caught – with who gets what within the criminal justice system. What happens in the courtroom forms the basis for much of the media reporting of crime for local and national newspapers and broadcasting; and the courtroom drama is a device regularly used to boost audience figures in soaps and as the basis of storylines in films and other productions.

In covering the 'who gets what' of criminal justice the chapter will start with an overview of the structure of the courts in England and Wales, the role of the Crown Prosecution Service and some of the key principles that inform the sentencing of offenders. The issue of impartiality in sentencing will be considered by looking at the extent to which race, gender and class, and in particular the race, gender and class of offenders, influences sentencing. The final part of the chapter examines those people who have the power to pass sentence on offenders – the judiciary; it considers the background, training and appointment of magistrates and judges.

The structure of the courts

The court structure in England and Wales (there are differences in the Scottish and Northern Irish criminal justice systems) is the result of hundreds of years of development, with some parts dating back over nine hundred years. It is based on a clear and recognisable

CHAPTER SIX

Table 6.1 The modern English court system

Court	Criminal functions	Civil functions	Number of courts	Case load (annual)	Composition
Magistrates' courts	Minor crime	Very limited	Several hundred	Vast	Part-time lay JPs, a few full-time stipendiary magistrates in large cities
County courts	None	Extensive case load	260	Approx. 2 million cases started – of which about 5% come to trial	Circuit and district judges
Crown courts	All	Limited	Technically one court with 90 locations	100,000-plus cases	Circuit judges and recorders
The High Court:					
Chancery Division	None	Trusts, tax law, wills, property, etc.		Approx. 700 trials	17 High Court judges
Family Division	None	Family law in general		2,000–3,000 defended cases	15 High Court judges
Queen's Bench	Some appeals from tribunals	All civil law apart from above – especially contract and tort		1,500–2,000 trials	63 High Court judges
Court of Appeal:					Lord Chief Justice and Master of the Rolls
Criminal Division	Most criminal appeals	None		6,000–7,000	Sits in benches of 1 or 2 judges from Court of Appeal and judges from Queen's Bench
Civil Division	None	Appeals from High Court, county court and tribunals		About 1,500	Sits in benches of 3 judges
House of Lords	Appeals from any court in England and Wales on any matter (and from Scotland and N. Ireland in many cases)			50–60	Benches of 5 from the 10–12 Lords of Appeal under the Lord Chancellor

Source: Adapted from Budge et al. (1998, pp. 476–477)

hierarchy, at the top of which sits the House of Lords as the 'highest court in the land' (although the supremacy of the House of Lords could be questioned, as British laws are now subject to the European Court in Luxembourg). However, there is not a straightforward pyramid structure; perhaps not surprisingly, given its ancient origins, there are all sorts of deviations and historical idiosyncrasies that affect the court structure.

There is, though, a basic dividing line between the criminal and the civil courts. On the criminal side, prosecutions are generally brought by the state against those whose behaviour has broken the criminal law. If found guilty, the individual is punished by the state. By contrast, civil cases are between private interests and involve one party suing another, usually for some harm caused or money owing. The police are not usually interested in such cases unless the behaviour also amounts to a crime. Different standards or degrees of proof are required in criminal and civil cases: in criminal cases there is a conviction only if the case is proved 'beyond reasonable doubt', whereas civil cases are won on 'the balance of probabilities' – in other words, a slightly lesser degree of proof is required. In addition, the titles and names used by the people involved in the different courts differ. For instance, the term 'plaintiff', for the person bringing an action, is used only in civil cases.

Another general and fundamental principle underlying the criminal justice system of England and Wales is that what happens in (adult) courts should be open and public; and apart from a few exceptions, for instance where there is felt to be a national security risk, any member of the public can see what goes on in court. Table 6.1 lists the main courts and their functions.

Magistrates' courts

The 460 or so magistrates' courts are the first layer of the court structure and can be found in most towns. Each of these courts has a 'bench' which is staffed by magistrates who are, in the main, part-time, unpaid laypersons. There are over 30,000 lay magistrates, known as Justices of the Peace (JPs). The fact that the vast majority of criminal cases are judged by these non-professional, part-time members of the community provides a unique aspect to the criminal justice system of England and Wales. In addition to JPs, there are a small number, around a hundred, of paid, legally qualified magistrates; now known as district judges, until 2000 these professional magistrates were called stipendiary magistrates. District judges are full-time members of the judiciary who have the same powers as benches of two lay magistrates. They usually sit in the bigger, urban courts with particularly heavy caseloads and tend to hear the lengthier and more complex cases that come before magistrates' courts. As well as district judges there are also deputy district judges who sit in magistrates' courts not as full-time professionals but on a fee-paid basis – and who can apply to become district judges after serving for a minimum of two years or 40 days in court. It is likely that there will be pressure to extend the professional magistracy in the future (an issue we will return to when looking at the appointment and background of the judiciary later in the chapter). However, in spite of this, it is important to remember that the vast majority of criminal cases in magistrates' courts are heard by a lay, part-time judiciary.

The main task of magistrates' courts is to deliver 'summary justice' to people charged with less serious crimes, and to decide which cases are serious enough to be sent for trial by judge and jury in a crown court (or for sentencing in the crown court if the offender has pleaded guilty). Having to send more serious cases to a higher court does not mean that magistrates have little power; they are able to send offenders to prison for up to six months (or 12 months when there are two sentences that are to run consecutively). Furthermore, although they deal only with less serious crime, the huge bulk of crime is of a relatively minor nature, which means that the vast majority of all criminal cases (something in the region of 98 per cent) start and end with the magistrates' courts. The great majority of defendants who come before magistrates' courts plead guilty, with the magistrates then having to pass sentence (or, as mentioned, to send them to the crown court if the offence merits a more severe punishment than magistrates can give). Those defendants who plead not guilty have the choice of trial by magistrates with no jury or of going to the crown court for a jury trial – however, there have been recent government moves to abolish the automatic right to a jury trial. Although not relating solely to magistrates' courts, in early 2003 the standing committee on the current criminal justice bill were considering proposals to restrict the right to trial by jury for cases deemed too lengthy or complex for a jury and where there was a risk of jury tampering.

QUESTION BREAK: JURY TRIALS?

Read the following extract from a letter written to the *Guardian* by two barristers and a solicitor defending the right to jury trial and consider the questions below.

For the first time it is being proposed that there should be exceptions to the right to be tried by a jury for serious criminal offences. Previous plans to curtail jury trial involved taking away the right to elect trial in the crown court and an extension to the list of offences which could only be tried in the magistrates' court.

Although it is true that long trials place a burden on a jury, and that in a tiny minority of cases there is a problem with the risk of jury tampering, there are other measures which can be taken to address these issues. We fear that once the principle of right to trial by jury is compromised, the list of exceptions will grow. These measurers represent a fundamental and unacceptable erosion of the democratic element in the justice system and we urge that they are vigorously opposed.

(C. Griffiths, H. Blaxland and A. Katzen, 'Defend Jury Trial',
Guardian Letters, 14 January 2003)

Questions
Why do you think the writers feel that restricting jury trial might lead to an 'erosion of the democratic element in the justice system'?

Suggest some arguments for and against jury trials.

As with all courts, there is a good deal of variation in sentencing practices across magistrates' courts, and to try to ensure that there is as much consistency as possible, each magistrates' bench is advised by a justice's clerk. These clerks are qualified lawyers with specialist training and, as well as advising magistrates on legal procedures, they are also responsible for training them. They also have a big role in pre-trial proceedings, including determining legal aid applications and organising court timetables. As regards sentencing in all the courts, offenders can appeal against their sentence, although in English law it is normal for sentences to commence immediately after they are given, even if the offender is going to appeal. The appeals process is so slow that those serving short sentences are likely to have finished or almost finished them by the time any appeal is heard. (This and the fact that crown courts can now increase sentences which offenders have appealed against makes appealing a high-risk strategy for offenders.)

Apart from their role as judges and sentencers, magistrates have also to make decisions as to whether to grant defendants bail or remand them in custody to wait for trial; and they have a wide range of powers in family matters (for instance, in decisions over maintenance payments to separated partners) and over decisions to grant drinks and opening hours licences.

Crown courts

Crown courts deal with the more serious criminal cases – the small percentage that get beyond the magistrates' courts – and are based at over ninety locations in England and Wales. The cases heard at crown courts are ranked according to seriousness, with the most serious heard by High Court judges and the majority of cases (those that are slightly less serious) dealt with by more junior judges – either circuit judges or recorders. (Crown courts deal with criminal cases. Their equivalent on the civil side of the court system are county courts, which deal with matters of civil law, so they are not the focus of our interest here in looking at the criminal justice system. There are around 260 county courts which hear cases concerning among other things, recovery of money. Most of these cases lead to settlements out of court.)

The crown courts hear in the region of 120,000 cases per year, in about a quarter of which the defendants plead not guilty. The most famous crown court is the Central Criminal Court or Old Bailey in London.

The High Court

Above the crown courts is the 'legal elite'. The High Court, which handles the most difficult and complex cases, is the most senior civil court. The High Court is a generic term which covers three separate kinds of courts, each with separate functions and each dating back hundreds of years. The three courts or divisions are the Queen's Bench, headed by the Lord Chief Justice, and the main civil court for disputes and wrongs; the Chancery Division, which deals with financial issues, including trade and industry disputes; and the Family Division, which hears all cases involving children and matrimonial issues.

The Court of Appeal

Appeals against convictions or sentences given in a lower court are heard by a higher court – so anyone convicted and sentenced by a magistrates' court can appeal to the crown court; and anyone convicted and sentenced by the crown court can appeal to the Court of Appeal. The Court of Appeal is staffed by the most senior judges, and the decisions these judges make influence and form the law of the country.

There are two divisions within the Court of Appeal: the Criminal Division, headed by the Lord Chief Justice; and the Civil Division, headed by the Master of the Rolls. The Criminal Division hears around 8,000 cases a year, most being appeals against sentence, and the Civil Division over 1,000, generally appeals against decisions of the High Court and certain tribunals (e.g. industrial tribunals). The Court of Appeal is unlike the lower courts in that it does not hear from witnesses except in exceptional cases; the decisions it makes are based on documents and transcripts from the particular case in question, occasionally supplemented with arguments from barristers.

The House of Lords

As mentioned earlier, the House of Lords is the highest court in the country. In this context, the House of Lords refers to the judicial committee of legal members of the House of Lords – twelve law lords who have reached the very summit of the legal profession. It is not the same as the parliamentary House of Lords. The House of Lords acts as the final arbiter of justice in Britain. However, there is no automatic right of appeal to it; the right to appeal is granted by the Court of Appeal. It handles only cases which are felt to have important implications for the impact of law on society.

There are other, more specialised courts and tribunals which relate to specific areas of the law – such as coroners' courts and employment appeal tribunals – but which we will not go into here. In addition, there are the two European courts which have a role to play in the English and Welsh criminal justice system. The decisions of the European Court in Luxembourg and the European Court of Human Rights in Strasbourg are theoretically even superior to those of the House of Lords. However, the extent to which the British government takes notice of and responds to their decisions is debatable. The European courts cannot be approached directly; all cases go to the European Commission first, and few ever reach the courts.

The Crown Prosecution Service

The Crown Prosecution Service (CPS) was established by the Prosecution of Offences Act of 1985. It takes over cases when the police have decided that it is advisable to prosecute and is therefore responsible for most public prosecutions in England and Wales. If the CPS does not agree with the police that the case should be prosecuted, it can be dropped, the charges can be changed or more evidence required. The CPS was set up to be an independent service – independent from both the police and the government so as to provide suspected offenders with an extra layer of protection. Although a national body, the CPS is organised into local areas which closely match up with the areas covered by regional police forces.

Rather than go into the organisational structure of the CPS, we will focus on how it decides whether or not to prosecute the cases that are handed over to it. Essentially this involves following what is known as the Code for Crown Prosecutors. As the code says in its introduction, prosecuting an individual or body is a serious step and so has to be as fair and effective as possible. The general principles guiding the CPS are that it ensures that the right person is prosecuted for the right offence and that it acts in a fair, independent and objective manner. In deciding whether to prosecute or not, the CPS applies what are know as the 'twin tests': the evidential test and the interests of justice test.

The evidential test is the first stage of the decision to prosecute and essentially means that a prosecution should be introduced and continued with only if there is a realistic chance of conviction. If there is not, then the evidential test is not passed and the prosecution should not go ahead. In deciding on how realistic a chance there is of conviction, the CPS considers what the defence case might be and how this is likely to affect the prosecution, and, then, whether a jury or magistrate (as the case may be) is more likely than not to convict the defendant or defendants. It may have to consider matters such as whether evidence that will be used in the case is reliable or not.

If the particular case does pass the evidential test, then the CPS has to decide that a prosecution would be in the public interest. In cases of any seriousness, a prosecution is usually expected unless public interest factors are particularly critical. Generally speaking, the more serious the offence, the more likely it is that a prosecution will be in the public interest. But the CPS might decide not to prosecute, on public interest grounds, if for example the offence is only likely to attract a very small penalty, if it was committed as a result of a genuine mistake or if there has been a long time lag between the offence and the date of the trial. However, none of these factors would be considered if the offence were serious enough – so, for instance, murder cases are often dealt with years after the offence as a result of new evidence coming to light. Other public interest factors considered include the age and health of the defendant and the effect that a prosecution may have on a victim's health.

We do not have the scope here to assess the effectiveness of the CPS. However, the decision to prosecute is a fundamental one, and it is important to bear in mind that the issues that the CPS has to weigh up provide scope for the different treatment of offenders and for the favouring of some interests rather than others.

Trials and sentencing: principles and issues

Criminal liability

It is a fundamental principle of criminal law that a person should be punished only if they have committed the act in question and if they are blameworthy – in other words, the offender has to have committed the act and be responsible for it. This requirement for there to be an action and intention is expressed in the legal terms *actus reus* (a Latin phrase meaning guilty act) and *mens rea* (guilty mind). While this might seem clear enough in theory, there are some crimes which do not involve or require a guilty mind, where there is not the same level of blame as in offences that are clearly intended. These might include certain driving offences such as speeding, for example. And although the most serious offence, murder, clearly involves intention, the law recognises that deaths can be caused in many circumstances which do not involve the same degree of intent and blame. So there are various categories of homicide that include manslaughter as well as murder; and murder charges can be reduced to manslaughter if, for instance, the offender was provoked or under pressure, or was suffering from diminished responsibility. What the criminal justice system is trying to do is to ensure that the law reflects the extent of moral blameworthiness. However, in doing so, difficulties can arise – among other examples, Davies *et al.* (1998) refer to careless driving, which can kill innocent people but which in many instances has no adverse consequences, or only very trivial ones. They ask what offence careless drivers should be charged with and what punishment they should be sentenced to when their actions kill other people.

Mitigation

After an offender is found guilty or has pleaded guilty, factors of mitigation can be offered in defence to suggest that he or she is less blameworthy than might appear, or to suggest that the offence itself was perhaps not as serious as it might have been. So, factors of mitigation may relate to the personal circumstances of the offender – they had lost their job or been deserted by their family, for instance – or to the offence itself – the offender was provoked or led into it. This aspect of the criminal justice process allows a convicted person an opportunity to argue for a more lenient sentence than they might otherwise be given.

Establishing guilt

The criminal justice system in England and Wales is adversarial, which means there are two sides, the defence and prosecution, who argue their case as best they can within certain ethical and, of course, legal limits. Rather than seeking to find the 'truth', each side aims to win its case by persuading the magistrates, judges or juries (depending on the particulars of the case) to find in its favour. Within this context, the rules surrounding court proceedings aim to protect the innocent from unfair conviction. This means that in theory the onus of proof is on the prosecution and that the defendant should be treated fairly. However, in the day-to-day practice of the court it is easy to assume that those who are accused (the defendants) are likely to be guilty; and to assume that the police must be pretty sure to bring them to court anyway. Given this tendency to assume that defendants have 'done something wrong', it is often a high-risk strategy to plead not guilty. If a defendant is found guilty after pleading not guilty, the sentence received will tend to be longer (for instance, it will be felt that the defendant has wasted the court's time and has subjected witnesses and victims to unnecessary pressure through cross-examination). In general terms, the Court of Appeal has indicated that a reduction of between one-quarter to one-third of the expected sentence is appropriate for a guilty plea. Furthermore, if a defendant is found guilty, it becomes more difficult to provide convincing mitigation to be taken into account in the sentence given (it is difficult to plead not guilty and then, if found guilty, to say, 'I'm sorry and I won't do it again'!).

A key decision facing a defendant is whether to plead guilty or not; and a decision to plead guilty can be affected by many considerations (as well as the 'truth'). A defendant may feel that to plead not guilty would protract the case, or that they did not commit the offence but it is only their word against that of the police, or that they are likely to get a lighter sentence if they plead guilty (which, as mentioned above, is the case). A guilty plea, then, involves weighing up a range of factors and may follow a bargaining process involving legal representatives. While not formally advocated, plea bargaining can save the expense of a contested trial, it can avoid the risk of a defendant being convicted for a more serious offence, it saves police time, and it reduces the uncertainty of the outcome following a not-guilty plea. Thus both sides could be said to benefit: the defendant is assured that the penalty will not be too harsh, and the police and prosecution are assured of a conviction.

QUESTION BREAK: GUILTY OR NOT?

The above section considered the decision to plead guilty or not. The two extracts that follow highlight other issues involved in determining guilt or innocence.

First, the comment from Lord Donaldson, Master of the Rolls from 1982 to 1992, makes the point that when defendants are acquitted it does not necessarily mean that they are innocent. Second, it is a basic, almost sacrosanct, feature of court proceedings that what happens in discussions among jurors should be kept absolutely secret.

Read the two extracts and consider the questions below.

> A 'guilty' verdict means that in the view of the jury the accused undoubtedly committed the offence. It is not only the innocent who are entitled to a 'not guilty' verdict. They are joined and, in my experience, are heavily outnumbered by the almost certainly guilty. This is as it should be because, as every law student is taught, it is far better that ten guilty men [sic] go free than that one innocent man be convicted.
>
> (Lord Donaldson, letter to *The Times*, 19 August 1994)

Imagine you are an Asian man on trial for arson, facing the prospect of years in jail if found guilty. Your fate is in the hands of 12 men and women chosen at random from the electoral roll. But what if some of those jurors are racist? Suppose they make disparaging remarks in the jury room about your appearance, your accent, your poor English and your business integrity. . . .

That's what happened during Sajid Qureshi's trail at Mold Crown Court in October 2000, according to one of the jurors who convicted him by an 11–1 majority and sent him down for four years. . . . In a letter to the court six days after his conviction, she claimed that some of her follow jurors seemed to have already decided their verdict from the start, that one juror fell asleep during the evidence . . . and that some tried to bully others. Enough, you might think, to raise serious doubts about whether Qureshi had a fair trail.

But not enough for the Court of Appeal . . . [which] refused him permission even to launch an appeal. The stumbling block was the Contempt of Court Act 1981, which bans anyone – and that includes judges – from inquiring into the secrets of the jury room.'

(C. Dyer, 'Jurors Behaving Badly', *Guardian*, 25 June 2002)

Questions

What arguments could be made against Lord Donaldson's conclusion?

What are the arguments for maintaining the absolute secrecy of jury deliberations? Do you agree with them?

Types of sentence

Before we list the different sentences available to the court, it is worth bearing in mind that the passing of a sentence occurs only in relation to a small proportion of the actual crimes that are committed. Aside from the massive amount of crime that is never reported, of those crimes which are reported, many are never recorded by the police as crimes and, even when they are recorded, never get 'cleared up' or solved. Many of the estimated 5 per cent of all crimes that are 'cleared up' are not followed up by any official action; it may be that the offender is too young or that there is not enough evidence to proceed, for example. On top of this, about one-third of offenders are cautioned rather than prosecuted, so that it is maybe only something like 2 per cent of all offences that lead to a conviction and a sentence from the court. This is not to say that sentencing is of no importance, and it certainly has strong symbolic importance, but such figures do highlight the need to be wary of expecting sentencing policy and practice to do much about altering patterns of behaviour of criminals.

There are a number of basic forms of sentence available to the courts and they can be grouped under four basic categories. First, there are discharges. These can be absolute, where the conviction is recorded but nothing will happen to the offender, or conditional, where the offender will receive no further punishment if they are not found guilty of any other offence for a certain period of time (they could be given a three-year conditional discharge, for example). In the latter case, if sentenced for another offence during that period, the offender can additionally be sentenced for the offence for which they were originally discharged. So the discharge is a sort of denunciatory sentence that does not seek to actually punish but which does have a deterrent effect in that if the offender offends again, they will be punished.

Second, the most common penalties are financial. These are subject to a maximum (of £5,000) in magistrates' courts, but there is no limit in crown courts. As well as financial penalties in the form of fines, there is also compensation that has to be considered by a court when cases involve personal injury or damage to property, and costs, which can be awarded against offenders. In terms of priority and order of payment, compensation has to be paid first, then fines and finally costs, with compensation to the victim thus taking priority.

QUESTION BREAK

What punishment should be given to someone who does not pay a fine?

Should persistent non-payment lead to imprisonment? Suggest reasons for and against such a course of action.

Third, there are community sentences. At the time of writing (2003), there are three main types of community sentences that are supervised by the Probation Service. These are Community Rehabilitation Orders (until recently known as Probation Orders), Community Punishment Orders (previously known as Community Service Orders) and Community Punishment and Rehabilitation Orders (a combination of the other two). For these sentences to be imposed, the offence has to be sufficiently serious and, usually, the offender has to agree to the particular order. The Community Rehabilitation Order can last from six months to three years and includes getting offenders to confront their behaviour and accept responsibility for their actions and the impact those actions have on others. A Community Punishment Order requires offenders to perform unpaid work for the benefit of the community of between 40 and 240 hours. As these brief comments indicate, community sentences can be seen to meet some of the key aims of punishment discussed in Chapter 1. Both kinds of orders are rehabilitative, with offenders hopefully acquiring new skills while following them; there is some denunciation if the community work undertaken is public and visible; and there are elements of reparation – if not always to the individual victim, then to the community.

Custodial sentences are the fourth main form of penalty. Shorter custodial sentences (of up to two years) can be suspended if there are 'exceptional circumstances'. Suspended sentences were introduced (by the 1967 Criminal Justice Act) to encourage the diverting away from prison of offenders. However, they did not succeed in lowering the prison population, with some courts seeming to use such sentences when they might not have passed a custodial sentence in the first place, rather than, as intended, as a substitute for custody. Although there are not fixed lengths of custody for particular offences, there are certain rules and guidelines that judges and magistrates have to follow. There is a mandatory life sentence for anyone guilty of murder and there are discretionary maximum sentences for other serious crimes. There is also a sort of 'going rate' or tariff for different offences that has built up on the basis of decisions made by the Court of Appeal. The starting point for deciding on length of sentence for serious offences is the time that a murderer would be expected to spend in prison. In the mid-1970s, for instance, the Lord Chief Justice, Lord Justice Lawton, took as a starting point that a murderer would spend fifteen years in prison, which would be the equivalent of two-thirds of a twenty-two year sentence (there was a one-third remission from prison sentences in the 1970s). What he termed 'wholly abnormal' offences such as political kidnapping and bomb attacks were placed just beneath this twenty-two-year guidance, with armed robbery next 'down' at eighteen years. Thus the Court of Appeal has developed 'guideline judgements' for different offences that take into account the likely remission that prisoners would receive from their initial sentences.

Although there have been various attempts through legislation to cut back, or at least restrain, the growth of custodial sentences, the prison population continues to grow (recent trends in the prison population will be examined on pp. 193–195). In a recent overview of sentencing in England and Wales, the Halliday Report (Home Office 2001) proposed that there be a 'custody plus' option to replace prison sentences of up to twelve months. This would involve offenders serving half their sentence and then being released on automatic unconditional release (AUR), when they would be expected to volunteer for some post-release supervision. This sort of combination type of sentence can be seen as 'tough and tender'; and in terms of the aims of punishment, it has been described as representing 'an important step forward in balancing rehabilitative and retributive aims in sentencing' (Ellis and Winstone 2001/2002). Introduced alongside the AUR for short sentences were different release dates for those serving longer sentences – so prisoners serving between twelve months and four years are released halfway through their sentences as an automatic conditional release (ACR), and those serving four years or longer have the possibility of discretionary conditional release (DCR) on parole after they have served half their sentence and must be released when they have served two-thirds of the sentence.

In May 2003 the Home Secretary, David Blunkett, advocated changes to the way murderers would be sentenced. He said that he intended to ask Parliament to approve a much tougher sentencing framework. This will include 'whole life' prison terms for cases involving child sex, terrorism and multiple murder, and a second tier of a minimum thirty years for contract killers, racist murderers and those who kill police officers, compared to the current minimum of twenty years. These proposed changes have been attacked by lawyers and the judiciary for interfering with judges' independence. The Bar Council, which represents barristers in England and Wales, said the plans were 'constitutionally a leap in the dark', with the Home Secretary accused of

> trying to institutionalise the grip of the executive around the neck of the judiciary . . . [in a manner that] will erode the separation of powers, which is something which has for hundreds of years been seen to be something which is a strength in our democracy.
>
> (quoted from *The Times*, 7 May 2003)

Sentencing procedure

There are various stages between establishing guilt and the passing of sentence. The sentence is not usually imposed immediately, unless the offence is of a very minor nature or if it is murder, for which life imprisonment is the mandatory, automatic sentence. The guilty defendant may ask for other offences to be taken into consideration, perhaps to indicate that a clean breast of past offences is being made. The defendant may personally or through legal representation put forward factors in mitigation (see p. 168). And the court may wish to look in more detail at the offender's circumstances, including mental and physical health. In addition, the court will consider reports from appropriate bodies such as the Probation Service and personal character references. So, there are a whole range of factors that are liable to influence the decision as to what sentence should be given, including the seriousness of the offence and the offender's previous record.

In spite of the sentencing guidelines, this leaves those who assign sentences – the judiciary – with a good deal of discretion – certainly compared to other countries, which have much more precise rules determining the passing of sentence. In the United States, sentencing guidelines have been established for more than a quarter of a century and have had a major influence on sentencing policy and practice. By introducing greater consistency into the sentencing process, guidelines have made it easier to predict sentencing outcome and the costs of these sentences. In most examples of these guidelines, two criteria are used to prescribe the punishment: the seriousness of the crime and the criminal history of the offender. Different states have their own guidelines, and they can be extremely detailed. North Carolina, for example, uses a matrix that separates its sentences into three categories: active punishments, including total confinement to prison; intermediate punishments, which might include sentences with elements of electronic monitoring or intensive supervision; and community punishments, which include probation, community service and fines. After an offender is placed within a range in the matrix, two further ranges are also used to take account of any aggravating or mitigating factors.

QUESTION BREAK

What factors do you feel should guide magistrates and judges in determining an appropriate sentence? Why should they?

Sentencing and social divisions

This section will consider the question of who gets sentenced – in particular, the influence that the ethnic, gender and class background of offenders has on the sentence they receive.

Race and sentencing

One of the most startling statistics regarding court sentences is the massive over-representation of ethnic minority populations among those who are sent to prison. Although ethnic minorities make up between 5 and 6 per cent of the population of England and Wales, data gathered by the Institute of Race Relations showed that in June 2000 ethnic minorities accounted for 19 per cent of the male prison population and 25 per cent of the female prison population. This over-representation is even more noticeable for specific ethnic minority groups. While around 1 per cent of the population are classified as of African or Caribbean origin, 12 per cent of male prisoners and 19 per cent of female prisoners are Afro-Caribbean (Institute of Race Relations 2002). The question this raises is whether these figures reflect a much greater propensity to commit crime among ethnic minority groups or whether they can be explained by other factors. Other factors that affect the prison statistics include the fact that the very high figure for Afro-Caribbean women is in part explained by the relatively large number of foreign nationals who are imprisoned for drug smuggling; plus the fact that women who are first-time offenders are more likely to be imprisoned than male first-time offenders. Demographic factors include the younger average age of the ethnic minority, and especially Afro-Caribbean, population – and young people are more likely to offend (or be caught, at least) than older people. In addition to this, Afro-Caribbean males are more likely to have other characteristics associated with higher offending rates – such as a greater chance of being unemployed, lower educational attainment on average, and a greater likelihood of living in an area with a high crime rate.

However, as regards sentencing practices, these points do not tell us whether the court system itself works differently for the different ethnic minority groups it deals with. Differential treatment in court is likely to occur as a result of black offenders pleading not guilty – for instance, 33 and 48 per cent of young black offenders plead not guilty in magistrates' and crown courts respectively, compared to 21 and 30 per cent for young white offenders. We have already seen that offenders are given heavier sentences if found guilty after entering a 'not guilty' plea – as a consequence of the 'discount' given for guilty pleas (see p. 169). Pleading not guilty can also influence the extent to which mitigating factors are taken into account in passing sentence. Pre-Sentence Reports (PSRs – previously known as SIRs) are prepared by the Probation Service and provide the courts with information on the circumstances of offenders. Pleading not guilty may affect whether an offender is provided with a PSR and also the recommendations made in such a report: it might be that pleading not guilty is interpreted as not facing up to one's guilt, which might influence the sort of sentence advocated in the report.

One of the largest and most detailed studies on sentencing in Britain was undertaken by Roger Hood (1992) for the Commission for Racial Equality. This study examined and tried to explain the over-representation of prisoners from an African or Caribbean background. The key issue Hood investigated was whether ethnic minority offenders are sentenced according to the same criteria as white offenders. Although it was difficult to pinpoint exact answers to that question, a number of relevant factors were highlighted. A higher proportion of black people were charged with offences that were deemed to be more serious and that could be dealt with only by the Crown Court – for instance, many more were charged with robbery. Although robbery is a nasty crime, it could be questioned whether it is any more serious than housebreaking or grievous bodily harm (GBH), both of which can be dealt with summarily by magistrates' courts if both parties consent. As regards the ranking of offences in terms of seriousness, black offenders were disproportionately charged with supplying drugs – and the insistence that offences involving trading in small or moderate amounts of cannabis should be committed to the crown court is also likely to influence the rate of imprisonment for black offenders. As well as being more likely to plead not guilty, black defendants were found to be more likely to be remanded in custody by magistrates – a factor which can, again, lead to a greater likelihood of a custodial sentence; it is difficult to prove that one has behaved well for a period of time after the offence if one is kept in custody.

Hood's research suggested that ethnic minority, and particularly black/Afro-Caribbean, defendants were subject to forms of indirect discrimination at least. The implications of a practice that favours so strongly those who plead guilty and the ways in which different offences are ranked in terms of where they should be tried, for example, would seem to work against the interests of ethnic minority offenders. Hood acknowledges that it is a complex issue, but on the basis of the detailed sample of almost three thousand crown court cases it would seem that some discrimination does occur in courts. And as Reiner (1997) argues, it does seem to be the case that with so many factors and people involved in decision making in the criminal justice system of England and Wales, even small degrees of ethnic bias and/or differential treatment could have a very large cumulative effect.

Gender and sentencing

The fact that about 94 per cent of prisoners in England and Wales are male can perhaps explain the common assumption that women are treated more leniently than men in the criminal justice system. This assumption is often referred to as the 'chivalry thesis', given that most criminal justice decision makers are male. A different interpretation sees the criminal justice system as treating women in a discriminatory and sexist manner which leads to women offenders being doubly punished – for breaking the law and for breaking from traditional expectations of gender role behaviour. This 'debate' will be introduced in this brief section.

Statistics seem at first sight to offer strong support for the chivalry notion. Even though the female prison population is the fastest growing of the whole prison estate, many more men than women are given custodial sentences – and longer ones as well. Similarly, males outnumber females in terms of crimes committed – in 1999, 511,000 people were found guilty or cautioned for indictable offences in England and Wales, and of these, almost 420,000 were male, around eight in ten (*Social Trends*, 2001).

Such figures do not, however, mean that women are necessarily dealt with more leniently than men, just that they are dealt with differently. In her study *Doubly Deviant, Doubly Damned*, Ann Lloyd (1995) examined the chivalry argument that the criminal justice system deals with women offenders in a more lenient manner than male offenders. She found that this might be the case for some women but not for all. In particular, chivalrous treatment from agencies such as the police and courts seemed to be limited to those women who were felt to conform to stereotypical views of how women should behave. In contrast, those women offenders who did not fit such a picture were treated with (even) less understanding than male offenders; they were seen as offending against the law and against generally held notions of 'good women'. Domesticity would appear to be a key issue as regards the sentencing of women: the family is often an important aspect of mitigation pleas, and the judiciary seem to be influenced by the impact of sentencing on children, although whether this influence works to the same extent for male as for female offenders is debatable.

QUESTION BREAK: WOMEN AND THE CRIMINAL JUSTICE SYSTEM

The extract below is taken from Ann Lloyd's study referred to in the previous sub-section.

The leniency or 'chivalry' argument is that women are treated more leniently by the courts simply because they are women. My argument is that while chivalry may well be extended to some women – those who conform to approved stereotypes – leniency will not be shown to 'deviant' women.

'If a woman conforms to a judge's idea of what is appropriate for a woman he will have trouble convicting her', Helena Kennedy told a conference at St. George's Medical School in 1991. 'Chivalry exists but it is very much limited to those women who are seen to conform.' She added that a woman who showed anger would be viewed as threatening by the court, which puts women who've been violent at particular risk of being treated more harshly than women who are perceived as conforming to notions of what constitutes proper womanhood. . . .

Another point to bear in mind when analysing statistics of conviction and sentencing rates is the influence of conventional stereotypical ideas and assumptions about women. . . .

Farrington and Morris noted that some factors (notably previous convictions) had an independent influence on sentence severity and reconviction for both men and women . . . others only had an influence for one sex. In particular, marital status, family background and children were more important for women than men. . . .

Working lawyers I've spoken to agree with these findings, and tell me that chivalry is very much limited to those women who are seen to conform. The criminal lawyer, the probation officer and the psychiatrist all know how the system works: judges and magistrates make decisions based on a division of 'good' and 'bad' women, so the defence team tailor what they do and say to try to ensure their clients approximate to that stereotype as closely as possible.

Lawyers may well be aware that these strategies are locking women into traditional stereotypes and may even question what they are doing to women in general. But their job is to do their best for the client. Helena Kennedy discusses these methods with women clients, trying to give them choices about what they want to do, telling them that if they turn up in a broderie anglaise blouse or a nice Marks and Spencer's dress they will be dealt with in a rather different way than if they turn up in bovver boots, sporting a spiky hair-do. . . .

[Also] where women can be shown to be mentally and emotionally unstable, they are likely to be treated more sympathetically than men. This viewing of women as unstable, though it may be advantageous to individual women, is a high price for all women to pay insofar as it is premised on a belief in women's inherent instability *per se*. It also raises questions about the unfairness of treating men as if they had no inner lives and therefore of denying psychiatric help to men who could benefit from it.

(Lloyd 1995, pp. 56–70)

Questions

Why do you think that Lloyd suggests that while treating women offenders in terms of stereo-typical views might benefit some women, 'it is a high price for all women to pay'?

To what extent should factors such as child-care influence the sentencing of women (and men)?

Look at recent press reports of crimes which involve both male and female defendants. Can you find any evidence for the chivalry argument?

Class and sentencing

As well as race and gender, it is important not to lose sight of the importance of social class background on justice received. However, social class is such a broad variable, and includes such a wide range of factors, including housing, income, wealth, status and power, that its influence is perhaps even more difficult to measure than that of race or gender. Issues around class and punishment were raised in examining theories of punishment (Chapter 2), and particularly arguments that there is 'one law for the rich and one for the poor'. In that context, class was considered in terms of the power some groups have to influence how certain types of behaviour are interpreted and defined as criminal. That said, social class position is conventionally determined by occupation, and we can raise a couple of points here with regard to its possible effect on sentencing.

Although attitudes towards unemployment may have changed as a result of mass unemployment in the 1970s and 1980s in particular, and while those passing sentence are probably more aware that unemployment is commonplace and not the individual's 'fault', traditional attitudes that 'people could find work if they really wanted to' might still be influential. There is a possibility that middle-class judges and magistrates (as the vast majority are) might see an employment record as evidence of stability and character and see unemployed people as lacking characteristics such as self-discipline and motivation. Furthermore, offenders who have jobs are likely to use their employment as a factor in mitigation, and it might seem sensible for sentencers to take account of the effect that losing a job would have on an offender (and his or her family) should he or she be sent to prison. If having a job is seen as a positive thing that might be used in mitigation, those who are unemployed might be deemed to have less to lose and therefore be sentenced more severely; while it is also more difficult to fine offenders who are not in work, so reducing the options available to sentencers.

QUESTION BREAK: CLASS IN COURT

Consider the following two cases: the theft of £500 worth of goods from a shop; and the embezzlement of £500 from a company's funds by a director.

Questions

How is each case likely to be dealt with?

How might this relate to social class?

Do you think that position in the community or 'respectability' should affect the sentence an offender receives?

(Adapted from McLaughlin and Muncie 1996, p. 148)

The judiciary

In this section we will look more closely at the appointment and background of the judiciary and at their role in the criminal justice system. There has been a massive increase in the number of judges and significant changes in the role of judges in the past thirty years or so, and certainly since the creation of the crown court in 1971. However, before looking at those judges who sit in the crown courts and higher courts, we will consider the judiciary who sit in the magistrates' courts.

Magistrates

As was detailed on p. 163, the judiciary in magistrates' courts is dominated by the 30,000-plus lay magistrates, known as JPs, who are supported by around one hundred full-time, professional magistrates, known as district judges. There has been a movement in the direction of a more professionalised magistracy in recent years, partly as a result of the increasing workload of magistrates' courts and the difficulty of recruiting enough lay magistrates. Although the number of district judges serving in magistrates' courts is relatively small, there have been concerns that in due course they will undermine the 'local' character of the English and Welsh justice system. In assessing the impact of stipendiary magistrates (the name given to professional magistrates up to 2000, when the term 'district judge' was introduced), Seago *et al.* (2000) found that they had had little impact on the work cultures or procedures in magistrates' courts. They dealt with cases more quickly than the lay magistrates, although this was due in part to the fact that as they sat alone in court, they had no need to confer with other magistrates, and as they were legally trained professionals, they had less need for advice from justices' clerks. Seago *et al.* argue that any wholesale replacement of lay magistrates by professionally trained magistrates would 'dilute the fundamental principles of citizenship and democracy', as well as being much more expensive.

QUESTION BREAK: LOCAL JUSTICE

Apart from its being more expensive, suggest the advantages and disadvantages of a more centralised and professional rather than local and 'lay' magistracy.

Magistrates are appointed in the name of the Queen by the Lord Chancellor, who is advised by almost one hundred advisory committees whose membership has traditionally been secret so as to prevent canvassing by would-be magistrates. In recent years this secrecy has been reduced, with successive Lord Chancellors trying to broaden and democratise the ranks of magistracy. There have been occasional advertisements in the press to encourage a wider range of candidates; however, personal recommendations from existing magistrates or locally respected organisations still play a major role in determining who is appointed. The selection process is, though, rigorous, with local advisory committees conducting interviews and turning down about three-quarters of applicants, often in the interests of getting a more balanced bench. While lay magistrates do undergo some training, it is not intended to turn them into professionals; indeed, magistrates are not encouraged to sit too often (or too infrequently), so as to prevent them from becoming 'case-hardened'.

Certain groups of the population are better suited to fitting in with the working patterns of lay magistrates than others in that not everyone can spare the time, or risk the financial loss, to sit as magistrates. As a result, groups who tend to be well represented on the bench include retired people, housewives with adult children, and the more senior teachers. That said, the ranks of JPs have broadened and include people from many different backgrounds and occupations.

Compared to the senior judiciary, there has been less research on the background and attitudes of magistrates. However, one study which did focus on the ideology of magistrates and how this influences their 'performance' in court in terms of their sentencing of offenders was undertaken by Parker et al. (1989) and is considered in the case study below.

DECIDING THE SENTENCE

In their study *Unmasking the Magistrates*, Parker et al. (1989) examined the factors that influence the way in which magistrates sentence offenders. On the basis of first-hand research across a number of magistrates' courts, they considered how magistrates sift and evaluate all the information they are presented with in court and how they arrive at a particular decision. Social Enquiry Reports (now called Pre-Sentence Reports) seemed to be treated with some misgivings by magistrates – an attitude that stemmed from an implicit criticism of the social work profession, based on very stereotypical views and illustrated by comments such as:

> 'Some social workers are very put out if you don't accept their recommendations, but they're often not realistic, recommending conditional discharges all the time. The best social workers have been

lost to early retirement. The new breed of whiz kids go to Keele for two years, have their brains removed, get a plastic card with their picture on it and think they're a social worker.'

(p. 95)

and

'I can remember that probation officer hitch-hiking round Europe with a guitar and a little rucksack. He had hair down to his shoulders and a beard to his navel. People of that kind are likely to take a lenient view of crime.'

(p. 95)

While possibly tongue-in-cheek, such comments from practising magistrates indicate rather narrow-minded and conservative attitudes. By contrast, school reports were generally well received by magistrates and seen as more reliable. Like social workers, defence lawyers were seen as not trustworthy and as being too much on the defendant's side.

As well as information from reports, there is also an element of assessment of the defendant's appearance and demeanour, with magistrates feeling they have the ability to assess a defendant's character almost at first sight. One of the interviewed magistrates said, '[T]hat girl had no intention of going to school ... she had her story off pat ... then when she turned away and I saw her split skirt and high heels, I thought, "you'll be on the game in a year or two".'

(p. 102)

While many factors interact and combine to determine a sentence, in particular the seriousness of the offence and the previous record of the offender, what is surprising is the weight magistrates gave to their own moral assessment of defendants. Parker *et al*. concluded that it is no wonder sentencing patterns are so difficult to explain. Although on one level it is true that 'every case is different', magistrates seemed to resist the principle of treating cases alike, and those interviewed in this study seemed to think that being consistent was being too rigid. The magistrates appeared to view sentencing as something of an art rather than a science and were very sceptical towards sentencing guidelines.

Judges

Although the judiciary, and especially the 'senior' judiciary, is an institution heavily steeped in tradition and very protective of its independence, the growth in the number of judges in recent years has helped to encourage a greater openness and democracy. In her examination of the effects of this expansion on the appointment, training and monitoring of what she terms the 'new judiciary', Malleson points out that 'the recent introduction of public advertisements, interview panels and job descriptions would have been almost unthinkable 30 years ago' (1999, p. 2). In spite of these changes and the fact that judges are more subject to media scrutiny and are more willing to engage in public debate, there is also a great reluctance to depart from traditional practices. In 1992, for instance, the Lord Chief Justice proposed the abolition of wigs – a suggestion that was swiftly defeated by opposition from other members of the senior judiciary. Such unwillingness to change is likely to reinforce the image of the judiciary as an archaic institution. In this section we will follow Malleson's approach and consider the appointment, background, training and accountability of judges.

Appointment and background

The appointment of judges is in the government's hands, through the Lord Chancellor's Department (the Lord Chancellor is a member of the government, although the Blair government is considering abolishing this office). As well as being responsible for appointing judges, including magistrates (see p. 179), the Lord Chancellor also decides which barristers are awarded the coveted title of Queen's Counsel (QC), and the great majority of senior judges are appointed from the ranks of QCs. Before recommending the appointment of a judge or a QC, the Lord Chancellor's Department will consult judges and senior legal figures for their opinions on the suitability of prospective candidates, these consultations being known as 'secret soundings'. This informal process originates from the time when the Lord Chancellor would personally know all the applicants because of the small group from which selection took place. However, in spite of the recent expansion of the judiciary and the increase in part-time appointments and the consequent growth in promotions within the judiciary, the appointment process is still typified by informality and secrecy.

With the increase in the number of judicial appointments, interview panels have become much more widespread and occur for all the 'lower' appointments – so district judges, assistant recorders, recorders and circuit judges all attend interview panels, although these panels are only one part of the appointment process and only make recommendations. As attempts are being made to broaden the spread of applicants, advertisements have also become more common, and there have even been adverts for High Court judges since 1998. Again, advertising has been seen as only a supplement to other information and not as a replacement for the traditional system of 'secret soundings' whereby likely candidates are asked to apply.

The appointment process has been criticised for encouraging self-replication among the judiciary; and in spite of the changes mentioned above, judges are still overwhelmingly white, male barristers over the age of fifty who have had a private education followed by an Oxbridge university education. The choice of senior judges is limited by the fact that they are invariably chosen from the most experienced barristers. This severely restricts access to the judiciary, as training to be a barrister has conventionally involved having to have a private means of funding for the early years of practice. However, it is becoming easier for newly qualified barristers to earn an adequate income, which should help encourage a less exclusive recruitment, as well as opening up access to the judiciary to solicitors as well as barristers.

The judiciary, and particularly the senior judges, remain a very privileged and atypical group. Of the first eighty-five judges appointed since the Labour Party's election to power in 1997, only seven were women and only one of these made it to the High Court bench. Ethnic minorities still account for fewer than 1 per cent of judges, with none at High Court level or above by 1999. And nearly 80 per cent of judges appointed or promoted between 1997 and 1999 were educated at public schools. Judges earn high salaries that have increased relative to average pay rises in recent years. It was announced in February 2003 that the Lord Chief Justice, for instance, will receive an additional £10,000 a year as well as a 7 per cent salary rise, taking his overall pay to over £200,000 a year. There were similar rises for other senior judges, with Appeal Court judges getting £166,394, High Court judges £147,198 and circuit judges £110,362. It has been argued these sorts of pay rises are necessary to attract suitable recruits to the judiciary, given that it is possible for top legal experts to earn substantially more money in other forms of legal work; and judges would argue that senior positions in other walks of life are also very well paid. Nonetheless, the restricted social background from which senior judges come and their high salaries do raise issues as to their understanding of and empathy with the wider population.

Of course, when we look at the senior judiciary it should be borne in mind that the same comments about background and exclusivity could be applied to the upper echelons of other key institutions in Britain, such as the army, Church and civil service. As regards judges, it is clear that the appointments system lacks transparency and helps to perpetuate a white, male judiciary drawn from a narrow social group. This has led to pressure for some form of judicial appointments committee, an idea which seems to have support from the current government and from Lord Falconer, the current Lord Chancellor, and Lord Irvine, his predecessor. Judicial appointments commissions are used in a number of countries and do appear to generate greater public confidence in the appointments process and in turn in the judges themselves. However, senior judges have spoken out against changes to the appointments system. In 1999, when he was Lord Chief Justice, Lord Bingham insisted that this system was 'as good as any to be found anywhere in the world' and dismissed arguments for a more transparent selection procedure with candidates being sifted by a judicial appointments commission. He described the present system as 'extraordinarily thorough and comprehensive and extraordinarily successful', adding that a system of selection which produces 'a high quality product cannot be as bad as suggested' (quoted in the *Guardian*, 1 June 1999).

QUESTION BREAK: BECOMING A QC

Read the following extract on how to become a QC

Smoothing the way to silk

- Applicants must be a barrister or solicitor with rights of advocacy in the higher courts. Should have at least 10 years' experience.
- Candidates should pay a fee of £720 and fill in a form which includes self-assessment and the names of up to six 'nominated consultees'.
- Details of all applicants sent to 300 automatic consultees – senior judges and leading members of the legal profession. All are asked to comment on the applicants' suitability.
- Officials from the Lord Chancellor's Department hold meetings with senior judges, leaders of the bar's circuits and officers of the Bar Council to obtain their views.

- Applications sifted by a senior official, who identifies candidates worthy of the Lord Chancellor's consideration, divided into an A list (strong support) and B list (less strong support but warranting consideration). Most candidates do not make it on to either list.
- Lord Chancellor is given a briefing on applicants on A and B list.
- Lord Chancellor discuss briefings with heads of the high courts divisions, attorney general and solicitor general before deciding on the successful applicants.

(*Guardian*, 8 October 2002, 'Judge Selection Found to Lack Transparency')

Questions

What effects will this process have on the make-up of the judiciary? (Try to consider both beneficial and less beneficial effects.)

Does the social background of judges matter? If so, why? (You might consider whether you think it will affect their interpretation of the law.)

Training

As the judiciary has grown and become (slightly) more open, so there have been developments in judicial training. Until around thirty years ago, training for judges was non-existent; it was felt to be unnecessary and a threat to the independence so valued by judges. Since the introduction of the Judicial Studies Board in 1979, training has become much more established and accepted. The Board is chaired and run by judges with some academic input and has become generally well regarded by judges. However, the amount of training undertaken by judges is still limited: crown court judges' training, for instance, amounts to a four-day residential course and the shadowing of an experienced judge for another ten days.

Malleson (1999) found that courses run by the Judicial Studies Board were generally felt to be of high quality and that judges were aware and supportive of the need for training, given the growing complexity of their jobs. The range of training has also needed to expand, given the speed of changes to the law and the growing diversity of the population; advice and training on matters of race are provided by the Board, for instance.

Accountability and independence

Judges have not been subject to the sort of accountability found in virtually all other professions and applied to senior officials in other spheres of public service. Their lack of accountability has been due to judges (in particular) arguing that accountability would threaten their independence. The principle of judicial independence is based on the notion that there should be a clear separation of powers between the executive (government), the legislature (Parliament) and the judiciary. This separation, it is argued, ensures that judges are able to balance competing interests and that they will not feel under pressure from the government, for example, to come to particular decisions because they fear their position may be threatened. Malleson argues that in practice this separation of powers is by no means clear-cut, with the government appointing and paying judges and with all senior judges being members of the House of Lords.

Like any powerful group, the judiciary have a vested interest in maintaining their independence and avoiding critical scrutiny. This does not mean they have anything to hide, and judges would argue that they are bound to make unpopular decisions, therefore there is always a danger of improper interference in their decision-making processes. Judges themselves might say that they are not free to express their views, that they are bound by precedent and duty. However, the law is often not clear, and judges do have a fair degree of discretion in terms of how it is interpreted. It is likely, and hardly surprising, that judges, like anyone else, will make decisions on the basis of their own values. And in the case of judges, given their backgrounds and training, these values are likely to be conventional and conservative. This is not to say that judges deliberately attempt to impose their views when judging, but it does raise the question of whether there can ever be a 'neutral' decision, as any choice will represent some set of values.

Although there may be a general level of respect for judges, confidence in them seems to have fallen in recent years, and criticism of judges for being too lenient or too harsh has encouraged a closer scrutiny. As with the appointing and training of judges, there have been moves towards greater openness with regard to judicial practice. And again as with these other areas, the introduction of greater accountability has mainly applied to the lower ranks of the judiciary, with the way they are 'appointed, trained and monitored [being] significantly different from that of the higher judiciary' (Malleson 1999, p. 233).

However, apart from in cases of extreme misconduct, judges are still virtually unaccountable for how they behave when sitting as judges, and the removal of a judge from office is almost impossible. The Lord Chancellor is able to admonish a judge with a public rebuke, but this again is an extremely rare occurrence. There have been changes in what judges can say in court, with rudeness and intolerance – for instance, sexist or racist behaviour – no longer acceptable. It remains the case, though, that 'judges remain almost immune from the consequences of all but the most extreme forms of misconduct or incompetent behaviour' (Malleson 1999, p. 230).

QUESTION BREAK: JUDICIAL ACCOUNTABILITY

Incompetent judges do not get the sack

Judges enjoy the privilege of being almost entirely unaccountable for poor work. . . .
Judges enjoy this immunity from the normal hazards of employment because of their constitutional position. Security of tenure underpins judicial independence and ensures that judges can rule against ministers or governments without an eye to promotion.

High Court judges can be removed from office only by the Queen after a vote by both Houses of Parliament and none ever has. Circuit judges can be dismissed for incapacity or misbehaviour by the Lord Chancellor.

That hardly ever happens. Only one, Judge Bruce Campbell, has been sacked this century, after pleading guilty to a smuggling offence.

(Adapted from F. Gibb, 'Incompetent Judges Do Not Get the Sack',
The Times, 9 July 1998)

Questions

Suggest the advantages and disadvantages that might come from greater judicial accountability.

What arguments are there for judges being 'above the law'? Do you agree with them?

A changing judiciary?

The size and influence of the judiciary have grown enormously in the past thirty or so years. In concluding her account of the developments that have taken place in the appointment, training and accountability of judges as a result of these changes, Malleson suggests that

Thirty years ago the judiciary was a largely self-selecting, self-regulating and self-taught body which operated its own informal rules almost entirely free of external scrutiny. . . . The consequence of pressure for changes has been that the elitism, secrecy and amateurism which were traditionally the hallmarks of the judiciary are slowly being replaced by diversification, openness and professionalism.

(1999, p. 233)

QUESTION BREAK

Using evidence from this section and from other sources, to what extent do you agree with Malleson's comment?

How much discretion do you feel judges should have?

SENTENCING ACTIVITY

The training for those who have been appointed as judges in the crown courts and higher courts involves doing 'sentencing exercises' in which they consider what sentence they would give for particular cases. The scenarios surrounding two cases are set out below. Read them and consider the issues listed after them. Then decide how, as a judge, you would sentence.

Susan's case

On a night out, Susan's husband gets into a fight in a club. At the end of the incident, Susan throws a half-pint glass across the room. It hits an innocent bystander, who is injured and loses the sight in one of his eyes.

Susan is charged with grievous bodily harm. She pleads not guilty. She has no previous convictions. She has children to look after. Her husband has already received a custodial sentence for his part in the incident.

Should Susan get either (a) a custodial sentence; (b) a suspended sentence; or (c) community service?

What issues do you need to taken into consideration?

Tyrone's case

When drunk, Tyrone followed a woman into a lift in a block of flats. He indecently assaulted her. Her screams led to his being arrested.

Tyrone is charged with indecent assault. He had previous convictions (including for rape). He pleaded guilty and is very remorseful. The assault was not premeditated. He says he has given up drink. He is receptive to treatment.

What sentence should Tyrone receive?

What issues do you need to take into consideration?

(*Answer*: These were based on real cases. Susan was given a twelve-month custodial sentence and Tyrone an eighteen-month sentence.)

Further reading

Griffiths, J. A. G. (1997) *The Politics of the Judiciary*, 5th edn, London: Fontana. First published in 1981 and now in its fifth edition, this has established itself as the definitive text on the role of the judiciary. Specific cases are used to question the impartiality of the judiciary.

Malleson, K. (1999) *The New Judiciary: The Effects of Expansion and Activism*, Dartmouth: Ashgate. A detailed examination of the developments in the appointment, training and scrutiny of judges as a result of the massive expansion in the size and power of the judiciary over the past thirty or so years. In particular, it highlights the tension between, on the one hand, the requirements that judges be independent, and, on the other, the need for them to be accountable.

Watkins, M. and Gordon, W. (2000) *The Sentence of the Court: A Handbook for Magistrates*, Winchester: Waterside Press. This is a very clear introduction to and outline of the law and practice of sentencing in magistrates' courts, where the vast majority of criminal trails are conducted.

The following Web sites provide plenty of current information on the judiciary. The Judicial Studies Board is the body which provides training and instruction for all judges, while the Magistrates Association applies particularly to magistrates.

www.jsboard.co.uk
www.magistrates-association.org.uk

7 Prisons and imprisonment

The history of prisons

When we examined the history of punishment (Chapter 3), a good deal of the focus was on the history of imprisonment. Essentially, this was because when considering history, punishment is often used almost synonymously with imprisonment – so, for example, an examination of the history of the different approaches to punishment, such as retribution and deterrence, is typically based around changes in the forms and styles of incarceration. We will not, therefore, need to delve into the origins and history of imprisonment in great detail in this chapter, or catalogue the various pieces of legislation. However, a brief overview of the key periods in the development of the prison in the past two hundred or so years will help provide the context for looking at the contemporary prison system and the major current issues that face it.

Prison histories of the past two hundred-plus years generally highlight three major periods which were characterised by differing rationales for prison and imprisonment. In the late eighteenth and early nineteenth centuries the emphasis was on reform – of both prisons and prisoners – and this period saw what Foucault described as the 'birth of the modern prison'. In the mid-nineteenth century a much more repressive approach was adopted. Partly as a reaction to this, by the end of the nineteenth century and into the twentieth century, new notions of reform and rehabilitation emerged. Of course, the history of imprisoning people goes back much further than the eighteenth century. Holding people before some form of trial, not necessarily in purpose-built prisons but perhaps in castles, goes back centuries. Private gaols existed from at least 1166 (when Henry II tried to set up a gaol in every English county) through to the eighteenth century; these were often privately run, commercial undertakings with prisoners charged for food and other services (including the hammering on and off of leg irons), and conditions – for those with no money, at least – dreadful.

Although our starting period here is the reforms of the late eighteenth century, there were examples of more humane, reformative approaches prior to this. While there are different interpretations for the emergence of the houses of correction in the sixteenth century, such a development certainly suggests an early reformative interest and agenda (see p. 64).

Early reforms: the late eighteenth century

Throughout the eighteenth century, prison conditions continued to be appalling. It was commonplace for there to be no segregation of men, women or children, no classifying of offenders (even between tried and untried), the sale of alcohol, and extortion by prison staff, among other things. These sorts of conditions were described most graphically by John Howard (examples of whose writings on the state of prisons can be found in most texts covering the history of prisons). Howard made a detailed survey of the state of prisons in the 1770s and argued that prisons should operate as secure but healthy and efficient institutions. His inspections and writings did have an impact. The 1779 Penitentiary Act, for instance, promoted the view that prison should have both a punitive and a reformative purpose – the very name 'penitentiary' implies prisoners being sorry or repentant for their behaviour, and thinking about it while doing some penance. More specifically, prisoners were to be put to hard work, with any profits earned from this work being used to improve prisons (with the notion of paying staff introduced). It was believed that the stress on hard physical work would be morally and physically helpful for offenders. Also, there was a move to start classifying prisoners into different categories. In highlighting the importance of the 1779 Act, Wilson (2002) commented that

> [It] synthesised everything that was believed at that time about what should be done with prisoners, in that they were to be subjected to solitary confinement, have regular religious instruction, be required to work – but not for profit, would have to wear a uniform, and be subjected to a coarse diet.

Following on from Howard's account of prison regimes and the 1779 Act, there was a spate of prison building in the late eighteenth and early nineteenth centuries. Another key factor behind the expansion of prisons at this time was the ending of transportation to America after the American Declaration of Independence in 1776. Transportation to Botany Bay, Australia, did not begin until 1787, and as an estimated 30,000 people had been transported to America between 1718 and 1775, the authorities were left with a problem as to what they should do with lawbreakers who would not be executed (Wilson 2002). The culmination of these developments was the opening in 1842 of Pentonville Prison in London. This was seen as the 'model prison' and demonstrated the transformation from the small, privately run prisons of the past. It had five hundred identical cells in which prisoners lived separately and in silence; they followed a detailed, meticulous routine, in line with that described by Foucault at the start of his famous account of the 'birth of the prison' in *Discipline and Punish* (1977). Foucault examined prisons alongside the development of other institutions, such as the new factories of the Industrial Revolution period, workhouses for the poor and asylums for the insane, and saw them as making up what he termed the 'great confinement' (see pp. 47–55 for a fuller discussion of Foucault's account). The better-regulated sort of prisons advocated by Howard can be compared to the sort of managerial changes going on in the mills and factories of the period, and often run by philanthropists with similar ideas to those of Howard, such as Arkwright (mills) and Wedgwood (pottery). The move away from public and local-ised punishments, including privately run local jails, to the 'reformed', state-financed and state-managed penitentiaries of the nineteenth century was completed by the Prison Act of 1877, which placed the entire penal system under state control.

There are two main theoretical positions that have put forward explanations for this move to reform prisons in the late eighteenth century: a *humanitarian* model that saw idealism and philanthropy as the key factors and a *radical* model that emphasised the regulation of dangerous groups. The basic question posed by the 'debate' between these two positions was whether the new prisons indicate a humanitarian idealism or a more insidious regulation of the 'deviant' lower classes.

The humanitarian explanation makes the point that the eighteenth-century penal reformers were invariably motivated by a strong religious faith and believed that they were pursuing an idealistic mission. In addition to this, a more general humanitarian mood was evidenced by the fact that there was also a good deal of public concern and even revulsion about the extent of capital and corporal punishments. This view of history is associated with the political position of the Whigs (a viewpoint which became almost synonymous with the Liberal Party after the early nineteenth century). Such an inter-pretation of history sees the ideas and visions of key individuals as being the major factor affecting social change and moving history along. Change and reform, then, are seen as motivated by benevolence and philanthropy, and histories advocating this approach tend to highlight and glorify the role played by a few great individuals. As regards the history of punishment and prisons, the starting point tends to be Beccaria's condemnation of unjust penalties (and particularly the death penalty) in his treatise *An Essay on Crimes and Punishments* (1764), the seminal text in the application of classicist and utilitarian philosophy to punishment and justice. Beccaria's legacy was taken on and practically applied to the criminal justice process by Jeremy Bentham; while other key figures in this humanitarian history included John Howard and Elizabeth Fry (see p. 69 for fuller discussion of the importance of these early penal reformers).

The radical explanation and model for the emergence of prisons has been seen as part of a more critical 'revisionist' history (Mathews 1999) that has seen the humanitarianism of this period as being more rhetoric than reality. The emphasis here is on social con-trol born out of class conflict and the attendant fears and the protecting of the vested interests of powerful groups in society. There are different variations of this broad approach, in particular an orthodox Marxist position, exemplified by Rusche and Kirchheimer's classic work (see pp. 40–43), whereby punishment is seen as helping to maintain a cheap and reliable workforce, and a position adopted by theorists such as Foucault and Ignatieff which focuses more on the ideological and political elements involved in establishing and maintaining order (Muncie 1996). Both Foucault (1977) and Ignatieff (1978) described the move from punishments of the body to those of the mind. Ignatieff emphasised the ideological and symbolic functions of the new forms of punishment centred around imprisonment (such as the treadmill and crank), and considered their role in maintaining order. Foucault's attention was more on the power of ideas, knowledge and discourses, and he interpreted the various reforms and penal developments as part of an emerging 'carceral society' (see p. 52).

The nineteenth century: (a return to) repressive measures

Following on from the pioneering work of John Howard and other early penal reformers, there were improvements to certain aspects of penal policy in the nineteenth century. However, although physical punishments, such as public whippings and corporal punishment in general, declined, there was also a clear decline in the support for the reformation of prisons. This reaction to the early reforms described above occurred in tandem with a strong push towards a greater centralisation of prisons, with a more uniform and rational prison regime introduced across the country. These developments were evidenced by the rigid application of strict rules and a strong emphasis on obedience, with the nineteenth-century prisons becoming impersonal and highly regimented institutions, characterised by an array of internal disciplinary procedures and punishments attached to all aspects of daily prison life (for example, prisoners being allowed to eat only after they had completed certain tasks – such as turning the crank a specified number of times). This repressive approach was well established and widely supported by the mid-1800s, helped by the panic over street crimes such as garrotting in the 1860s and given governmental backing by the Carnarvon Report (1864), which highlighted an 'insufficiency of penal discipline'. The language of this report, while typical of the time, was indicative of this more repressive approach: 'the large majority of criminals were low and brutish, mainly swayed by self gratification and animal appetite' (quoted in Muncie 1996, p. 186).

The mid-nineteenth century also saw the establishment of the separate cell system. In general terms, then, prisons were extremely harsh and austere establishments up until the 1890s, and completely lacking the religious and moral overtones of the early nineteenth century. Of course, these comments provide only the overall picture and highlight the general tenor of the time. It is important to remember that even at the same time as an overall move to greater discipline and repression was taking place, there were still some reformist moves and developments, such as attempts to classify and categorise different groups of prisoners, reflecting a realisation that not all fitted the 'brutish animal' stereotype.

QUESTION BREAK: HARD LABOUR IN VICTORIAN PRISONS

The extract that follows is taken from Priestley's study of Victorian prison lives and refers to one of the common forms of hard labour expected of prisoners: oakum picking (oakum was the old tarred ropes of ships' rigging, from an inch upwards in thickness).

Three images dramatise Victorian prison work in the popular imagination: men climbing the endless staircase of the treadwheel; convicts breaking rocks; and the picking of Oakum. Oakum was picked by prisoners in cells and workhouses for the greater part of the nineteenth century. . . .

Oakum was extremely dirty: after working for an hour or so one's fingers would be covered with tar, and stick to everything you touched. . . .

To the dirt and the difficulty was added, under the threat of punishment, the daily 'task', that of picking 'three pounds per diem' ... [and] every day several [were] reported just by way of keeping the discipline up to the recognised standard of severity. ...

Oakum was a difficult and dirty and distressing occupation. ... But it went on being picked, because of its simplicity and its tediousness and because no one could think of any better way of keeping so many unskilled hands from idleness. ... Its great convenience, though, was as cell tasks for men in separate confinement, where it continued to keep afloat the leaky vessel of penal labour policy until into the twentieth century.

(Priestley 1985, pp. 121–123)

Questions

How might hard prison labour be seen to provide the potential to reform prisoners?

What sort of theoretical explanations could be offered for forcing prisoners to engage in hard labour for no other purpose than to keep them busy?

New approaches to reform and rehabilitation: the late nineteenth and early twentieth centuries

As mentioned above, at the same time as the imposition of harsh and repressive regimes within prisons, there was also the introduction of some reformative measures. In the latter part of the nineteenth century there were attempts to classify prisoners and, in particular, to focus on young offenders and to ensure that they were not subject to the same regimes as older prisoners. A key figure here is Mary Carpenter, who campaigned for young offenders to be placed in educational homes and who helped establish 'reformatory schools' as a separate class of penal institution, and one that developed into the approved schools at the start of the twentieth century. Apart from juveniles, there was little differentiation of prisoners, even between male and female regimes, up until the 1890s. However, by the end of the nineteenth century the harsh prison regime was being questioned, fuelled in part by the high cost of prisons and continued high rates of recidivism. These concerns were clearly evident in the Gladstone Report of 1895, which emphasised reformation and rehabilitation, and helped pave the way for a more scientific, treatment-based model and regime to emerge.

Changes to the prison regime from 1900 included the replacement of unproductive labour for the sake of it with more useful work, with particular prison industries being developed, the phasing out of the separate system and an increase in association between prisoners. The Borstal system, based around indeterminate sentences (see p. 23) and the notion that juveniles should leave custody when they had demonstrated that they had been rehabilitated, was introduced for young offenders. As well as changes within the prison regime, the most significant developments in punishment and criminal justice in the early years of the twentieth century occurred outside of the prison, with the Probation Service being established by the Probation of Offenders Act of 1907. Building on the work of police court missionaries, probation was made available for those found guilty of all offences except murder and treason, and involved the offender being supervised by a probation officer, whose basic duty, according to the Act, was 'to advise, assist and befriend' the offender (see p. 212 for more detail).

This brief history of the emergence of the modern prison system should not necessarily be interpreted as an uninterrupted movement from harshness to greater humanitarianism. While being in a nineteenth-century prison might be considered preferable to being faced with the 'Bloody Code' of the late eighteenth century when there were so many capital offences, whether the mid-Victorian prison regimes based around solitary confinement and hard unproductive labour were 'better' than the houses of correction of the seventeenth century (see p. 64) is perhaps debatable. Indeed, this raises the general issue of whether punishment aimed at the mind is any more rational and humane than that aimed at the body.

Prisons and imprisonment: the current context

Probably the most crucial current issue facing the prison service is the massive increase in the prison population in recent years. Moreover, there seems to be a general assumption and an acceptance of the fact that the number of prisoners will continue to rise. However, the continual year-on-year rise in these numbers is not inevitable. As recently as the 1980s, the prison population remained relatively stable, and it is only since 1993 and the hardline policy promoted by the then Home Secretary, Michael Howard, that the prison population in England and Wales has risen at what can only be described as a phenomenal rate. This situation mirrors to some extent that of the United States and raises the question as to whether the United Kingdom will follow the sort of 'mass incarceration' being experienced there. With that in mind, it would be useful to say something about the United States' jail situation by way of comparison.

In terms of the major aims of punishment, it would seem that deterrence, reform and even retribution have become less important than just incarceration as a basic justification for imprisonment. The United States contains roughly 5 per cent of the world's population yet is responsible for about 25 per cent of the world's prisoners and has a higher proportion of its citizens in prison than any other country. This type of mass imprisonment has been justified on a sort of cost–benefit basis. As crime rates in the United States have fallen in the past few years, and with estimates of the cost of the average crime put at $300, with the average criminal committing fifteen crimes a year, it can be seen how an 'economic argument' might be made for putting more offenders in prison. In addition, the fact that prisons in the United States are quite efficient adds another element to this utilitarian calculation and approach.

A containment strategy, though, is very different from the 'traditional' aims of punishment and imprisonment. Deterrent, retributive and reformist justifications for imprisonment recognise the human nature of offenders and their capacity for choice. Containment and incapacitation require little acknowledgement of the human and moral nature of offenders – rather, they represent a sort of social hygiene approach that assumes it is not worth bothering to try to intervene or influence them. Of course, it may be that indefinite containment is the only option for certain offenders from whom the wider public need to be protected. However, on a widespread scale, such an approach and policy is based on a pretty depressing picture of humanity and on the notion that people do not change much (and that even if they may change for the better, it is impossible to know for sure that this has happened and so it is safer and easier to assume they cannot).

QUESTION BREAK: INCAPACITATION

There would appear to be a lot of public support for a hardline, containment-style policy both in the United States and in the United Kingdom.

Questions

Why do you think a containment/incapacitation approach might be popular?

What arguments can you think of to suggest that people (a) can change and be reformed; and (b) are essentially unchangeable?

To return to the British context, it is commonly held that the expansion of the prison population constitutes a 'penal crisis'. We will consider this notion of a crisis in relation to four main areas: numbers and cost; conditions; security and containment; and legitimacy. This will provide a structure for examining some of the major current issues that are faced by the Prison Service. Before we look at the prison population, a brief comment on the notion of 'penal crisis' might be appropriate. For many years, commentators have described the British prison system as being in crisis – over twenty years ago, for instance, Bottoms wrote a study entitled *The Coming Penal Crisis* (1980); and reference to the British prison system as being in such a state would seem to be generally and widely accepted. This, though, does beg the question of what constitutes a crisis in the prison context. If a crisis is viewed as something that is relatively rare and takes place over a short period of time (Sparks 1996), it is perhaps debatable how useful it is to describe the current situation. As Cavadino (1992) put it, 'how long can a situation remain at crisis point before it is not a crisis?'. However accurate or appropriate the term 'crisis' might be, it is clear that the British prison service has faced many problems throughout its existence and that now, in the twenty-first century, these problems are arguably greater than ever. And whether we use the dramatic term 'crisis' or not, it is important to examine the current state of the prison system and how the different problems it faces relate to one another.

Numbers and cost

The size of the prison population is commented on regularly in the press, and in recent years these figures have been setting new records on an almost weekly basis. Official figures can be found in Home Office publications such as the *Annual Abstract of Statistics* and *Social Trends*. Here we can provide only a snapshot picture of the current situation.

Despite different initiatives over the years, there has been little effect on the size of the prison population or on rates of reoffending, both of which have risen inexorably. Although there have been slight dips in the prison population from time to time, for instance in the late 1980s, the overall trend has been a regular and pretty continual rise. In January 2003, Alan Travis, *Guardian* Home Affairs editor, reported that 'the lord chancellor admitted yesterday that the record jail population of 72,522 in England and Wales was insupportable' (*Guardian*, 7 January 2003). While projecting the future prison population is a tricky task, recent estimates from the Office for National Statistics suggest that it will rise to over 100,000 before the end of the current decade. This sort of rise is likely because of the government's target of ensuring that more offenders are 'brought to book' (and if there are more convictions, there will inevitably be more people sent to prison). These record numbers demonstrate quite a change from the situation just over fifty years ago, when there were roughly 15,000 prisoners in forty prisons. In terms of more recent comparisons, the number of prisoners in England and Wales has increased by over 25,000 during the past ten years; and when the Labour government took office in May 1997, the prison population was 60,131 (over 12,000 less than it is at the time of writing – early 2003).

Within the overall prison population figures there are different categories of prisoner, and one area of particular 'growth' has been in the number of women prisoners. Between 1992 and 2002 the female prison population rose from 1,577 to 4,408, an increase of 179 per cent (we will consider women prisoners as a separate group – see pp. 205–208). As regards the overall numbers, much of the recent rise can be explained by the increase in the numbers of long-term prisoners, including those serving life sentences.

Long-term prisoners

Although most prison sentences are relatively short, the number of long-term prisoners has increased enormously over the past few years. There were 24,520 male prisoners serving four years or over in June 2002, compared to 14,000 in 1991; and the number of life-sentence prisoners increased from less than 4,000 in 1998 to 5,150 by June 2002. Over a slightly longer period, 88 new prisoners were sentenced to ten or more years in 1965, compared to 556 in 1995 and 862 in 2000. As well as there being more long-term and life-sentence prisoners, those who are sentenced to life serve longer in prison than they used to: the average time for a lifer in 1985 was just under eleven years, whereas in 1999/2000 it was around fourteen years (figures from Prison Reform Trust; and see Morgan 2002). More recently, and in an attempt to halt this upward drift in the number of years served by life-sentence prisoners, in 2002 the Lord Chief Justice published guidelines cutting the minimum sentence for offenders convicted of murders to twelve years rather than fourteen. However, the effects of this are likely to be mitigated because adult murderers involved in the most serious cases will now serve a longer minimum term of sixteen years and those convicted of the most serious murders will be given a minimum term with little or no hope of release – so serial killers, for instance, will serve a minimum of thirty years.

The Lord Chief Justice's guidelines were undermined by the Home Secretary, David Blunkett, in May 2003 in an attack on 'inconsistent' judges in which he insisted that

Parliament must have the right to lay down the principles of sentencing. The Home Secretary said that anyone who abducts and murders a child should die in jail, rather than face the current penalty of a twenty-year minimum sentence, with similar 'whole life' terms also to be imposed on terrorist or multiple murderers and on murderers who have killed before. Other serious crimes such as the murder of a police or prison officer or a race-motivated murder would lead to a minimum thirty-year sentence, an increase of ten years on current practice. His comments were opposed by leading figures from within the criminal justice system. The Bar Council said David Blunkett was trying to ensure that the government tightened its grip around 'the neck of the judiciary', while the Howard League for Penal Reform said that such measures would increase the present number of life-sentence prisoners by 50 per cent. The Assistant General Secretary of the probation officers' union, Harry Fletcher, commented that 'The proposals suggest that there could never be room for redemption. Each case and release date must remain with the parole authorities to reflect remorse, change in the offender and the risk they may pose.'

As well as the fact that life-sentence prisoners are serving longer sentences, the number of life sentences has been extended, as a result of the Crime Sentences Act 1997, to include those convicted of a second serious violent or sexual offence. In their study *Murderers and Life Imprisonment*, Cullen and Newell (1999) highlight the different offences that can lead to life imprisonment. It is a mandatory sentence for murder committed by someone aged 21 or over and a discretionary maximum sentence for a number of other serious offences, including manslaughter, arson, robbery and rape. Also, as mentioned above, it is now a mandatory sentence under the 'two strikes' provision of the 1997 Act. This 'two strikes' legislation has attracted a good deal of concern and is worth commenting on briefly. It is based on the policy introduced in California in 1994 giving a life sentence to any offender who committed three indictable offences of any severity. This led to some absurd cases where offenders were getting life sentences for committing minor thefts or burglaries. Nonetheless, the British government proposed an automatic life sentence for offenders convicted for the second time of a serious violent or sexual offence (unless there were very exceptional circumstances). Of course, a life sentence does not mean that the prisoner will remain in prison for life. However, this legislation has undoubtedly increased the length of sentence for many offenders and so increased the prison population figures. As well as the resource implications of legislation that increases the prison population, such developments also raise issues of justice and fairness (see the extract from *The Times* in the following question break).

QUESTION BREAK: LONG-TERM PRISONERS

It is long-term prisoners who tend to dominate the routines of prisoner life rather than those who are in prison for only a few months. This creates a dilemma for the Prison Service, which has to cater for most prisoners who have a brief, transitory experience of prison, while at the same time having to accommodate more and more prisoners who will be inside for many years.

Questions

List the main differences between the needs of long-term and shorter-term prisoners.

What tensions might there be between the two groups?

How might these factors affect the administration and management of prisons?

Read the extract that follows and suggest the advantages and disadvantages of the 'two strikes' policy.

What ethical issues does it raise?

Robber gets life for his second serious offence

A robber has been jailed for life for stealing £520 under the 'two strikes and you're out' law.

It was Noel Boylan's second serious offence in four years: in 1994 he was jailed for four years for a robbery he committed with a pistol-shaped cigarette lighter.

Judge Jeremy Griggs told Truro Crown Court that there was no alternative to a mandatory life sentence for Boylan under the 1997 Crime Sentence Act. He would normally have jailed him for nine years, which, with good behaviour, would have entitled him to release after six years. . . .

The 1997 Act . . . was inspired by the similar American 'three strikes and you're out' law which became notorious after a vagrant was jailed for life for stealing a pizza.

The sentence was condemned by civil liberties groups. Paul Cavadino of the National Association for the Care and Resettlement of Offenders said: 'This was a serious offence but we do not think it is right to require courts to pass a life sentence regardless of the circumstances. It is clear the offender deserved a severe sentence but the judge should have been able to decide its length.

'There is a risk the new law will deter offenders from pleading guilty, which could lead to unnecessary trials and the possible acquittal of some dangerous offenders. It will also provide an incentive to plea-bargaining to avoid the automatic sentence.'

(S. De Bruxelles, 'Robber Gets Life for his Second Serious Offence',
The Times, 8 October 1998)

Cullen and Newell (1999) also consider the question of how many life-sentence prisoners might be innocent. While it is impossible to ascertain the numbers, it is an important issue in that innocent life-sentence prisoners are likely to serve longer than other lifers as they are seen as not admitting their guilt and demonstrating remorse. And the likelihood that such prisoners will protest their innocence often leads to their being seen as more awkward than other prisoners. The Criminal Cases Review Commission was set up in 1995 to investigate suspected miscarriages of justice and, according to Cullen and Newell, receives new cases at the rate of five a day. Although, again, it is impossible to establish how many who claim to be innocent are 'genuinely' innocent, even the Prison Officers Association estimated in 1992 that there could be around 700 innocent convicted prisoners. Of course, any estimates are liable to be on the low side as there are many reasons for prisoners not to maintain their innocence, with parole and transfer to other prisons possibly depending on a willingness to own up to crimes and admit guilt. As Cullen and Newell put it, 'It is quite clear that to get parole any sex offender would have to admit guilt, and participate in programmes to work on his offence and any cognitive distortions' (1999, p. 65). They also cite a comment from the former *Observer* journalist David Rose that 'for the life sentenced prisoners, protesting innocence is a sure-fire way to remain in gaol forever'.

The various high-profile and infamous miscarriages of justice in recent years have illustrated the extent of this issue. However, it could be argued that the innocence or not of prisoners is not really an area where the Prison Service can get involved, as it is the courts that convict and sentence offenders. Cullen and Newell argue that such a view is short-sighted in that prisons are an integral part of the criminal justice system; and prisoners who feel they are innocent are more likely to refuse to accept the realities of prison life and more likely to engage in protest about their conditions.

There is an obvious link between the numbers of prisoners and the costs of running the prison service. It is not cheap to keep someone in prison: Morgan (2002) estimates that it costs around £27,500 per prisoner per year, or about £530 a week. On top of this there is the phenomenal cost of building new prisons to cope with the rising prison population. According to Prison Reform Trust figures, since 1995 over 12,000 additional prison places have been provided at a cost of £1.28 billion, an average of about £100,000 per prison place.

Before we turn to prison conditions, it is important to bear in mind when considering the prison numbers that the prison population is not determined by levels of crime; essentially it is politically determined and it could be considerably smaller, as it is in other European countries, or, presumably, larger, as it is in the United States. And if there is no clear political drive to restrain the current expansion, then prison numbers will undoubtedly continue to rise. As a final point, in this section we have referred to different categories of prisoners, for instance lifers, but one area where there is potential to greatly reduce the prison population is with regard to the number of fine defaulters sent to prison each year. These offenders were not originally sentenced to prison, presumably because their crime did not merit it. When they default on their fines and end up in prison, the government does not get the money from the fine anyway, and there is the additional (and, as we saw above, heavy) cost of keeping the offender in prison. And the number of people sent to prison for not paying fines is considerable – making up roughly a quarter of all people imprisoned per year.

Conditions

It is probably fair to say that the material conditions in which prisoners live are better nowadays, in terms of food and hygiene for instance, than they have ever been. Although the old Victorian prison buildings are still in use, there are also many new, purpose-built prisons, and daily life in prisons has changed, with there no longer being rows of prisoners working in silence. However, it is only in recent years that some very degrading practices have been eliminated. It was not until the Strangeways prison riot of 1990 and the subsequent Woolf Report that a target date was set for ending 'slopping out'; this daily ritual whereby prisoners were allowed out of their cells to empty the buckets which they had used for toilets the previous night was only finally ended in 1994. Slopping out will probably be looked back on as an archaic, even barbaric, relic – like the crank and treadmill of nineteenth-century prisons, but one which lasted until the end of the twentieth century.

The recent improvements, though, do not mean that bad conditions and repressive regimes in prisons are a thing of the past. There is still a lack of constructive activities for most inmates and, in large part as a result of the massive increase in numbers, many prisoners spend longer alone in their cells and consequently less time working outside of them. Other pressures come from the longer periods served in prison and from the overcrowding consequent on rising numbers – so while many prison cells may be better equipped than in the past, this is perhaps scant consolation if prisoners spend ever-longer periods of time in them. It is clear that poor conditions remain a major area of concern and dispute for prisoners and so work against the smooth running of prisons.

In terms of day-to-day prison life, fear is a prominent and pervasive feature. For instance, there are more and more drugs of all kinds in prisons, and the consequent violence and intimidation that stem from them exacerbate this fear. The quality of prison life is also affected by pressure on prison staff – and the extra demands on staff caused by ever-increasing numbers can lead to cancellation of work and can limit the opportunities for inmates to engage in useful activities, such as educational programmes, and in leisure activities. Although it is easier to manage with fewer staff if prisoners are locked in their cells, again this will affect the quality of life for prisoners and thereby increase degrees of dissatisfaction. A report by the Chief Inspector of Prisons, Anne Owers, into Norwich Prison published in January 2003 showed that more than 200 out of 250 inmates on one wing had no access to meaningful work or education, while on the prison's 'training wing' only eight of forty-five inmates were in education and none was undertaking what might be termed meaningful work (Travis 2003).

It is difficult to assess the extent of prison overcrowding accurately: the data will fluctuate as offenders enter and leave prisons and as prisoners themselves are moved around the system. According to a report from the Howard League for Penal Reform, in 2002 more than 60 per cent of prisons in England and Wales were overcrowded; the report published a 'league table' of the most overcrowded prisons – Preston, with 661 inmates in its 356 spaces, came out as 'top', followed by Shrewsbury (331 in 184 spaces), Leicester (351 in 199 spaces) and Dorchester (258 in 153 spaces).

QUESTION BREAK: PRISON OVERCROWDING

The current level of overcrowding is undesirable but very limited. Only 20% of prisoners are currently having to double up in a cell designed for one. Regimes are still being delivered, and prisoners are still receiving education, purposeful activity, offending behaviour programmes, and getting exercise and time out of their cells. . . . No prison is being required to take more than its operational capacity and we are committed to ensuring that overcrowding does not impact on safety in any way, and we recognise the pressures it creates for prisoners and staff.

(Hilary Benn, Prisons Minister, quoted in *The Times*, 29 August 2002)

Our prisons are becoming no more than warehouses once again. . . . The consequences of overcrowding are jeopardising both the safe running of the prison system and the rehabilitation of individual offenders. . . . Although 20% of inmates are 'doubling up' in cells designed for one the prison service does not collect data on overcrowding in other types of cells, such as when three inmates have to share facilities designed for two.

(Frances Crook, Director of the Howard League, quoted in *The Times*, 29 August 2002)

Compare the comments of the Prisons Minister and the Howard League with the report of the Chief Inspector of Prisons on Norwich Prison (p. 198) on the extent and impact of overcrowding, then answer the following questions:

Questions

Which interpretation of the same data do you find more convincing? Why?

What additional problems is overcrowding likely to lead to for (a) the management of prisons; (b) the rehabilitation of prisoners?

As well as affecting the day-to-day quality of life in prisons, poor conditions, exacerbated by overcrowding, have been linked with prison disturbances and with increased suicides within prisons. While perhaps not as spectacular as the prison riots of the early 1990s at Strangeways Prison in Manchester and elsewhere, there have been a number of disturbances in British prisons in recent years. The Prison Service admitted to there being 'disturbances and acts of indiscipline' at four prisons in August 2002. Four days of disturbances at Holme House Prison, Teesside, led to thirty-four cells being damaged beyond use after about sixty inmates refused to return to their cells, and there were similar disturbances and damage at Swaleside Prison in Kent, Pentonville in London, and Ashfield in Bristol. The Prison Service acknowledged that overcrowding and staff shortages were at least partly to blame. The deputy head of the Prison Service, Phil Wheatley, referred to the record prison population as having 'increased instability and contributed to a small but significant number of incidents of mass disorder'; he went on to highlight the 'real risk that such incidents could escalate to involve large numbers of prisoners leading to a riot' (quoted in A. Travis, 'Crowding Fuels Prison Violence', *The Times*, 29 August 2002). Prior to these disturbances, in June 2002, the Lord Chief Justice, Lord Woolf, had warned that 'the intolerable conditions in Britain's overcrowded jails risk further prison riots like those that occurred in the early 1990s' (*Guardian*, 21 June 2002). These sorts of fears were realised in the full-scale riot that occurred at Lincoln Prison in October 2002. Prisoners forced the twenty-five prison officers on duty (in a prison holding 571 inmates) to withdraw to the prison gates and effectively controlled the prison for three hours on 24 October. After a prison officer had been assaulted and his keys taken, hundreds of prisoners were unlocked and went on the rampage, smashing cells and furnishings and lighting fires in two of the prison's wings. The riot ended after 250 prison officers from seventeen jails and equipped with riot gear took back control of the prison, wing by wing. The general secretary of the Prison Officers' Association, Brian Caton, said:

> 'We have been warning the Prison Service that unless they resourced us correctly for the very large increase in the prison population . . . these kind of events would become more frequent. We believe that there are many overcrowded prisons now that are reaching crisis point.'
>
> (*The Times*, 25 October 2002)

Poor conditions and increased overcrowding have also been linked to the increased suicide rate within prisons. This suicide rate has increased more rapidly than the increase in the prison population: it was 116 for every 100,000 inmates in 2002, compared to 89 for every 100,000 the previous year. As Anne Owers, the Chief Inspector of Prisons, said in her first annual report:

> Recently there were eight suicides in one week, five of them within twenty-four hours. These shocking statistics are, of course, directly connected to prison overcrowding and the consequential 'churn' as prisoners continually move into and out of prisons throughout the estate.
>
> (quoted in *The Times*, 11 December 2002)

Her concerns were endorsed by the director general of the Prison Service, Martin Narey, who told the Commons Home Affairs Select Committee that 'the increased population and high population turnover, particularly in local prisons, is making it more difficult to identify the suicidal and intervene and help them' (*The Times*, 11 December 2002). In a more general consideration of how prisoners adapt to imprisonment, Mathews (1999) points to the tendency to explain suicides in prison 'as a function of the mental instability of some prisoners with histories of psychiatric disorder'. However, those who commit suicide in prison are less likely to have a history of psychiatric disorder than suicides among the general population: 'whereas some 90 per cent of the recorded suicides in the community have a history of psychiatric disorder, only a third of those who commit suicide in prison have similar histories' (Mathews 1999, p. 70). Mathews suggests that explaining suicides in prison in individualistic terms ignores the effects of the prison regimes and the control strategies in prisons, with little attention being paid to the depersonalising nature of prison life and the range of activities and social stimuli that are available to prisoners. He argues that 'those most likely to attempt suicide are those who are physically and socially isolated in prisons with few activities and with little contact with home and family' (ibid.).

Security and containment

Another aspect of prison life that is affected by increased numbers and poor conditions is prison security, with overcrowding leading to many inmates being held in unsuitable parts of prisons and in the wrong security conditions. Prison security and containment became a prominent issue in the 1960s with a number of spectacular escapes by high-profile prisoners, including the Great Train Robbers Ronnie Biggs and Charlie Wilson in 1965 and the spy George Blake in 1966. Until then, security considerations had been relatively low on the prison agenda, but these escapes led to the Mountbatten Report (Home Office 1966), which highlighted weaknesses in prison security and established a new categorisation of all prisoners in terms of their security risk. This categorisation, which determines where prisoners are allocated to serve their sentences, is still in place today in much the same form as suggested by Mountbatten.

As suggested, the escape of George Blake, in particular, was a key factor in these developments and is worth referring to briefly here. Blake was employed by MI6 after the Second World War and, while serving in Berlin, offered his services to the KGB. After twelve years of spying for the Soviet Union he was sentenced to forty-two years' imprisonment in 1961, the longest ever determinate sentence passed in Britain. Essentially, George Blake seems to have managed to escape from Wormwood Scrubs five years later without meeting any real obstacles; an accomplice threw a rope ladder over the prison wall and then drove Blake to a house a few minutes away from the prison. He was smuggled out of the country and to East Berlin in December 1966 and is still alive and living in Moscow with a Russian wife, son and grandson.

At the time of Blake's escape, prisoners were classified as either 'stars' (first-time prisoners) or 'ordinaries' (those who had served at least one previous sentence). The categorisation system introduced by the Mountbatten Report included four categories of prisoner according to the level of security felt necessary to hold them in custody. These categories were defined as follows:

- Category A. Prisoners who must in no circumstances be allowed to get out either because of security considerations affecting spies, or because their violent behaviour is such that members of the public or the police would be in danger of their lives if they were to get out.
- Category B. Prisoners for whom the very high expenditure on the most modern escape barriers may not be justified, but who ought to be kept in secure conditions.
- Category C. Prisoners who lack the resource and will to make escape attempts, [but] have not the stability to be kept in conditions where there is no barrier to escape.
- Category D. Prisoners who can reasonably be entrusted to serve their sentences in open conditions.

(Home Office 1966)

As mentioned, this security categorisation is still in place today, and is perhaps the most important of the prison's internal procedures. As Price puts it,

[I]t structures the use of the prison estate, acting as a first line of defence against escapes, determining living conditions and allocation possibilities for convicted prisoners. Almost every other internal procedure within the prison system is conditional on the results of this one decision.

(2000, p. 3)

However, it is a decision and a procedure that offer the prisoner little opportunity to question or appeal against.

One of the main issues addressed by the Mountbatten Inquiry was that of what to do with the category A prisoners. It recommended one, specially built maximum security prison, which was going to be known as 'Vectis'. However, this did not become policy.

The Home Office was not in favour of one fortress-type prison for a number of reasons: in the wake of the Blake escape there was a concern about the consequences of a mass break-out, and there were misgivings around issues of staffing and control in such a prison. Instead, a further inquiry by the Advisory Council on the Penal System (1968) proposed that the most dangerous prisoners be spread around a number of high-security prisoners, most of whose inmates would be categories B or C. It is understandable that the Prison Service is particularly concerned about containing and controlling a small number of very dangerous prisoners, and the advantages and disadvantages of either the concentration or the dispersal of such prisoners have been an ongoing area of debate. Indeed, discussion of how a prisoner comes to be classified as a maximum security risk in the first place has been overshadowed by the debate about what to do with such prisoners (Price 2000).

Problems of security and control in prison are not necessarily one and the same. For instance, there will be prisoners who may well have the connections and capacity to organise an escape but who will pose few problems in terms of day-to-day control within prison and might be very compliant prisoners. This raises the question of how to distinguish between a prisoner who is a security risk and one who is a control risk, and highlights a particular problem with the fourfold categorisation of prisoners. The categories A and B relate to the risk and danger if a prisoner escapes, while C and D refer to the likelihood of an escape. As Price (2000) points out, this leaves 'a large hole in the centre of the four categories', in that category B is defined as being almost but not quite A and category C as not quite the same as D, but the distinction between categories B and C is much less clear. And how the categories are applied in practice often becomes rather subjective, even depending on which part of the country prisoners serve their sentence. In 1981, for instance, a Prison Department Working Party found that the Midland region placed over 22 per cent of its prison population in category D, open, conditions and just 11 per cent in category B, while the South-West had close to 30 per cent in category B conditions and 10 per cent in category D, open prisons. These differences were simply due to the different levels of prison accommodation available in the different regions.

Since the mid-1960s there have been few escapes by prisoners who pose a genuine danger, although many prisoners who are deemed lower risk do walk out of open prison conditions or abscond when working outside prison. However, there were two exceptional and dramatic escapes from high-security prisons in the 1990s. Six prisoners escaped from the secure unit of Whitemoor Prison in Cambridgeshire in 1994, injuring a prison officer with one of two guns used in the escape. In 1995, three prisoners from Parkhurst Prison, who were identified by the Prison Service as some of the most dangerous in the prison system, managed to make a master key and a ladder that could be dismantled into smaller parts in the prison workshops, to obtain wire cutters, pliers and a gun, to evade the CCTV cameras and dog patrols at the prison perimeter, and break through two fences without setting off any alarms. They were at large on the Isle of Wight for four days before being spotted by an off-duty prison officer and recaptured.

These escapes led to separate inquiries, the Woodcock Report (1994) into the Whitemoor escape and the Learmont Report (1995) into that at Parkhurst. Both recommended, and have led to, increases in prison security and surveillance, and to more restrictions on long-term prisoners, with the Learmont Report stressing that custody should be the primary purpose of the Prison Service. But while it is clear that some prisoners are dangerous and need to be held securely at all times, the vast majority of prisoners are not; and there is a danger that in reacting to specific situations with harsher restrictions, opportunities that may help prisoners to settle into outside life after their release, such as pre-release home leaves, might well be missed.

Legitimacy

The Woolf Report (1991) highlighted the sense of injustice held by inmates as a key factor behind the Strangeways disturbances of 1990. This sense of injustice was related to internal prison practices and procedures. As Woolf put it,

> a recurring theme in the evidence from prisoners who . . . were involved in the riots was that their actions were a response to the manner in which they were treated by the prison system. Although they did not always use these terms, they felt a lack of justice.

The report argued that the Prison Service should seek to achieve and maintain a balance between justice, security and control. This justice should not be seen as some sort of privilege or award for good behaviour; rather, it should be a basic requirement that prisoners would receive humane treatment, be subject to fair procedures and be provided with reasoned explanations for decisions made that affected their situation. Although not explicitly referring to the term 'legitimacy', the Woolf Report advocated what could be seen as a 'theory of legitimacy' (Cavadino and Dignan 2002):

> The evidence is that prisoners will not join in disturbances in any numbers if they feel conditions are reasonable and relationships are satisfactory. These are matters which the prison service must address more closely. They are fundamental to maintaining a stable prison system which is able to withstand and reject the depradations of disruptive and violent prisoners. These are matters which must be resolved if we are to have peace in our prisons.

As regards the balance between justice and security and control, the emphasis since the Woolf Report has been on implementing the security recommendations, such as installing metal detectors and X-ray machines. This emphasis has been sharpened by the Woodcock and Learmont inquiries into the prison escapes of the mid-1990s (see p. 202), and has led to some incredibly detailed monitoring of inmates' possessions. The *Prisons Handbook* illustrates the detailed control over prisoners' property:

> The basic rule is that the standard limit, for all prisoners, for all property held in possession is that which fits into two volumetric control boxes. The volumetric control box measures 0.7m × 0.55m × 0.25m and has a volume of 0.9625 cubic metres.
> (Leech and Cheney 1999, p. 242)

In contrast, there has been much slower progress made on other recommendations of the Woolf Report, such as on action to end overcrowding and to improve relationships between prison officers and inmates. It would seem that security has become the top priority and that another detailed and thoughtful inquiry, with some useful recommendations, has become a further missed opportunity.

Woolf found that the standard response when dealing with prison disorders was to identify the 'troublemakers' and to subject them to some form of punishment, such as solitary confinement, or to ship them out to another prison. There was little attempt to investigate the inmates' grievances. This sort of approach illustrates a general concern of prisoners that the grievance procedures within prisons are inadequate. In addition, the internal prison disciplinary system is felt to operate in a manner that works against the interests of prisoners. As regards internal disciplinary offences, prison governors carry out the initial investigation and deal with the vast majority of cases themselves – a procedure which is perhaps unlikely to be viewed very positively by prisoners. More serious offences can be referred to the police if they also constitute a crime (cases of assault or possession of drugs, for example). Until 1992, the prison Boards of Visitors used to be involved with more serious disciplinary cases. This was felt by the Woolf Report to compromise the impartiality of the Boards of Visitors, and their main role now is to find out about and draw attention to any abuse of prisoners. Boards of Visitors were established by the Prison Act of 1895. They changed their name to Independent Monitoring Boards in April 2003, with each Board being responsible for a particular prison. They are meant to act as independent watchdogs, safeguarding the well-being and rights of prisoners. However, although they are meant to be independent of the Prison Service, members are appointed by the Home Office, they tend to be local dignitaries (including magistrates) and usually they do not inspire a great deal of confidence in prisoners themselves.

Justice within prison does not just refer to how grievances or disciplinary offences are dealt with. The emphasis on prisoners having to 'earn' privileges and, in particular, to earn remission from their sentences raises further concerns about justice in prison. The Crime Sentences Act 1997 proposed that prisoners would have to 'earn' their early release, rather than its being a right. However, it is difficult to apply such a policy with justice, and in a way that is felt by prisoners to be legitimate, as such decisions will almost inevitably involve day-to-day appraisal by prison officers. Hence these decisions about early release or not are bound to cause all sorts of ill feelings. They might result in many extra months of a sentence being served by some prisoners but not by others.

QUESTION BREAK: RELEASE FROM PRISON

While the idea of prisoners having to earn remission from a sentence is not new – it is similar to the indeterminate sentence idea that has been used in the past (see p. 22) – it can increase tension among inmates and raises awkward questions.

Questions
What do you think should determine a prisoner's release from prison?

List the arguments for and against linking the release date for prisoners to their behaviour while in prison.

Imprisonment: experiences and issues

Now that we have considered the current situation in British prisons in relation to numbers, conditions, security and legitimacy, the focus of this section is on the 'experiences of prison life'. This is obviously a vast area, and here we will focus on two particular areas: the experiences of female prisoners, and the question of whether prison can 'work' in terms of rehabilitating those convicted for serious offences.

Women and prison

According to data from the Prison Service, out of a prison population of just over 73,000 on 2 May 2003, just under 4,500 (roughly 6 per cent) were female. So, with around 94 per cent of prisoners being male, it is perhaps not surprising that the prison system has been dominated by the needs of male rather than female prisoners. Although a figure of 6 per cent may seem very low, given that just over half the total population of England and Wales is female, the female prison population has been growing at a much faster rate than the male prison population in recent years: between 1991 and 2001 there was a 150 per cent increase in the number of female prisoners compared to a 40 per cent increase for men (Morgan 2002). In a report from the Prison Reform Trust into Newton Hall Prison, Durham, overcrowding was highlighted as a real cause for concern, with the report, which appeared in 2003, finding almost half of the female prisons in England and Wales suffering from overcrowding. It made the point that few women offenders are a 'real risk' to the public, with the director of the Prison Reform Trust, Juliet Lyon, commenting that 'for all but the most serious and violent offenders, support and supervision centres in local communities offer the best chance for women offenders to get out of trouble'. However, as we have seen in looking at prison numbers generally, attempts to reduce the prison population do not seem to have much success. The Youth Justice Board, for instance, has recommended that all girls aged 16 and younger should be removed from prisons but has said that these plans have been frustrated by an increase in the number of teenagers being jailed.

As regards the make-up of the female prison population, there are some differences from male prisoners. A higher proportion of female prisoners are on remand awaiting trial (21 per cent compared to 17 per cent for males), while sentenced female prisoners are usually older and serving shorter sentences, and are substantially less likely to be reconvicted (Morgan 2002). Another development that has affected the female prison population has been the increase in foreign nationals held in British prisons, many for drug-related offences, including drug smuggling, which tend to carry relatively long sentences (Mathews 1999). According to a Prison Reform Trust press release, in 2001, 40 per cent of female prisoners were held for drug offences and 15 per cent were classed as foreign nationals; by contrast, only 15 per cent were held for violent offences. The rise in the number and proportion of women in prison for drug offences is particularly striking: in 1992, 24 per cent of the female sentenced prison population had committed drug offences compared to the 40 per cent figure for 2001.

The increase in the number of women in prison and the fact that the prison service tries to place women in female-only institutions affects the experience of female prisoners. As Morgan (2002) points out, with only 19 out of the 137 prison establishments accommodating women, it is difficult to place female prisoners near to their homes. And as almost two-thirds of female prisoners have at least one child below the age of 18, being in a prison close to their home is the highest priority for most such prisoners. These sorts of practical issues are likely to intensify the tensions that occur in women's prisons.

Although the female prison population has risen dramatically in recent years, the proportion of female prisoners has not always been as low as it is now. During the Victorian era, women made up around one in five of those sent to local prisons, and between 1860 and 1890 the average daily population of women in local prisons increased from 4,567 to 4,840 – higher numbers than today, and in relation to a male prison population of less than 20,000 at the end of the nineteenth century (Zedner 1991). The female prison population was declining at the end of the nineteenth century and continued to do so into the twentieth, partly because of a decline in the number of women prosecuted for public order offences such as prostitution and also because of a growing emphasis on explaining female offending in terms of 'feeblemindedness', alongside a policy of sending those prosecuted for drunkenness to reformatories rather than prisons. Between 1898 and 1914 a number of inebriate reformatories for female drunkards were founded (Zedner 1991). The female prison population continued to fall in the first half of the twentieth century and was less than 2,000 by the 1960s. As mentioned above, the figures have increased from that low in recent years.

However, it was during the Victorian era that approaches to female imprisonment (as well as female offending) that are still in vogue today were introduced – for instance, the notion that women should be held separately from men and that women prisoners would benefit from the sort of personal attention that was best provided by prison officers of their own sex (Mathews 1999). There was also a different approach to prison labour for female prisoners; while it was agreed that all prisoners should engage in some form of work to aid their reform, the following contemporary comment indicates the different regime advocated for women prisoners:

> The work done by the women prisoners is, of course, of different character to that performed [at] the hulks . . . the hard labour of prisoners working in the arsenal and dockyard is here replaced by the more feminine occupation of the laundry.
>
> (Mayhew and Binny 1860, in Mathews 1999, p. 18)

While there will clearly be common aspects and some overlap between the experiences of and responses to imprisonment for male and female prisoners, there are some issues which relate more strongly to female prisoners. And, as Heidensohn (2002) points out, while there may be some debate as to how 'gendered' women's experience of imprisonment is, there is a general consensus that women offenders should be treated differently. She refers to the Prison Reform Trust inquiry led by Dorothy Wedderburn, which pointed to the prison system's failure to provide for the particular needs of women and highlighted four distinctive characteristics of women prisoners: different patterns of offending from men and lower risk to the public; their role as mothers and primary carers; their history of psychiatric illness; and the effects of the proportionately low numbers of women prisoners ('Justice for Women: The Need for Reform', Prison Reform Trust 2000, in Heidensohn 2002).

The point about the small proportion of the prison population was referred to earlier as leading to female prisoners typically being held some distance from their homes, with consequent difficulties for arranging visits and so maintaining family contact. A further implication of this is that women's prisons have to cope with a wider range of offenders than men's prisons; and that the range of work, training and educational opportunities is likely to be more limited (Mathews 1999). These sorts of 'structural' factors attendant on numbers and space will also affect the 'culture' within women's prisons. The fact that the majority of female prisoners are mothers affects the nature of and culture within women's prisons. As mentioned above, roughly two-thirds of female prisoners are mothers, and according to estimates from the Prison Reform Trust, each year up to 20,000 children are affected by the imprisonment of their mother. Only around 5 per cent of women prisoners' children remain in their own home once their mother is sent to prison, with most being looked after by their grandmothers, other family members or friends. The question break that follows considers how women respond to their imprisonment.

QUESTION BREAK: WOMEN BEHIND BARS

The first extract below is taken from the section of Mary Eaton's study *Women after Prison*, which considers how women responded to their imprisonment. The second is from an article by journalist Libby Brooks in which she questions why ever more women offenders are being sent to prison.

The women described ways of coping with the regimes in which they were held. . . .

1 Withdrawal
To preserve something of the sense of self with which one entered prison it is necessary to withhold that self from engagement with the world of the prison. In withdrawing from the situation, women may feel that they are keeping the institution at a distance, however, they are actively conforming to the regime which defines docility as an appropriate characteristic for women. . . .

2 Retaliation
I used to get into every kind of skulduggery that was going – like making drink – alcohol. . . . That was the way I did my prison sentence – messing around and getting them back all the time. . . .

For some women, confrontation with the prison authorities was one way of preserving a sense of self-dignity. . . .

3 Incorporation
. . . Women may play an active part in maintaining the hierarchy that characterizes prison life, and so endorse the relative positions within that hierarchy. Experiencing exclusion themselves they practise exclusion on others. Being subject to power, they wield a limited

power. 'What I hated more than anything was that there was so much bad feeling and aggression between the women'.... Prison life does not encourage the creation of community.... In such a situation many women felt that they changed in response to perceived aggression from others. If there was to be a hierarchy to be reinforced then they determined not to be at the bottom, not to be victims.... 'I abhor physical violence, but in prison I was totally different.... It was more like being in care where if you didn't physically stand up to someone who you thought could possibly bully you then you were going to be in trouble.'

(Eaton 1993, pp. 41–47)

We know that the vast majority of women offenders pose a low risk to the public ... Most women in prison are not that dangerous.... We know, too, that because inmates are held far from home, imprisoning mothers has a disproportionate disruptive effect on family life. We know that women react more adversely to custody than men, not least because of the higher incidence of mental health problems among female prisoners. We know that more than half the women in prison have experienced physical or sexual abuse.

(L. Brooks, 'Women behind Bars', *Guardian*, 26 February 2002)

Questions

What do you think are the major differences and similarities between the responses of the women interviewed by Eaton and those of male prisoners?

In what other ways might prisoners, and particularly female prisoners, respond to imprisonment?

Why do you think women 'react more adversely to custody than men'?

Can prison work?

This sub-section will consider some contemporary examples of treatment programmes designed to rehabilitate long-term, dangerous prisoners. David Rose (2002) studied the effects of a year-long Cognitive Self-Change Programme (CSCP) run at Channings Wood Prison, Devon. Seven of the eight prisoners on the programme that he examined were serving life sentences and all were judged by psychologists as at risk of offending again. The programme aims to reduce those risks and is one example of rehabilitative programmes that are in place across the majority of prisons in the United Kingdom. The existence of these programmes is seen by Rose as part of the 'radical transformation in philosophy and practice now sweeping the British prison system'. In 2001, over 6,000 prisoners completed offending behaviour programmes, more than eleven times as many as in 1994, with the figure set to rise substantially in the next few years. This new rehabilitative emphasis is strongly supported by the director-general of the Prison Service, Martin Narey: 'Like many who work in the service, I've never seen my job as being about just locking people up. . . . If we can get people off drugs, on to offending behaviour programmes and into education, then we're going to reduce crime' (quoted in Rose 2002). Not all the prisoners were so enthusiastic about the CSCP programme; some expressed a degree of scepticism, as illustrated by the following comment from one of the participants:

'The psychology department have to put you through a stringent risk assessment. It's a year on a microscope slide. If you get your rubber stamp at the end of it, you're OK for D cat [open prison]. If not . . .'

However, most of the prisoners were positive. As one of the lifers said,

'I didn't want to do this course, but it has given me a lot of insights: why I killed the person I killed and why I've committed violent offences through my life. It's given me a lot of tools that I'm already using, to assess my own and other people's actions.'

As well as programmes for serious offenders, there are also less intensive courses for prisoners serving shorter sentences. The Enhanced Thinking Skills (ETS) course, for instance, is used in seventy-nine jails. Rose refers to research by prison psychologist Caroline Friendship which demonstrated the relative success of such courses. Offenders who had followed a rehabilitation programme were found to be significantly less likely to be reconvicted within two years than were offenders matched in terms of offence and social background but who had not followed any programme.

However, these positive developments are threatened by the ever-increasing prison population and the consequent overcrowding, with many prisoners disappearing from courses just as they get going on them. As well as affecting the living standards within prisons, large rises in the prison population make it more difficult for prison staff to supervise and work with prisoners in tackling reoffending.

Grendon is Britain's only therapeutic prison. It opened in 1962 and is a category B prison taking only the most difficult and dangerous offenders, but ones who it is felt might benefit from the psychological treatment offered. The therapeutic process at Grendon is based around group therapy sessions in which prisoners confront their crimes and learn to take responsibility for their actions and the effects those actions have on others. According to Weale (2001), it is proof that prison can be 'humane, constructive and life-changing' and can work. Mark Leech, now an author (he is editor of the *Prisons Handbook*, for instance) and campaigner for penal reform, served twenty years in prison and is an ex-Grendon prisoner. He agrees with Weale, saying, 'It certainly worked for me. . . . Grendon made me realise there were other options I could choose.'

Certainly, reconviction rates from Grendon inmates are encouraging: the 24 per cent reoffending rate for life prisoners in general contrasts with an 8 per cent rate at Grendon, while for non-lifers the reoffending rate is 10 per cent lower at Grendon than elsewhere. Grendon is run as a democratic community that sets its own rules based around three policies that everyone is expected to follow: no drugs, no sex and no violence. Such a regime does not suit all prisoners, and the comparative freedom within the prison comes as a culture shock to many – prison cells are open all day from 8 a.m. until lock-up at 9 p.m., allowing prisoners to eat and talk together freely. While this relative freedom might seem like a soft option to some prisoners, staff and inmates regularly refer to it as being the toughest way to 'do your bird', with the therapy being intensive and gruelling. However, not all prisoners respond positively to Grendon's regime. Convicted sex offender Gary Watkins volunteered for Grendon, but within a month of his release kidnapped and sexually assaulted a 17-year-old girl, saying at his trial that he had maintained fantasies of assaulting and killing a young girl throughout his treatment.

As Grendon's director of research and development, John Shine, commented, 'Some people here make enormous changes. Other people we have to be extremely cautious about. . . . We don't know what goes on in their head.' In concluding her examination of the Grendon regime, Weale (2001) makes the point that while Grendon could certainly be seen as a success, it should not distract from the bigger issue of why we keep expanding our prison system when we know it creates more problems than it solves.

To some extent, examples such as Grendon and other offending behaviour programmes could be seen as merely papering over the cracks of Britain's prison system. In responding to David Rose's positive review of rehabilitation programmes, the director of the Prison Reform Trust, Juliet Lyon (2002), argues that while prison regimes have improved over recent years, it is misleading to claim that 'prison works' on the basis of a review of therapeutic programmes for long-term prisoners when the 'immense pressure of prison overcrowding' means that 'purposeful activity has increased for each prisoner by just ten minutes a day in ten years' and 'prisons are being turned back into human warehouses'. In concluding her article, Lyon comments that

> the debate on whether prison works or not is futile. What matters is that prison is allowed to take its proper place in the criminal justice system, one of excellent last resort, properly equipped and able to cope with those who really need to be there.

QUESTION BREAK: PRISON INSPECTIONS

The following extracts are taken from reviews of reports into prison between 1996 and 2003.

An unannounced short inspection at Aldington prison revealed that it was 'not operating successfully as a resettlement prison and is providing a "poor" standard of throughcare'. . . . Too few prisoners received any meaningful training and the prison did not fulfil any of the criteria necessary for resettling prisoners into the community at the end of their sentences. It was remote from any external employment, education and training facilities and there was little purposeful activity for inmates within the prison. The accommodation was 'flimsy', grubby and failed security standards. There had been little improvement since the 1992 inspection.'
(*Howard Journal of Criminal Justice*, 1996, 35 (3), 274)

The inspection at HMP Chelmsford disclosed 'a collective failure over a period of time of a number of senior members of the Prison Service to recognise and eliminate too many unacceptable practices and deficiencies in the running of the prison'. Among elements making Chelmsford 'dreadful' were 'the appalling and 19th century attitude to the treatment of young offenders' which the chief inspector felt may breach the UN convention on children's rights, and finance/staffing problems. Adult and young offenders were freely mixing in the same accommodation and 'it was not difficult to find young men of 17 clearly lost and often afraid within the prison'.
(*Howard Journal of Criminal Justice*, 1998, 37 (1), 105)

The jail overcrowding crisis, poor industrial relations, and a lack of a clear purpose have led to an 'unacceptable regime' at Liverpool prison, the largest in Britain, according to the chief inspector of prisons.

The report by Anne Owers published today said conditions for new inmates were among the worst her inspectors had seen – with cockroaches, broken windows, and dirty cells and toilets. . . .

Prisoners were able to shower and change their underwear once a week and in some cases not even that frequently, according to the report.

[. . .]

There were fewer opportunities for work and education despite criticism in the 1999 inspector's report. 'Only 18% of prisoners had access to education, though the prison's own statistics showed that 95% needed help with basic literacy and numeracy. No national vocational qualifications were being offered,' Ms Owers said.

The inspectors also found that, like many local prisons, Liverpool suffered severely from overcrowding.

'Many single cells held two prisoners with an unscreened toilet, and there was considerable difficulty in safely managing the large number of prisoners coming through reception every day.'
(A. Travis, 'Regime at Biggest Jail Found Wanting', *Guardian*, 28 May 2003)

Questions

In spite of numerous critical reports, why do you think prison conditions are still found to be of such poor standard?

Suggest the possible long-term effects on prisoners and prison officers of experiences and institutions such as those illustrated above.

How might those who favour (a) retribution, and (b) rehabilitation respond to these extracts?

Community penalties

In the final part of this chapter we will look briefly at non-custodial, community penalties, often referred to as 'alternatives to prison'. Imprisonment is the most severe penalty available within Britain's criminal justice system and has tended therefore to attract much greater interest than 'less severe' penalties. There is a vast amount of literature on prisons yet relatively little on non-custodial punishments. As Worrall (1997) puts it in the introduction to her study on community punishment, 'there is no market for the autobiographies of offenders' experiences of community service'. She suggests that academic and political debate 'tends to assume that penalty is synonymous with prison'. However, it is important to remember that the vast majority of offenders will never be given a custodial sentence.

Although non-custodial, including community, penalties might be thought of as a relatively recent addition to our criminal justice system, they are by no means new, and in this section we will briefly trace their history. Before the twentieth century, fines and release on recognisances were the only sentences apart from imprisonment that were regularly used by the courts, although non-payment of fines led to many people being imprisoned anyway. A recognisance was a bond by which the offender agreed to do, or refrain from doing, something; often it involved the offender being required simply to 'keep the peace'. By the mid-nineteenth century, release on recognisance normally involved some form of surety guaranteeing the future behaviour of the offender; these guarantees were often given by Police Court Missionaries, a body founded in 1876 and seen as the forerunners of the modern probation service (Worrall 1997). The Probation of First Offenders Act in 1887 recognised the role of these missionaries in helping the courts identify suitable offenders for probation (Brownlee 1998).

So, probation has its origins in the nineteenth century, when minor offenders could be bound over if a suitable person could be found to supervise their future conduct. This sort of supervision in place of another punishment was seen as providing the offender with an opportunity to 'prove' themselves, hence the term 'probation'.

A system of supervision based around missionary work was developed in the United States in the mid-nineteenth century and was followed by penal reformers in Britain, and can be seen in the 1907 Probation of Offenders Act, which spelled out the role of the probation officer as being 'to advise, assist and befriend [the person under supervision] and, when necessary, to endeavour to find him suitable employment' (from Brownlee 1998). However, it took many more years before a system of paid, full-time probation officers was in place.

The first half of the twentieth century saw a move away from the 'missionary' aspect of probation to a 'treatment model' based around therapeutic work related to the offender's needs and motivations. This reflected developments in criminology and the notion that crime was something which might be 'cured' through treating the social and psychological conditions and needs of offenders. The Probation Service itself became a more bureaucratic and professional organisation based around therapeutic treatment of offenders. Although religious and philanthropic elements of the nineteenth century continued to influence both the recruitment to and the organisation of the Probation Service in the first decades of the twentieth century, increased professionalism led to a gradual move away from the old view of the probation officer as being someone who saw the job as a religious calling. This trend continued through the twentieth century. The development of the welfare state after the Second World War ensured that the principle of diagnosing and treating individuals was firmly established as basic probation practice in the 1950s and 1960s. During this post-war period the Probation Service expanded enormously. The numbers of probation officers increased from 1,006 in 1950 to 5,033 in 1976, while the number of offenders supervised rose from just over 55,000 in 1951 to more than 120,000 by 1971 (Brownlee 1998).

By the end of the 1970s the treatment model was being criticised on both empirical and ethical grounds (Raynor 2002). Studies into the effectiveness of punishments in general provided disappointing results, and the 'nothing works' philosophy came to the fore. The 'treatment' model was also criticised on ethical grounds as dehumanising individuals. This encouraged a move back to a more retributivist approach. Although the phrase 'nothing works' is associated with an American writer, Martinson, and his 1974 article

'What Works? Questions and Answers about Prison Reform', the notion was more widely applied and accepted in Britain. By the 1980s there was, according to Raynor, greater emphasis on avoiding unnecessary harm to offenders through imprisonment – with probation seen essentially as a means of reducing imprisonment, reflecting a move away from the earlier emphasis on 'doing good' through treatment.

Greater optimism about rehabilitation began to be found in the late 1980s and into the 1990s, with moves being made to avoid what had become almost a competition between community sentences and prisons – illustrated by the phrase 'alternatives to prison'. As Raynor puts it, cooperation across criminal justice agencies 'would not be helped if one service continued to define its mission as saving people from the other'. These changes were reflected in the 1991 Criminal Justice Act, which advocated a key role for the Probation Service.

The new developments are characterised by a shift in focus to 'what works' rather than the 'nothing works' philosophy. These rehabilitative-based approaches have been centred largely around the work of psychological criminologists. In his overview, Raynor (2002) highlights Andrews and Bonta's theory of offending, which relates social disadvantage to personality traits in developing a model of how offending occurs and develops. Social disadvantages such as poverty are seen as making it difficult for families to provide a supportive environment for children; while personality characteristics such as impulsiveness can be reinforced by peer pressure, which may provide access to illegitimate opportunities and delinquent activities and may work against succeeding in formal education. This sort of approach, bringing in both social and psychological factors, has encouraged intervention strategies based on trying to reduce the 'risk' factors faced by potential offenders.

As the 'what works' approach of the 1990s developed, examples of community penalty programmes which seemed to have a positive effect in reducing reoffending came to the fore. As Raynor puts it, 'rather than being the focus of interest for only a few researchers and practitioners [by the end of the 1990s there was] an officially recognized and endorsed strategy . . . prompting a considerable reorganization of the process of supervising offenders' (2002, p. 1192). Brownlee summarises the changing role of the Probation Service as proceeding,

> from its earliest days as a branch of the Church's missionary work among the alcoholic and destitute, through its quasi-medical diagnostic and normalising phase, to its current position as an integral part of a systematised criminal justice apparatus, having special responsibility for the supervision of punishment in the community.
>
> (1998, p. 98)

The Probation Service does not just supervise offenders who are 'on probation', but also oversees a number of other community penalties. The current range of community penalties were detailed in Chapter 6 (p. 171). The 1991 Criminal Justice Act attempted to clarify the concept of community penalty through defining six 'community orders': probation order, community service order, combination order, curfew order, supervision order and an attendance centre order. This framework is the basis of the current situation, although the well-established term 'probation order' has been replaced by 'Community Rehabilitation Order', and the community service order has become a 'Community Punishment Order'. This latter order involves the offender undertaking some penalty in the community rather than in custody, with the offender having to comply with various requirements concerning their behaviour.

The continued growth of community penalties is shown in figures provided by Raynor (2002). The Probation Service is responsible for supervising over 200,000 offenders at any particular time, including about 61,000 on Community Rehabilitation Orders, 46,000 on Community Punishment Orders and 29,000 on Community Punishment and Rehabilitation Orders. In addition, it supervises about 80,000 who have been released from prison and other custodial institutions – for instance, all young offenders who receive custodial sentences are supervised after their release, and although such supervision is not a community penalty, it involves the Probation Service.

Community penalties are an established and important part of the British sentencing system and clearly have a future; however, there will always be need to deal with the 'high-risk' offenders, and this may lead to an increase in 'bifurcation' – providing very different types of services according to (a risk analysis of) the dangerousness of the offender. Of course, any changes and developments are dependent on the political climate of the day, and there is always a danger that notions of community penalty are not perceived as grabbing the popular imagination (or vote!) as much as hardline rhetoric and approaches.

This 'danger' highlights the difficulties for establishing and developing community penalties. Brownlee (1998) suggests that there are four 'obstacles' to community punishment. First, as suggested above, there is the public and media perception that community penalties are 'soft' and that prison is the only appropriate punishment. Second, there is the problem of unfair or inconsistent sentencing. Community sentences tend to be given to those who are socially advantaged (and deemed by probation officers to be able to 'benefit' from supervision), whereas less advantaged groups seem to be over-represented in prison. Third, there is a danger that an increase in 'alternatives to custody' will lead to more and more people being drawn into the 'net' of the criminal justice system – so that rather than keeping people out of prison, community penalties will increase the numbers of people with criminal records. Finally, Worrall highlights the problems with enforcing community penalties. Probation and community orders are fine if followed by the offenders, but if not, then such penalties have to be 'backed up' with prison – which can lead to the use of such penalties actually increasing the prison population (although Worrall does point out that probation officers do not lightly institute proceedings against offenders who do not comply with community penalties and are reluctant to return offenders to court if they can possibly avoid it).

In concluding his overview, Raynor suggests that a way forward is to include reparative elements in a wider range of community sentences, so as to emphasise (to the population and government) that rehabilitation is basically restorative and that it benefits the community as well as the offender – in other words, to try to change public perceptions of rehabilitation as being 'soft' and only 'offender focused'.

Further reading

Leech, M. and Cheney, D. (1999) *The Prisons Handbook 2000*, Winchester: Waterside Press. This is an annual guide to the prison service in England and Wales. Supported by the Prison Service, it offers practical information and advice for prisoners and those who work with them. It provides a brief description of every penal establishment and is a mine of useful information.

Liebling, A. and Price, D. (2001) *The Prison Officer*, London: HM Prison Service. The focus of the discussion in this chapter has been on prison and prisoners and, as its title implies, this text looks at the role of the prison officer – although a vitally important role for the running of Britain's prison system, an area which is often ignored in studies of prison and imprisonment.

Mathews, R. (1999) *Doing Time: An Introduction to the Sociology of Imprisonment*, London: Palgrave. This text provides a clear introduction to the main sociological debates surrounding imprisonment. After examining the history of and current practices within prisons, it examines the impact of imprisonment on different social groups, including young people, women and ethnic minorities.

Rawlings, P. (1999) *Crime and Power: A History of Criminal Justice, 1688–1998*, Harlow: Longman. Chapters 4 and 6 of this general historical text provide detail on the early prisons of the eighteenth and nineteenth centuries.

Raynor, P. (2002) 'Community Penalties: Probation, Punishment and "What Works"', in Maguire, M., Morgan, R. and Reiner, R. (eds) *The Oxford Handbook of Criminology*, 3rd edn, Oxford: Oxford University Press. An up-to-date review of the history and contemporary practice of community punishment that highlights the obstacles faced in trying to provide rehabilitative punishments.

Two useful Web sites that focus specifically on prisons are:
www.hmprisonservice.gov.uk
www.guardian.co.uk/prisons

References

Advisory Council on the Penal System (1968) *The Regime for Long-Term Prisoners in Conditions of Maximum Security* (the Radzinowicz Report), London: HMSO.

Alford, F. (2000) 'What Would It Matter if Everything Foucault Said about Prison Were Wrong? Discipline and Punish after Twenty Years', *Theory and Society*, 29:1, pp. 125–146.

Amir, M. (1971) *Patterns in Forcible Rape*, Chicago: University of Chicago Press.

Anderson, D. M. and Killingray, D. (1991) *Policing the Empire: Government Authority and Control, 1830–1940*, Manchester: Manchester University Press.

Anderson, S., Grove-Smith, C., Kinsey, R. and Wood, J. (1990) *The Edinburgh Crime Survey*, Edinburgh: Scottish Office.

Aron, R. (1970) *Main Current in Sociological Thought 2*, Harmondsworth: Pelican.

Ballinger, A. (2000) *Dead Woman Walking: Executed Women in England and Wales, 1900–1955*, Dartmouth: Ashgate.

Barbalet, J. M. (1993) 'Citizenship, Class Inequality and Resentment', in Turner, B. S. (ed.) *Citizenship and Social Theory*, London: Sage.

Barton, A. R. (2001) 'Fragile Moralities and Dangerous Sexualities: A Case Study of Women and Semi-penal Institutions on Merseyside, 1823–1994', PhD thesis, Liverpool John Moores University.

Beck, U. (1992) *Risk Society: Towards a New Modernity*, London: Sage.

Becker, H. S. (1963) *Outsiders: Studies in the Sociology of Deviance*, New York: Free Press.

Bottoms, A. E. (1980) *The Coming Penal Crisis*, Edinburgh: Scottish Academic Press.

Bowling, B. and Phillips, C. (2002) *Racism, Crime and Justice*, Harlow: Longman.

Box, S. (1983) *Power, Crime and Mystification*, London: Tavistock.

Braithwaite, J. (1984) *Corporate Crime in the Pharmaceutical Industry*, London: Routledge.

Brown, J. (1997) 'Equal Opportunities and the Police in England and Wales: Past, Present and Future Possibilities', in Francis, P., Davies, P. and Jupp, V. (eds) *Policing Futures: The Police, Law Enforcement and the Twenty-first Century*, London: Macmillan.

Brownlee, I. (1998) *Community Punishment: A Critical Introduction*, Harlow: Longman.

Budge, I., Crewe, I., MacKay, D. and Newton, K. (1998) *The New British Politics*, Harlow: Longman.

Calavita, K. and Pontell, H. N. (1994) 'The State and White-Collar Crime', *Law and Society Review*, 28:2.

Cavadino, M. (1992) 'Explaining the Penal Crisis', *Prison Service Journal*, 87.

Cavadino, M. and Dignan, J. (2002) *The Penal System: An Introduction*, 3rd edn, London: Sage.

Chan, J. (1996) 'Changing Police Culture', *British Journal of Criminology*, 36:1.

Clark, L. M. G. and Lewis, D. J. (1977) *Rape: The Price of Coercive Sexuality*, Toronto: Women's Press.

Coffey, J. (2000) *Persecution and Toleration in Protestant England, 1558–1689*, Harlow: Longman.

Cohen, S. (1980) *Folk Devils and Moral Panics*, 2nd edn, Oxford: Oxford University Press.

Cohen, S. (1996) 'Human Rights and Crimes of the State', in Muncie, J., McLaughlin, E. and Langan, M. (eds) *Criminological Perspective: A Reader*, London: Sage.

Cohen, S. and Scull, A. (eds) (1985) *Social Control and the State: Historical and Comparative Essays*, Oxford: Oxford University Press.

Colman, C. and Moyniham, J. (1996) *Understanding Crime Data: Haunted by the Dark Figure*, Milton Keynes: Open University Press.

Cook, D. (1989) *Rich Law, Poor Law: Different Responses to Tax and Supplementary Benefit Fraud*, Milton Keynes: Open University Press.

Cox, B., Shirley, J. and Short, M. (1977) *The Fall of Scotland Yard*, Harmondsworth: Penguin.

Croall, H. (1992) *Understanding White Collar Crime*, Milton Keynes: Open University Press.

Cullen, E. and Newell, T. (1999) *Murderers and Life Imprisonment: Containment, Treatment, Safety and Risk*, Winchester: Waterside Press.

Davies, H., Croall, H. and Tyrer, J. (1998) *Criminal Justice*, 2nd edn, Harlow: Longman.

Dobash, R. P. and Dobash, R. E. (1998) *Rethinking Violence Against Women*, London: Sage.

Dobash, R. P., Dobash, R. E. and Gutteridge, S. (1986) *The Imprisonment of Women*, Oxford: Blackwell.

Dowie, M. (1977) 'Pinto Madness', reprinted in Hills, S. J. (ed.) *Corporate Violence: Injury and Death for Profit*, Totowa, NJ: Rowman and Littlefield.

Draper, R. and Burgess, P. (1989) 'The Explanations of Violence: The Role of Biological, Behavioural and Cultural Selection', in Ohlin, L. and Tonry, M. (eds) *Family Violence*, Chicago: University of Chicago Press.

Durkheim, E. (1960 (1893)) *The Division of Labour in Society*, New York: Free Press.

Durkheim, E. (1964 (1895)) *The Rules of Sociological Method*, New York: Free Press.

Durkheim, E. (1984 (1901)) 'The Two Laws of Penal Evolution', in Lukes, S. and Scull, A. (eds) *Durkheim and the Law*, Oxford: Blackwell.

Eaton, M. (1993) *Women after Prison*, Milton Keynes: Open University Press.

Edwards, S. (1989) *Policing Domestic Violence: Women, the Law and the State*, London: Sage.

Ellis, T. and Winstone, J. (2001/2002) 'Halliday, Sentencers and the National Probation Service', *Criminal Justice Matters*, 46, pp. 20–21.

Emsley, C. (1996a) *The English Police: A Political and Social History*, 2nd edn, Harlow: Longman.

Emsley, C. (1996b) *Crime and Society in England, 1750–1900*, 2nd edn, Harlow: Longman.

Fattah, E. A. (1986) 'Prologue on Some Visible and Hidden Dangers of the Victims Movement', in Fattah, E. A. (ed.) *From Crime Policy to Victim Policy*, London: Macmillan.

Faulkner, D. (2001) *Crime, State and Citizen: A Field Full of Folk*, Winchester: Waterside Press.

Finlay, L. (1996) 'The Pharmaceutical Industry and Women's Reproductive Health', in Szockyj, E. and Fox, J. G. (eds) *Invisible Crimes: Their Nature and Control*, London: Macmillan.

Foucault, M. (1977) *Discipline and Punish: The Birth of the Prison*, London: Allen Lane.

Garland, D. (1985) *Punishment and Welfare: A History of Penal Strategies*, Aldershot: Gower.

Garland, D. (1990) *Punishment and Modern Society: A Study in Social Theory*, Oxford: Clarendon.

Garland, D. (1999) Editorial: 'Punishment and Society Today', *Punishment and Society*, 1:1.

Gatrell, V. A. C. (1994) *The Hanging Tree: Execution and the English People, 1770–1868*, Oxford: Clarendon Press.

Geis, G. (1967) 'The Heavy Electrical Equipment Antitrust Cases of 1961', in Ermann, M. D. and Lundman, R. (eds) (1992) *Corporate and Governmental Deviance*, Oxford: Oxford University Press.

Gerber, J. and Weeks, S. L. (1992) 'Women as Victims of Corporate Crime: A Case for Research on a Neglected Topic', *Deviant Behaviour*, 13:4.

Giddens, A. (1984) *The Constitution of Society*, Cambridge: Polity Press.

Gilchrist, E. and Blisset, J. (2002) 'Magistrates' Attitudes to Domestic Violence and Sentencing', *Howard Journal of Criminal Justice*, 41:4.

Gill, M. (1999) 'Crimes, Victims and Workplace', *Criminal Justice Matters*, 35.

Gilroy, P. (1987) *'There Ain't No Black in the Union Jack': The Cultural Politics of Race and Nation*, London: Hutchinson.

Goffman, E. (1959) *The Presentation of Self in Everyday Life*, Harmondsworth: Penguin.

Grace, S. (1995) 'Policing Domestic Violence in the 1990s', London: HMSO.

Griffiths, J. A. G. (1997) *The Politics of the Judiciary*, 5th edn, London: Fontana.

Grove, T. (2002) 'A Light on the Lay Magistracy', *Criminal Justice Matters*, 49, pp. 24–25.

Hall, S., Critcher, C., Jefferson, T., Clarke, J. and Roberts, B. (1978) *Policing the Crisis: Mugging, the State and Law and Order*, London: Macmillan.

Hawkings, D. T. (1992) *Criminal Ancestors: A Guide to Historical Criminal Records in England and Wales*, Lewes: Sutton.

Hay, D., Linebaugh, P., Rule, J. G., Thompson, E. P. and Winslow, C. (1977) *Albion's Fatal Tree: Crime and Society in the Eighteenth Century*, Harmondsworth: Penguin.

Health and Safety Commission (1997) *Annual Report of Accounts 1996/97*, London: The Stationery Office.

Heidensohn, F. (1998) 'Women in Policing', *Criminal Justice Matters*, 32.

Heidensohn, F. (2002) 'Gender and Crime', in Maguire, M., Morgan, R. and Reiner, R. (eds) *The Oxford Handbook of Criminology*, 3rd edn, Oxford: Oxford University Press.

Henriques, U. R. Q. (1979) *Before the Welfare State: Social Administration in Early Industrial Britain*, Harlow: Longman.

Hentig, H. von (1948) *The Criminal and his Victim*, New Haven, Conn.: Yale University Press.

Hills, S. L. (1987) *Corporate Violence: Injury and Death for Profit*, Totowa, NJ: Rowman and Littlefield.

Hindelang, M. J., Gottfredson, M. R. and Garofalo, J. (1978) *Victims of Personal Crime: An Empirical Foundation for a Theory of Personal Victimization*, Cambridge, Mass.: Ballinger.

Hobsbawm, E. (1964) *Labouring Men*, London: Weidenfeld and Nicolson.

Home Office (1966) Inquiry into Prison Escapes and Security (Mountbatten Report), London: HMSO.

Home Office (1990) *Crime, Justice and Protecting the Public*, London: HMSO.

Home Office (2001) *Making Punishments Work: Report of a Review of the Sentencing Framework* (Halliday Report), London: HMSO.

Hood, R. (1992) *Race and Sentencing: A Study in the Crown Court. A Report for the Commission for Racial Equality*, Oxford: Clarendon.

Hough, J. M. and Mayhew, P. (1983) *The British Crime Survey*, London: Home Office Research and Statistics Department.

Howarth, G. and Rock, P. (2000) 'Aftermath and the Construction of Victimisation: The Other Victims of Crime', *Howard Journal of Criminal Justice*, 39:1.

Hoyle, C. (1999) *Negotiating Domestic Violence*, Oxford: Clarendon.

Hudson, B. (2003) *Understanding Justice: An Introduction to Ideas, Perspectives and Controversies in Modern Penal Theory*, 2nd edn, Milton Keynes: Open University Press.

Ignatieff, M. (1978) *A Just Measure of Pain: The Penitentiary in the Industrial Revolution, 1750–1850*, London: Macmillan.

Jefferson, T. (1990) *The Case against Paramilitary Policing*, Milton Keynes: Open University Press.

Jefferson, T. and Shapland, J. (1990) 'Criminal Justice and the Production and Order of Control: Trends since 1980 in the UK', paper presented to GERN Seminar on the Production of Order and Control, Paris: CESDIP.

Jenkins, P. (1986) 'From Gallows to Prison? The Execution Rate in Early Modern England', *Criminal Justice History*, 7.

Jones, T., McClean, B. and Young, J. (1986) *The Islington Crime Survey*, Aldershot: Gower.

Karman, A. (1990) *Crime Victims: An Introduction to Victimology*, Pacific Grove, Calif.: Brookes Cole.

Kempe, C. H. and Kempe, R. E. (1981) *The Battered Child*, 2nd edn, Chicago: University of Chicago Press.

Kinsey, R. (1984) *Merseyside Crime Survey: First Report*, Merseyside Metropolitan Council.

Langbein, J. (1983) 'Albion's Fatal Flaws', *Past and Present*, 98.

Laub, J. H. (1990) 'Patterns of criminal victimization in the United States', in Lurigio, A. J., Skogan, W. G. and Davis, R. C. (eds) *Victims of Crime*, Beverly Hills, Calif.: Sage.

Lea, J. and Young, J. (1993) *What's to Be Done about Law and Order*, 2nd edn, London: Pluto Press.

Learmont Report (1995) *Review of Prison Service Security in England and Wales and the Escape from Parkhurst Prison on Tuesday 3 January 1995*, Cmnd 3020, London: HMSO.

Leech, M. and Cheney, D. (1999) *The Prisons Handbook 2000*, Winchester: Waterside Press.

Leishman, F., Loveday, B. and Savage, S. (eds) (2002) *Core Issues in Policing*, 2nd edn, Harlow: Longman.

Levi, M. (1987) *Regulating Fraud: White Collar Crime and the Process*, London: Tavistock.

Levi, M. (1992) 'White Collar Crime Victimisation', in Schlegel, K. and Weisburd, D. (eds) *White Collar Crime Reconsidered*, Boston: North Eastern University Press.

Liebling, A. and Price, D. (2001) *The Prison Officer*, London: HM Prison Service.

Lloyd, A. (1995) *Doubly Deviant, Doubly Damned: Society's Treatment of Violent Women*, Harmondsworth: Penguin.

Lombroso, C. (1876) *L'uomo delinquente*, Milan: Hoepli.

Lukes, E. (1973) *Emile Durkheim: His Life and Work*, Harmondsworth: Penguin.

Lyon, J. (2002) 'The Last Resort', *Observer*, 19 May.

Lytton, C. (1988 (1914)) *Prisoners: The Stirring Testimony of a Suffragette*, London: Heinemann.

McGowan, R. (1998) 'The Well-Ordered Prison: England, 1780–1865', in Morris, N. and Rothman, D. J. (eds) *The Oxford History of the Prison: The Practice of Punishment in Western Society*, Oxford: Oxford University Press.

Mackinnon, C. A. (1989) *Towards a Feminist Theory of the State*, Cambridge, Mass.: Harvard University Press.

McLaughlin, E. (1996) 'Political Violence, Terrorism and Crimes of the State', In Muncie, J. and McLaughlin, E. (eds) *Social Problems and the Family*, Milton Keynes: Open University Press.

McLaughlin, E. and Muncie, J. (eds) (1996) *Controlling Crime*, London: Sage.

McLaughlin, E., Fergusson, R., Hughes, G. and Westmarland, L. (eds) (2003) *Restorative Justice: Critical Issues*, London: Sage.

Macpherson, W. (1999) *The Stephen Lawrence Inquiry: Report of an Inquiry by Sir William Macpherson*, London: HMSO.

Maguire, M., Morgan, R. and Reiner, R. (eds) (2002) *The Oxford Handbook of Criminology*, 3rd edn, Oxford: Oxford University Press.

Malleson, K. (1999) *The New Judiciary: The Effects of Expansion and Activism*, Dartmouth: Ashgate.

Martin, C. (1996) 'The Impact of Equal Opportunities Policies on the Day-to-Day Experience of Women Police Constables', *British Journal of Criminology*, 36:1, pp. 510–527.

Martinson, R. (1974) 'What Works? Questions and Answers about Prison Reform', *The Public Interest*, 35, pp. 22–54.

Mathews, R. (1999) *Doing Time: An Introduction to the Sociology of Imprisonment*, London: Palgrave.

Mawby, R. and Walklate, S. (1994) *Critical Victimology: International Perspectives*, London: Sage.

Mayhew, P., Elliott, D. and Dowds, L. (1989) *The 1988 British Crime Survey*, London: HMSO.

Mendelsohn, B. (1963) 'The Origin and Doctrine of Victimology', reprinted in Rock, P. (ed.) (1993) *Victimology*, Aldershot: Dartmouth.

Miers, D. (1978) *Responses to Victimisation*, Abingdon: Professional Books.

Miers, D. (1989) 'Positivist Victimology', *International Review of Victimology*, 2.

Miers, D. (1990) 'Victimology: A Critique', *International Review of Victimology*, 3.

Mills, C. W. (1970) *The Sociological Imagination*, Harmondsworth: Penguin.

Mirlees-Black, C., Mayhew, P. and Percy, A. (1996) *The 1996 British Crime Survey*, London: HMSO.

Moore, L. (2000) *Conmen and Cutpurses: Scenes from the Hogarthian Underworld*, London: Penguin.

Morgan, R. (2002) 'Imprisonment: A Brief History, the Contemporary Scene and Likely Prospects', in Maguire, M., Morgan, R. and Reiner, R. (eds) *The Oxford Handbook of Criminology*, 3rd edn, Oxford: Oxford University Press.

Morgan, R. and Newburn, T. (1997) *The Future of Policing*, Oxford: Oxford University Press.

Morley, R. and Mullender, A. (1994) 'Preventing Domestic Violence to Women', Crime Prevention Unit, Paper 48, London: Home Office Police Department.

Morris, N. and Rothman, D. J. (eds) (1998) *The Oxford History of the Prison: The Practice of Punishment in Western Society*, Oxford: Oxford University Press.

Muncie, J. (1996) 'Prison Histories: Reform, Repression and Rehabilitation', in McLaughlin, E. and Muncie, J. (eds) *Controlling Crime*, London: Sage.

Newburn, T. (ed.) (2003) *A Handbook of Policing*, Cullompton, Devon: Willan Publishing.

Newburn, T. and Hayman, S. (2001) 'Keeping Watch', *Police Review*, 5 October.

Nozick, R. (1981) *Philosophical Explanations*, Oxford: Clarendon Press.

Parker, H., Sumner, M. and Jarvis, G. (1989) *Unmasking the Magistrates*, Milton Keynes: Open University Press.

Pearce, F. (1990) *Second Islington Crime Survey: Commercial and Conventional Crime in Islington*, London: Middlesex Polytechnic, Centre for Criminology.

Pearce, F. and Tombs, S. (1998) *Toxic Capitalism: Corporate Crime and the Chemical Industry*, Aldershot: Ashgate.

Pearson, G. (1983) *Hooligan: A History of Respectable Fears*, London: Macmillan.

Perry, S. and Dawson, J. (1985) *Nightmare: Women and the Dalkon Shield*, New York: Macmillan.

Peters, E. M. (1998) 'Prison before the Prison: The Ancient and Medieval Worlds', in Morris, N. and Rothman, D. J. (eds) *The Oxford History of the Prison: The Practice of Punishment in Western Society*, Oxford: Oxford University Press.

Phillips, D. (1983) 'A Just Measure of Crime, Authority, Hunters and Blue Locusts: the "Revisionist" Social History of Crime and Law in Britain, 1780–1850', in Cohen, S. and Scull, A. (eds) *Social Control and the State: Historical and Comparative Essays*, Oxford: Oxford University Press.

Pizzey, E. (1974) *Scream Quietly or the Neighbours Will Hear*, Harmondsworth: Penguin.

Pollard, C. (1998) 'Keeping the Queen's Peace', *Criminal Justice Matters*, 31, pp. 14–16.

Price, D. (2000) 'The Origins and Durability of Security Categorisation: A Study in Penological Pragmatism or Spies, Dickie and Prison Security', in *British Criminology Conference: Selected Proceedings*, vol. 3, Liverpool (edited by Mair, G. and Tarling, R.).

Priestley, P. (1985) *Victorian Prison Lives: English Prison Biography, 1830–1914*, London: Methuen.

Punch, M. (1996) *Dirty Business: Exploring Corporate Misconduct*, London: Sage.

Quinney, R. (1972) 'Who Is the Victim?', *Criminology*, November.

Radzinowicz, L. (1968) *A History of the English Criminal Law*, vol. 4, London: Stevens.

Rafter, N. H. (1983) 'Chastising the Unchaste: Social Control Functions of a Women's Reformatory, 1894–1931', in Cohen, S. and Scull, A. (eds) *Social Control and the State: Historical and Comparative Essays*, Oxford: Oxford University Press.

Rawlings, P. (1999) *Crime and Power: A History of Criminal Justice, 1688–1998*, Harlow: Longman.

Rawlings, P. (2002) *Policing: A Short History*, Cullompton, Devon: Willan Publishing.

Raynor, P. (2002) 'Community Penalties: Probation, Punishment and "What Works"', in Maguire, M., Morgan, R. and Reiner, R. (eds) *The Oxford Handbook of Criminology*, 3rd edn, Oxford: Oxford University Press.

Reiner, R. (1997) 'Policing and the Police', in Maguire, M., Morgan, R. and Reiner, R. (eds) *The Oxford Handbook of Criminology*, 2nd edn, Oxford: Oxford University Press.

Reith, C. (1938) *The Police Idea*, Oxford: Oxford University Press.

Reith, C. (1943) *British Police and the Democratic Idea*, Oxford: Oxford University Press.

Rock, P. (1990) *Helping the Victims of Crime*, Oxford: Clarendon Press.

Rock, P. (1999) 'Acknowledging Victims' Needs and Rights', *Criminal Justice Matters*, 35.

Rose, D. (2002) 'It's Official: Prison Does Work after All', *Observer*, 5 May.

Rusche, G. and Kirchheimer, O. (1939) *Punishment and Social Structure*, New York: Columbia University Press.

Rybrant, L. and Kramer, R. (1995) 'Hybrid Nonwomen and Corporate Violence: The Silicone Implant Case', *Violence against Women*, 1:3.

Sanders, A. and Young, R. (2000) *Criminal Justice*, 2nd edn, London: Butterworth.

Scarman Report (1982) *The Brixton Disorders, 10–12 April 1981: Report of an Enquiry by the Rt Hon. Lord Scarman*, London: HMSO.

Scraton, P., Sim, J. and Skidmore, P. (1991) *Prisons under Protest*, Milton Keynes: Open University Press.

Seago, P., Walker, C. and Wall, D. (2000) 'The Professionalisation of Local Courts' Justice', *Criminal Justice Matters*, 38.

Sharpe, J. A. (1999) *Crime in Early Modern England*, 1550–1750, 2nd edn, Harlow: Longman.

Smith, B. L. (1985) 'Trends in the Victims' Rights Movement and Implications for Future Research', *Victimology*, 10.

Smith, D. J. and Gray, J. (1983) *The Police and People in London IV: The Police in Action*, London: Policy Studies Institute.

Snell, J. E., Rosenwald, R. J. and Robey, A. (1964) 'The Wife Beater's Wife: A Study of Family Interaction', *Archives of General Psychiatry*, 11.

Sparks, R. F. (1996) 'Prisons, Punishment and Penality', in McLaughlin, E. and Muncie, J. (eds) *Controlling Crime*, London: Sage.

Sparks, R. F., Genn, D. and Dodd, D. J. (1977) *Surveying Victims*, Chichester: John Wiley.

Stanko, E. (1990) *Everyday Violence*, Pandora: London.

Stanley, E. (1990) *Feminist Praxis: Research, Theory and Epistemology in Feminist Research*, London: Routledge.

Stedman Jones, G. (1984) *Outcast London. A Study in the Relationship between Classes in Victorian Society*, Harmondsworth: Penguin.

Storch, R. D. (1975) 'The Plague of Blue Locusts: Police Reform and Popular Resistance in Northern England, 1840–57', *International Review of Social History*, 20.

Strauss, M. A. (1980) 'Sexual Inequality and Wife Beating', in Strauss, M. A. and Hotaling, G. T. (eds) *The Social Causes of Husband–Wife Violence*, Minneapolis: University of Minnesota Press.

Strong, B. and DeVault, C. (1995) *The Marriage and Family Experience*, 6th edn, St Paul: West.

Sutherland, E. (1949) *White Collar Crime*, New York: Holt, Rinehart and Winston.

Taylor, N. (1999) 'Fixing the Price for Spoiled Lives', *Criminal Justice Matters*, 35.

Thomas, K. (1978) *Religion and the Decline of Magic*, Perthshire: Peregrine.

Thompson, E. P. (1985) *Whigs and Hunters: The Origins of the Black Act*, Harmondsworth: Penguin.

Tobias, J. J. (1967) *Crime and Industrial Society in the 19th Century*, London: Batsford.

Tombs, S. (1990) 'Industrial Injuries in British Manufacturing Industry', *Sociological Review*, 38:2.

Travis, A. (2003) 'Record Jail Numbers Insupportable Says Lord Irvine', *Guardian*, 7 January.

Valier, C. (2002) *Theories of Crime and Punishment*, Harlow: Longman.

Waddington, D., Jones, K. and Critcher, C. (1989) *Flashpoints: Studies in Public Disorder*, London: Routledge.

Waddington, P. (1991) *The Strong Arm of the Law: Armed Police and Public Order Policing*, Oxford: Oxford University Press.

Waddington, P. (1993) *Calling the Police: The Interpretation of, and Responses to, Calls for Assistance from the Public*, Aldershot: Avebury.

Waddington, P. (2000) 'Public Order Policing: Citizenship and Moral Ambiguity', in Leishman, F., Loveday, B. and Savage, S. (eds) *Core Issues in Policing*, 2nd edn, Harlow: Pearson.

Walker, N. (1991) *Why Punish?*, Oxford: Oxford University Press.

Walklate, S. (1989) *Victimology: The Victim and the Criminal Justice Process*, London: Unwin Hyman.

Walklate, S. (1990) 'Researching Victims of Crime: Critical Victimology', *Social Justice*, 17:2.

Walklate, S. (2000) 'Reflections on "New Labour" or "Back to the Future"?', *Criminal Justice Matters*, 38, pp. 7–8.

Walkowitz, J. R. (1982) *Prostitution and Victorian Society: Women, Class and the State*, Cambridge: Cambridge University Press.

Wall, D. (1999) 'Getting to Grips with Cybercrime', *Criminal Justice Matters*, 36, pp. 17–19.

Walsh, M. and Schram, D. (1980) 'The Victims of White-Collar Crime: Accuser or Accused?', in Geis, G. and Stotland, E. (eds) *White-Collar Crime*, Beverly Hills, Calif.: Sage.

Watkins, M. and Gordon, W. (2000) *The Sentence of the Court: A Handbook for Magistrates*, Winchester: Waterside Press.

Weale, S. (2001) 'Prison – the Therapeutic Way', *Guardian*, 2 February.

Weber, M. (1978 (1920)) *Economy and Society*, ed. Roth, G. and Wittich, C., Berkeley: University of California Press.

Wells, C. (1989) 'What about the Victim?', *The Investigator*, 5, pp. 26–27.

Wertham, F. (1949) *The Show of Violence*, New York: Doubleday.

Wilson, D. (2002) 'Millbank, the Panopticon and their Victorian Audiences', *Howard Journal of Criminal Justice*, 41:4, pp. 364–381.

Wolfgang, M. E. (1958) *Patterns in Criminal Homicide*, Philadelphia: University of Pennsylvania Press.

Wolfgang, M. E. (1998) 'We Do Not Deserve to Kill', *Crime and Delinquency*, 44:1, pp. 19–31.

Woodcock Report (1994) *Report of the Enquiry into the Escape of Six Prisoners from the Special Secure Unit at Whitemoor Prison on Friday 9 September 1994*, Cmnd 2741, London: HMSO.

Woolf Report (1991) *Prison Disturbances April 1990: Report of an Inquiry by the Rt Hon. Lord Justice Woolf*, London: HMSO.

Worrall, A. (1997) *Punishment in the Community: The Future of Criminal Justice*, Harlow: Longman.

Young, J. (1986) 'The Failure of Criminology: The Need for a Radical Realism', in Mathews, R. and Young, J. (eds) *Confronting Crime*, London: Sage.

Young, J. (1996) 'The Failure of Criminology: The Need for a Radical Realism', reprinted in McLaughlin, J., Muncie, E. and Langan, M. (eds) (1996) *Criminological Perspectives: A Reader*, London: Sage.

Young, J. (1997) 'Left Realist Criminology: Radical in its Analysis, Realist in its Policy', in Maguire, M., Morgan, R. and Reiner, R. (eds) *The Oxford Handbook of Criminology*, 2nd edn, Oxford: Oxford University Press.

Zedner, L. (1991) *Women, Crime and Custody in Victorian England*, Oxford: Clarendon Press.

Zedner, L. (1992) 'Sexual Offences', in Casale, S. and Stockdale, E. (eds) *Criminal Justice under Stress*, London: Blackstone.

Zedner, L. (1998) 'Wayward Sisters: The Prison for Women', in Morris, N. and Rothman, D. J. (eds) *The Oxford History of the Prison: The Practice of Punishment in Western Society*, Oxford: Oxford University Press.

Index

Page references for tables are in *italics*

eBooks

eBooks – at www.eBookstore.tandf.co.uk

A library at your fingertips!

eBooks are electronic versions of printed books. You can store them on your PC/laptop or browse them online.

They have advantages for anyone needing rapid access to a wide variety of published, copyright information.

eBooks can help your research by enabling you to bookmark chapters, annotate text and use instant searches to find specific words or phrases. Several eBook files would fit on even a small laptop or PDA.

NEW: Save money by eSubscribing: cheap, online access to any eBook for as long as you need it.

Annual subscription packages

We now offer special low-cost bulk subscriptions to packages of eBooks in certain subject areas. These are available to libraries or to individuals.

For more information please contact webmaster.ebooks@tandf.co.uk

We're continually developing the eBook concept, so keep up to date by visiting the website.

www.eBookstore.tandf.co.uk